The Life of John Ruskin

PREFACE TO THE SEVENTH EDITION

This book in its first form was written nearly twenty years ago with the intention of contributing a volume to a series of University Extension Manuals. For that purpose it included a sketch of Ruskin's "Work," with some attempt to describe the continuous development of his thought. It had the advantage—and the disadvantage—of being written under his eye; that is to say, he saw as much of it as his health allowed; and it received his general approval.

To explain my venturing upon the subject at all, I may perhaps be allowed to state that I became his pupil in 1872 (having seen him earlier), and continued to be in some relation to him—as visitor, resident assistant, or near neighbour—until his death.

After his death the biographical part of my book was enlarged at the expense of the description of his writings; and in revising once more I have thrown out much relating to his works, chiefly because they are now accessible as they were not formerly.

W.G.C.
CONISTON, *May 1911*

CONTENTS

PREFACE TO THE SEVENTH EDITION 7

BOOK I
THE BOY POET (1819-1842)

CHAPTER I 15
   HIS ANCESTORS
CHAPTER II 23
   THE FATHER OF THE MAN (1819-1825)
CHAPTER III 30
   PERFERVIDUM INGENIUM (1826-1830)
CHAPTER IV 35
   MOUNTAIN-WORSHIP (1830-1835)
CHAPTER V 47
   THE GERM OF "MODERN PAINTERS" (1836)
CHAPTER VI 53
   A LOVE-STORY (1836-1839)
CHAPTER VII 57
   "KATA PHUSIN" (1837-1838)
CHAPTER VIII 64
   SIR ROGER NEWDIGATE'S PRIZE (1837-1839)
CHAPTER IX 69
   THE BROKEN CHAIN (1840-1841)
CHAPTER X 75
   THE GRADUATE OF OXFORD (1841-1842)

BOOK II
THE ART CRITIC (1842-1860)

CHAPTER I 81
    "TURNER AND THE ANCIENTS" (1842-1844)
CHAPTER II 87
    CHRISTIAN ART (1845-1847)
CHAPTER III 95
    "THE SEVEN LAMPS"
CHAPTER IV 108
    "STONES OF VENICE" (1849-1851)
CHAPTER V 117
    PRE-RAPHAELITISM (1851-1853)
CHAPTER VI 127
    THE EDINBURGH LECTURES (1853-1854)
CHAPTER VII 133
    THE WORKING MEN'S COLLEGE (1854-1855)
CHAPTER VIII 139
    "MODERN PAINTERS" CONTINUED (1855-1856)
CHAPTER IX 147
    "THE POLITICAL ECONOMY OF ART" (1857-1858)
CHAPTER X 156
    "MODERN PAINTERS" CONCLUDED (1838-1860)

BOOK III
HERMIT AND HERETIC (1860-1870)

CHAPTER I 163
    "UNTO THIS LAST" (1860-1861)
CHAPTER II 171
    "MUNERA PULVERIS" (1862)

CHAPTER III 176
   THE LIMESTONE ALPS (1863)
CHAPTER IV 180
   "SESAME AND LILIES" (1864)
CHAPTER V 184
   "ETHICS OF THE DUST" (1865)
CHAPTER VI 189
   "THE CROWN OF WILD OLIVE" (1865-1866)
CHAPTER VII 199
   "TIME AND TIDE" (1867)
CHAPTER VIII 207
   AGATES, AND ABBEVILLE (1868)
CHAPTER IX 214
   "THE QUEEN OF THE AIR" (1869)
CHAPTER X 220
   VERONA AND OXFORD (1869-1870)

BOOK IV
PROFESSOR AND PROPHET (1870-1900)

CHAPTER I 229
   FIRST OXFORD LECTURES (1870-1871)
CHAPTER II 240
   "FORS" BEGUN (1871-1872)
CHAPTER III 249
   OXFORD TEACHING (1872-1875)
CHAPTER IV 262
   ST. GEORGE AND ST. MARK (1875-1877)
CHAPTER V 275
   DEUCALION AND PROSERPINA (1877-1879)
CHAPTER VI 285
   THE DIVERSIONS OF BRANTWOOD (1879-1881)

CHAPTER VII 295
    "FORS" RESUMED (1880-1881)
CHAPTER VIII 303
    THE RECALL TO OXFORD (1882-1883)
CHAPTER IX 312
    THE STORM-CLOUD (1884-1888)
CHAPTER X 320
    DATUR HORA QUIETI (1889-1900)

BOOK I

THE BOY POET (1819-1842)

CHAPTER I

HIS ANCESTORS

If origin, if early training and habits of life, if tastes, and character, and associations, fix a man's nationality, then John Ruskin must be reckoned a Scotsman. He was born in London, but his family was from Scotland. He was brought up in England, but the friends and teachers, the standards and influences of his early life, were chiefly Scottish. The writers who directed him into the main lines of his thought and work were Scotsmen—from Sir Walter and Lord Lindsay and Principal Forbes to the master of his later studies of men and the means of life, Thomas Carlyle. The religious instinct so conspicuous in him was a heritage from Scotland; thence the combination of shrewd common-sense and romantic sentiment; the oscillation between levity and dignity, from caustic jest to tender earnest; the restlessness, the fervour, the impetuosity—all these are the tokens of a Scotsman of parts, and were highly developed in John Ruskin.

In the days of auld lang syne the Rhynns of Galloway—that hammer-headed promontory of Scotland which looks towards Belfast Lough—was the home of two great families, the Agnews and the Adairs. The Agnews, of Norman race, occupied the northern half, centring about their island-fortress of Lochnaw, where they became celebrated for a long line of hereditary sheriffs and baronets who have played no inconsiderable part in public affairs. The southern half, from Portpatrick to the Mull of Galloway, was held by the Adairs (or, as formerly spelt, Edzears) who took their name from Edgar, son of Dovenald, one of the two Galloway leaders at the Battle of the Standard. Three hundred years later Robert Edzear—who does not know his descendant and namesake, Robin Adair?—settled at Gainoch, near the head of Luce Bay; and for another space of 300 years his children kept the same estate, in spite of private feud, and civil war, and religious persecution, of which they had more than their share.

At the beginning of the eighteenth century, John Adair, the laird of Little Genoch, was married to Mary Agnew, a near kinswoman of the celebrated Sir Andrew, colonel of the Scots Fusiliers at Dettingen. The exact relationship of Mary Agnew to "the bravest man in the British army" remains undecided, but letters still extant from the Lady Agnew of the day address her as "Dear Molly," and end, "Your affectionate cousin" or "kinswoman." Her son Thomas succeeded his father in 1721, and, retiring with his captaincy, settled on the estate. He married Jean, daughter of Andrew Ross of Balsarroch and Balkail, a lady noted for her beauty, her wit, and her Latin scholarship, and a member of a family which has given many distinguished men to the army and navy. Among them Admiral Sir John Ross, the Arctic explorer, Sir Hew Dalrymple, and Field-Marshal Sir Hew Dalrymple Ross, were all her great-nephews, and her son, Dr. John Adair, was the man in whose arms Wolfe died at the taking of Quebec; it is he who is shown in Benjamin West's picture supporting the General.

Dr. Adair's sister Catherine, the daughter of Thomas Adair and Jean Ross, married the Rev. James Tweddale, minister of Glenluce from 1758 to 1778, representative of an old Covenanting family, and holder of the original Covenant, which had been confided to the care of his great-aunt Catherine by Baillie of Jarviswood on his way to execution in the "killing time." The document was sold with his library at his death, his children being then under age, and is now in the Glasgow Museum. One of these children, Catherine, married a John Ruskin.

The origin of the name of Ruskin is English, dating from the middle ages. Soon after the dissolution of Furness Abbey, Richerde Ruskyn and his family were land-owners at Dalton-in-Furness. One branch, and that with which we are especially concerned, settled in Edinburgh.

John Ruskin—our subject's grandfather—when he ran away with Catherine Tweddale in 1781, was a handsome lad of twenty. His portrait as a child proves his looks, and he evidently had some charm of character or promise of power, for the escapade did not lose him the friendship of the lady's family. Major Ross, her uncle and guardian, remained a good friend to the young couple. She herself was only sixteen at her marriage—a bright and animated brunette, as her miniature shows, in later years ripening to a woman of uncommon strength, with old-fashioned piety of a robust, practical type, and a spirit which the trials of her after-life—and they were many—could not subdue. Her husband set up in the wine trade in Edinburgh. For many years they lived in the Old Town, then a respectable neighbourhood, among a cultivated and well-bred society, in which they moved as equals, entertaining, with others, such a man as Dr. Thomas Brown, the professor of philosophy, a great light in his own day, and still conspicuous in the constellation of Scotch metaphysicians.

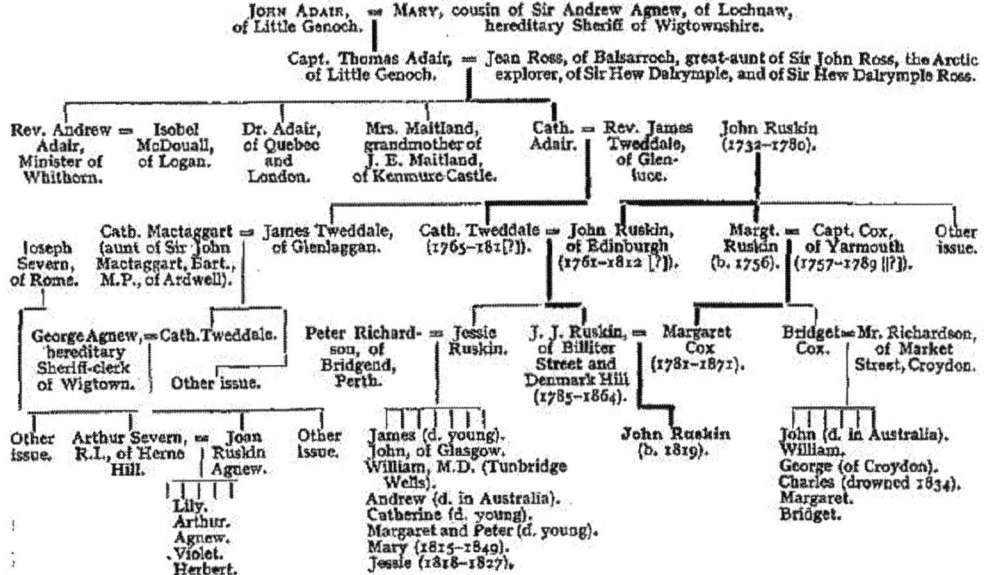

Their son, John James Ruskin (born May 10, 1785), was sent to the famous High School of Edinburgh, under Dr. Adam, the most renowned of Scottish head-masters, and there he received the sound old-fashioned classical education. Before he was sixteen, his sister Jessie was already married at Perth to Peter Richardson, a tanner living at Bridge End, by the Tay; and so his cousin, Margaret Cox, was sent for to fill the vacant place.

She was a daughter of old Mr. Ruskin's sister, who had married a Captain Cox, sailing from Yarmouth for the herring fishery. He had died in 1789, or thereabouts, from the results of an accident while riding homewards to his family after one of his voyages, and his widow maintained herself in comfort by keeping the old King's Head Inn at Croydon Market-place. Of her two daughters the younger married another Mr. Richardson, a baker at Croydon, so that, by an odd coincidence, there were two families of Richardsons, unconnected with one another except through their relationship to the Ruskins.

Margaret, the elder daughter, who came to keep house for her uncle in Edinburgh, was then nearly twenty years of age. She had been the model pupil at her Croydon day-school; tall and handsome, pious and practical, she was just the girl to become the confidante and adviser of her dark-eyed, active, and romantic young cousin.

Some time before the beginning of 1807, John James, having finished his education at the High School, went to London, where a place had been found for him by his uncle's brother-in-law, Mr. MacTaggart. He was followed by a kind letter from Dr. Thomas Brown, who advised him to keep up his Latin, and to study political economy, for the Professor looked upon him as a young man of unusual promise and power. During some two years, he worked as a clerk in the house of Sir William Gordon, Murphy and Co., where he made friends, and laid the foundation of his prosperity; for along with him at the office there was a Mr. Peter Domecq, owner of the Spanish vineyards of Macharnudo, learning the commercial part of his business in London, the headquarters of the sherry trade. He admired his fellow-clerk's capacity so much as to offer him the London agency of his family business. Mr. MacTaggart found the capital in consideration of their taking his relative, Mr. Telford, into the concern. And so they entered into partnership, about 1809, as Ruskin, Telford and Domecq: Domecq contributing the sherry, Mr. Henry Telford the capital, and Ruskin the brains.

How he came by his business capacity may be understood—and in some measure, perhaps, how his son came by his flexible and forcible style—from a letter of Mrs. Catherine Ruskin, written about this time; in which, moreover, there are a few details of family circumstances and character, not without interest. John James Ruskin had been protesting that he was never going to marry, but meant to devote himself to his mother; she replied:

"... But my son an old Batchelor—believe me my beloved Child I feel the full force and value of that affection that could prompt to such a plan—dear as your society is to me it would then become the misery of my existence—could I see my Child so formed for domestick happiness deprived of every blessing on my account. No my Dr John I do not know a more unhappy being than an old Batchelor ... may God preserve my Child from realizing the dreary picture—as soon as you can keep a Wife you must Marry with all possible speed—that is as soon as you find a very Amiable woman. She must be a good daughter and fond of Domestick life—and pious, without ostentation, for remember no Woman without the fear of God, can either make a good Wife or a good Mother—freethinking Men are shocking to nature, but from an Infidel Woman Good Lord deliver us. I have thought more of it than you have done—for I have two or three presents carefully [laid] by for her, and I have also been so foresightly as to purchase two Dutch toys for your Children in case you might marry before we had free intercourse with that country ... Who can say what I can say 'here is my Son—a hansome accomplished young man of three and twenty—he will not Marry that he may take care of his Mother—here is my Dr Margaret, hansome, Amiable and good and she would not leave her *Ant* (I mean Aunt) for any Man on Earth.' Ah My Dear and valuable children, dear is your affection to my heart, but I will never make so base a use of it. I entreat my Dr John that you will not give yourself one moment's uneasiness about me—I will at all events have £86 a year for life that your Father cannot deprive me of, and tho' I could not live very splendidly in a Town on this, yet with a neat little House and Garden in the country, it would afford all the means of life in fullness to Meggy myself and our servant. You forget, my Dr how much a woman can do without in domestick affairs to save Money—a Woman that has any management at all can live with more comfort on £50 a year than a Man could do on two hundred. There was a year of my life that I maintained myself and two children on twenty pound, the bread too was 1/2 the loave that year: we did not indeed live very sumptuously nor shall I say our strength improved much but I did not contract one farthing of debt and that to me supplyed the want of luxuries. Now my Dr John let me never hear a fear expressed on my account; there is no fear of me; make yourself happy and all will be well, and for God sake my beloved Boy take care of your health, take a good drink of porter to dinner and supper and a little Wine now and then, and tell me particularly about yr new Lodgings," etc.

He returned home to Edinburgh on a visit and arranged a marriage with his cousin Margaret, if she would wait for him until he was safely established; and then he set to work at the responsibilities of creating a new business. It was a severer task than he had anticipated, for his father's brain and business, as the above letter hints, had both gone wrong; he left Edinburgh and settled at Bower's Well, Perth, ended tragically, and left a load of debt behind him, which the son, sensitive to the family honour, undertook to pay before laying by a penny for himself. It took nine years of assiduous labour and economy. He worked the business entirely by himself. The various departments that most men entrust to others he filled in person. He managed the correspondence, he travelled for orders, he arranged the importation, he directed the growers out in Spain, and gradually built up a great business, paid off his father's creditors, and secured his own competence.

This was not done without sacrifice of health, which he never recovered, nor without forming habits of over-anxiety and toilsome minuteness which lasted his life long. But his business cares were relieved by cultured tastes. He loved art, painted in water-colours in the old style, and knew a good picture when he saw it. He loved literature, and read aloud finely all the old standard authors, though he was not too old-fashioned to admire "Pickwick" and the "Noctes Ambrosianæ" when they appeared. He loved the scenery and architecture among which he had travelled in Scotland and Spain; but he could find interest in almost any place and any subject; an alert man, in whom practical judgment was joined to a romantic temperament, strong feelings and opinions to extended sympathies. His letters, of which there are many preserved, bear witness to his character, taste, and intellect, curiously anticipating, on some points, those of his son. His portraits give the idea of an expressive face, sensitive, refined, every feature a gentleman's.

So, after those nine years of work and waiting, he went to Perth to claim his cousin's hand. She was for further delay; but with the minister's help he persuaded her one evening into a prompt marriage in the Scotch fashion, drove off with her next morning to Edinburgh, and on to the home he had prepared in London at 54, Hunter Street, Brunswick Square (February 27, 1818).

The heroine of this little drama was no ordinary bride. At Edinburgh she had found herself, though well brought up for Croydon, inferior to the society of the Modern Athens. As the affianced of a man of ability, she felt it her duty to make herself his match in mental culture, as she was already in her own department of practical matters. Under Dr. Brown's direction, and stimulated by his notice, she soon became—not a bluestocking—but well-read, well-informed above the average. She was one of those persons who set themselves a very high standard, and resolve to drag both themselves and their neighbours up to it. But, as the process is difficult, so it is disappointing. People became rather shy of Mrs. Ruskin, and she of them, so that her life was solitary and her household quiet. It was not merely from narrow Puritanism that she made so few friends; her morality and her piety, strict as they were within their own lines, permitted her most of the enjoyments and amusements of life; still less was there any cynicism or misanthropy. But she devoted herself to her husband and son. She was too proud to court those above her in worldly rank, and she was not easily approached except by people fully equal to her in strength of character, of whom there could never be many. The few who made their way to her friendship found her a true and valuable friend.

CHAPTER II

THE FATHER OF THE MAN (1819-1825)

Into this family John Ruskin was born on February 8, 1819, at half-past seven in the morning. He was baptised on the twentieth by the Rev. Mr. Boyd.

The first account of him in writing is in a letter from his mother when he was six weeks old. She chronicles—not without a touch of superstition—the breaking of a looking-glass, and continues: "John grows finely; he is just now on my knees sleeping and looking so sweetly; I hope I shall not get proud of him." He was a fine healthy baby, and at four months was "beginning to give more decided proofs that he knows what he wants, and will have it if crying and passion will get it." At a year his mother resolves that "this will be cured by a good whipping when he can understand what it is," and we know that she carried out her Spartan resolve.

This, and the story in "Arachne," how she let him touch the tea-kettle; and the reminiscences in "Præterita" of playthings locked up, and a lone little boy staring at the water-cart and the pattern on the carpet—all these give a gloomy impression of his mother, against which we must set the proofs of affection and kindliness shown in her letters. In these we can see her anxiously nursing him through childish ailments, taking him out for his daily walk to Duppas Hill with a captain's biscuit in her muff, for fear he should be hungry by the way; we hear her teaching him his first lessons, with astonishment at his wonderful memory, and glorying with Nurse Anne over his behaviour in church; and all these things she retails in gossiping letters to her husband, while Mr. Richard Gray gives two-year-old John "his first lesson on the flute, both sitting on the drawing-room floor, very deeply engaged." "I am sure," she says, "there is no other love, no other feeling, like a mother's towards her first boy when she loves his father;" and her pride in his looks, and precocity, and docility—"I never met with a child of his age so sensible to praise or blame"—found a justification in his passionate devotion to the man who was so dear to them both.

Though he was born in the thick of London, he was not City-bred. His first three summers were spent in lodgings in Hampstead or Dulwich, then "the country." So early as his fourth summer he was taken to Scotland by sea to stay with his aunt Jessie, Mrs. Richardson of Perth. There he found cousins to play with, especially one, little Jessie, of nearly his own age; he found a river with deep swirling pools, that impressed him more than the sea, and he found the mountains. Coming home in the autumn, he sat for his full-length portrait to James Northcote, R.A., and being asked what he would choose for background, he replied, "Blue hills."

Northcote had painted Mr. and Mrs. Ruskin, and, as they were fond of artistic company, remained their friend. A certain friendship too, was struck up between the old Academician, then in his seventy-seventh year, the acknowledged cynic and satirist, and the little wise boy who asked shrewd questions, and could sit still to be painted; who, moreover, had a face worth painting, not unlike the model from whom Northcote's master, the great Sir Joshua, had painted his famous cherubs. The painter asked him to come again, and sit as the hero of a fancy picture, bought at the Academy by the flattered parents. There is a grove, a flock of toy sheep, drapery in the grand style, a mahogany Satyr taking a thorn out of the little pink foot of a conventional nudity—poor survivals of the Titianesque. But the head is an obvious portrait, and a happy one; far more like the real boy, so tradition says, than the generalized chubbiness of the commissioned picture.

In the next year (1823) they quitted the town for a suburban home. The spot they chose was in rural Dulwich, on Herne Hill, a long offshoot of the Surrey downs; low, and yet commanding green fields and scattered houses in the foreground, with rich undulating country to the south, and looking across London toward Windsor and Harrow. It is all built up now; but their house (later No. 28) must have been as secluded as any in a country village. There were ample gardens front and rear, well stocked with fruit and flowers—quite an Eden for a little boy, and all the more that the fruit of it was forbidden. It was here that all his years of youth were spent. Here, under his parents' roof, he wrote his earlier works, as far as vol. i. of "Modern Painters." To the adjoining house, as his own separate home, he returned for a period of his middle life; and in the old home, handed over to his adopted daughter, he still used to find his own rooms ready when he cared to visit London.

So he was brought up almost as a country boy, though near enough to town to get the benefit of it, and far enough from the more exciting scenes of landscape nature to find them ever fresh, when summer after summer he revisited the river scenery of the West or the mountains of the North. For by a neat arrangement, and one fortunate for his education, the summer tours were continued yearly. Mr. John James Ruskin still travelled for the business, then greatly extending. "Strange," he writes on one occasion, "that Watson [his right-hand man] went this journey without getting one order, and everyone gives me an order directly." In return for these services to the firm, Mr. Telford, the capitalist partner, took the vacant chair at the office, and even lent his carriage for the journeys. There was room for two, so Mrs. Ruskin accompanied her husband, whose indifferent health gave her and his friends constant anxiety during long separations. And the boy could easily be packed in, sitting on his little portmanteau, and playing horses with his father's knees; the nurse riding on the dickey behind.

They started usually after the great family anniversary, the father's birthday, on May 10, and journeyed by easy stages through the South of England, working up the west to the north, and then home by the east-central route, zigzagging from one provincial town to another, calling at the great country seats, to leave no customer or possible customer unvisited; and in the intervals of business seeing all the sights of the places they passed through—colleges and churches, galleries and parks, ruins, castles, caves, lakes, and mountains—and seeing them all, not listlessly, but with keen interest, noting everything, inquiring for local information, looking up books of reference, setting down the results, as if they had been meaning to write a guide-book and gazetteer of Great Britain. *They*, I say, did all this, for as soon as the boy could write, he was only imitating his father in keeping his little journal of the tours, so that all he learned stayed by him, and the habit of descriptive writing was formed.

In 1823 they seem to have travelled only through the south and south-west; in 1824 they pushed north to the lakes, stayed awhile at Keswick, and while the father went about his business, the child was rambling with his nurse on Friar's Crag, among the steep rocks and gnarled roots, which suggested, even at that age, the feelings expressed in one of the notable passages in "Modern Painters." Thence they went on to Scotland, and revisited their relatives at Perth. In 1825 they took a more extended tour, and spent a few weeks in Paris, partly for the festivities at the coronation of Charles X., partly for business conference with Mr. Domecq, who had just been appointed wine-merchant to the King of Spain. Thence they went to Brussels and the field of Waterloo, of greater interest than the sights of Paris to six-year-old John, who often during his boyhood celebrated the battle, and the heroes of the battle, in verse.

Before he was quite three he used to climb into a chair and preach. There is nothing so uncommon in that. Of Robert Browning, his neighbour and seven-years-older contemporary, the same tale is told. But while the incident that marks the baby Browning is the aside, *à propos* of a whimpering sister, "Pew-opener, remove that child," the baby Ruskin is seen in his sermon: "People, be dood. If you are dood, Dod will love you; if you are not dood, Dod will not love you. People, be dood."

At the age of four he had begun to read and write, refusing to be taught in the orthodox way—this is so accurately characteristic—by syllabic spelling and copy-book pothooks. He preferred to find a method out for himself, and he found out how to read whole words at a time by the look of them, and to write in vertical characters like book-print, just as the latest improved theories of education suggest. His first letter may be quoted as illustrating his own account of his childhood, and as proving how entirely Scotch was the atmosphere in which he was brought up. The postmark gives the date March 15, 1823. Mrs. Ruskin premises that John was scribbling on a paper from which he proceeded to read what she writes down (I omit certain details about the whip):

"MY DEAR PAPA,

"I love you. I have got new things. Waterloo Bridge—Aunt Bridget brought me it. John and Aunt helped to put it up, but the pillars they did not put right, upside down. Instead of a book bring me a whip, coloured red and black . . . To-morrow is Sabbath. Tuesday I go to Croydon. I am going to take my boats and my ship to Croydon. I'll sail them on the pond near the burn which the bridge is over. I will be very glad to see my cousins. I was very happy when I saw Aunt come from Croydon. I love Mrs. Gray and I love Mr. Gray. I would like you to come home, and my kiss and my love."

[First autograph in straggling capitals]

"JOHN RUSKIN"

When once he could read, thenceforward his mother gave him regular morning lessons in Bible-reading and in reciting the Scotch paraphrases of the Psalms and other verse, which for his good memory was an easy task. He made rhymes before he could write them, of course.

At five he was a bookworm, and the books he read fixed him in certain grooves of thought, or, rather, say they were chosen as favourites from an especial interest in their subjects—an interest which arose from his character of mind, and displayed it. But with all this precocity, he was no milksop or weakling; he was a bright, active lad, full of fun and pranks, not without companions, though solitary when at home, and kept precisely, in the hope of guarding him from every danger. He was so little afraid of animals—a great test of a child's nerves—that about this time he must needs meddle with their fierce Newfoundland dog, Lion, which bit him in the mouth, and spoiled his looks. Another time he showed some address in extricating himself from the water-butt—a common child-trap. He did not fear ghosts or thunder; instead of that, his early-developed landscape feeling showed itself in dread of foxglove dells and dark pools of water, in coiling roots of trees—things that to the average English fancy have no significance whatever.

At seven he began to imitate the books he was reading, to write books himself. He had found out how to *print*, as children do; and it was his ambition to make real books, with title-pages and illustrations, not only books, indeed, but sets of volumes, a complete library of his whole works. But in a letter of March 4, 1829, his mother says to his father: "If you think of writing John, would you impress on him the propriety of not beginning too eagerly and becoming careless towards the end of his *works*, as he calls them? I think in a letter from you it would have great weight. He is never idle, and he is even uncommonly persevering for a child of his age; but he often spoils a good beginning by not taking the trouble to think, and concluding in a hurry."

The first of these sets was imitated in style from Miss Edgeworth; he called it, "Harry and Lucy Concluded; or, Early Lessons." Didactic he was from the beginning. It was to be in four volumes, uniform in red leather, with proper title, frontispiece, and "copper-plates," "printed and composed by a little boy, and also drawn." It was begun in 1826, and continued at intervals until 1829. It was all done laboriously in imitation of print, and, to complete the illusion, contained a page of errata. This great work was, of course, never completed, though he laboured through three volumes; but when he tired of it, he would turn his book upside down, and begin at the other end with other matters; so that the red books contain all sorts of notes on his minerals and travels, reports of sermons, and miscellaneous information, besides their professed contents; in this respect also being very like his later works.

There you have our author ready made, with his ever-fresh interest in everything, and all-attempting eagerness, out of which the first thing that crystallizes into any definite shape is the verse-writing.

CHAPTER III

PERFERVIDUM INGENIUM (1826-1830)

The first dated "poem" was written a month before little John Ruskin reached the age of seven. It is a tale of a mouse, in seven octosyllabic couplets, "The Needless Alarm," remarkable only for an unexpected correctness in rhyme, rhythm, and reason.

His early verse owes much to the summer tours, which were prolific in notes; everything was observed and turned into verse. The other inspiring source was his father—the household deity of both wife and child, whose chief delight was in his daily return from the city, and in his reading to them in the drawing-room at Herne Hill. John was packed into a recess, where he was out of the way and the draught; he was barricaded by a little table that held his own materials for amusement, and if he liked to listen to the reading, he had the chance of hearing good literature, the chance sometimes of hearing passages from Byron and Christopher North and Cervantes, rather beyond his comprehension, for his parents were not of the shockable sort: with all their religion and strict Scotch morality, they could laugh at a broad jest, as old-fashioned people could.

So he associated his father and his father's readings with the poetry of reflection, as he associated the regular summer round with the poetry of description. As every summer brought its crop of description, so against the New Year (for, being Scotch, they did not then keep our Christmas) and against his father's birthday in May he used always to prepare some little drama or story or "address" of a reflective nature, beginning with the verses on "Time," written for New Year's Day, 1827.

That year they were again at Perth, and on their way home some early morning frost suggested the not ungraceful verses on the icicles at Glenfarg. By a childish misconception, the little boy seems to have confused the real valley that interested him so with Scott's ideal Glendearg, and, partly for this reason, to have found a greater pleasure in "The Monastery," which he thereupon undertook to paraphrase in verse. There remain some hundreds of doggerel rhymes; but his affection for that particular novel survived the fatal facility of his octosyllabics, and reappears time after time in his later writings.

Next year, 1828, their tour was stopped at Plymouth by the painful news of the death of his aunt Jessie, to whom they were on their way. It was hardly a year since the bright little cousin, Jessie of Perth, had died of water on the brain. She had been John's especial pet and playfellow, clever, like him, and precocious; and her death must have come to his parents as a warning, if they needed it, to keep their own child's brain from over-pressure. It is evident that they did their best to "keep him back"; they did not send him to school for fear of the excitement of competitive study. His mother put him through the Latin grammar herself, using the old Adam's manual which his father had used at Edinburgh High School. Even this old grammar became a sort of sacred book to him; and when at last he went to school, and his English master threw the book back to him, saying, "that's a Scotch thing," the boy was shocked and affronted, as which of us would be at a criticism on *our* first instrument of torture? He remembered the incident all his life, and pilloried the want of tact with acerbity in his reminiscences.

They could keep him from school, but they did not keep him from study. The year 1828 saw the beginning of another great work, "Eudosia, a Poem on the Universe"; it was "printed" with even greater neatness and labour; but this, too, after being toiled at during the winter months, was dropped in the middle of its second "book." It was not idleness that made him break off such plans, but just the reverse—a too great activity of brain. His parents seem to have thought that there was no harm in this apparently quiet reading and writing. They were extremely energetic themselves, and hated idleness. They appear to have held a theory that their little boy was safe so long as he was not obviously excited; and to have thought that the proper way of giving children pocket-money was to let them earn it. So they used to pay him for his literary labours; "Homer" was one shilling a page; "Composition," one penny for twenty lines; "Mineralogy," one penny an article.

The death of his aunt Jessie left a large family of boys and one girl to the care of their widowed father, and the Ruskins felt it their duty to help. They fetched Mary Richardson away, and brought her up as a sister to their solitary son. She was not so beloved as Jessie had been, but a good girl and a nice girl, four years older than John, and able to be a companion to him in his lessons and travels. There was no sentimentality about his attachment to her, but a steady fraternal relationship, he, of course, being the little lord and master; but she was not without spirit, which enabled her to hold her own, and perseverance, which sometimes helped her to eclipse, for the moment, his brilliancy. They learnt together, wrote their journals together, and shared alike with the scrupulous fairness which Mrs. Ruskin's sensible nature felt called on to show. And so she remained his sister, and not quite his sister, until she married, and after a very short married life died.

Another accession to the family took place in the same year (1828); the Croydon aunt, too, had died, and left a dear dog, Dash, a brown and white spaniel, which at first refused to leave her coffin, but was coaxed away, and found a happy home at Herne Hill, and frequent celebration in his young master's verses. So the family was now complete—papa and mamma, Mary and John and Dash. One other figure must not be forgotten, Nurse Anne, who had come from the Edinburgh home, and remained always with them, John's nurse and then Mrs. Ruskin's attendant, as devoted and as censorious as any old-style Scotch servant in a story-book.

The year 1829 marked an advance in poetical composition. For his father's birthday he made a book more elaborate than any, sixteen pages in a red cover, with a title-page quite like print: "Battle of Waterloo | a play | in two acts | with other small | Poems dedicated to his father | by John Ruskin | 1829 Hernhill *(sic)* Dulwich."

To this are appended, among other pieces, fair copies of "Skiddaw," and "Derwentwater." A recast of these, touched up by some older hand, and printed in *The Spiritual Times* for February, 1830, may be called his first appearance in type.

An illness of his postponed their tour for 1829, until it was too late for more than a little journey in Kent. He has referred his earliest sketching to this occasion, but it seems likely that the drawings attributed to this year were done in 1831. He was, however, busy writing poetry. At Tunbridge, for example, he wrote that fragment "On Happiness" which catches so cleverly the tones of Young—a writer whose orthodox moralizing suited with the creed in which John Ruskin was brought up, alternating, be it remembered, with "Don Quixote."

Coming home, he began a new edition of his verses, on a more pretentious scale than the old red books, in a fine bound volume, exquisitely "printed," with the poems dated. This new energy seems to have been roused by the gift from his Croydon cousin Charles, a clerk in the publishing house of Smith, Elder, and Co., of their annual "Friendship's Offering." Mrs. Ruskin, in a letter of October 31, 1829, finds "the poetry very so-so"; but John evidently made the book his model.

He was now growing out of his mother's tutorship, and during this autumn he was put under the care of Dr. Andrews for his Latin. He relates the introduction in "Præterita," and, more circumstantially, in a letter of the time, to Mrs. Monro, the mother of his charming Mrs. Richard Gray, the indulgent neighbour who used to pamper the little gourmand with delicacies unknown in severe Mrs. Ruskin's dining-room. He says in the letter—this is at ten years old: "Well, papa, seeing how fond I was of the doctor, and knowing him to be an excellent Latin scholar, got him for me as a tutor, and every lesson I get I like him better and better, for he makes me laugh 'almost, if not quite'—to use one of his own expressions—the whole time. He is so funny, comparing Neptune's lifting up the wrecked ships of Æneas with his trident to my lifting up a potato with a fork, or taking a piece of bread out of a bowl of milk with a spoon! And as he is always saying [things] of that kind, or relating some droll anecdote, or explaining the part of Virgil (the book which I am in) very nicely, I am always delighted when Mondays, Wednesdays, and Fridays are come."

Dr. Andrews was no doubt a genial teacher, and had been a scholar of some distinction in his University of Glasgow; but Mrs. Ruskin thought him "flighty," as well she might, when, after six months' Greek, he proposed (in March, 1831) to begin Hebrew with John. It was a great misfortune for the young genius that he was not more sternly drilled at the outset, and he suffered for it through many a long year of struggles with deficient scholarship.

The Doctor had a large family and pretty daughters. One, who wrote verses in John's note-book, and sang "Tambourgi," Mrs. Orme, lived until 1892 in Bedford Park; the other lives in Coventry Patmore's "Angel in the House." When Ruskin, thirty years later, wrote of that doubtfully-received poem, that it was the "sweetest analysis we possess of quiet, modern, domestic feeling," few of his readers could have known all the grounds of his appreciation, or suspected the weight of meaning in the words.

CHAPTER IV

MOUNTAIN-WORSHIP (1830-1835)

Critics who are least disposed to give Ruskin credit for his artistic doctrines or economical theories unite in allowing that he taught his generation to look at Nature, and especially at the sublime in Nature—at storms and sunrises, and the forests and snows of the Alps. This mission of mountain-worship was the outcome of a passion beside which the other interests and occupations of his youth were only toys. He could take up his mineralogy and his moralizing and lay them down, but the love of mountain scenery was something beyond his control. We have seen him leave his heart in the Highlands at three years old; we have now to follow his passionate pilgrimages to Skiddaw and Snowdon, to the Jungfrau and Mont Blanc.

They had planned a great tour through the Lakes and the North two years before, but were stopped at Plymouth by the news of Mrs. Richardson's death. At last the plan was carried out. A prose diary was written alternately by John and Mary, one carrying it on when the other tired, with rather curious effect of unequally-yoked collaboration. We read how they "set off from London at seven o'clock on Tuesday morning, the 18th May," and thenceforward we are spared no detail: the furniture of the inns; the bills of fare; when they got out of the carriage and walked; how they lost their luggage; what they thought of colleges and chapels, music and May races at Oxford, of Shakespeare's tomb, and the pin-factory at Birmingham; we have a complete guide-book to Blenheim and Warwick Castle, to Haddon and Chatsworth, and the full itinerary of Derbyshire. "Matlock Bath," we read, "is a most delightful place"; but after an enthusiastic description of High Tor, John reacts into bathos with a minute description of wetting their shoes in a puddle. The cavern with a Bengal light was fairyland to him, and among the minerals he was quite at home.

Then they hurried north to Windermere. Once at Lowwood, the excitement thickens, with storms and rainbows, mountains and waterfalls, boats on the lake and coaching on the steep roads. This journey through Lakeland is described in the galloping anapæsts of the "Iteriad," which was simply the prose journal versified on his return, one of the few enterprises of the sort which were really completed.

To readers who know the country it is interesting as giving a detailed account in the days when this "nook of English ground" was "secure from rash assault." One learns that, even then, there were jarring sights at Bowness Bay and along Derwentwater shore, elements unkind and bills exorbitant. Coniston especially was dreary with rain, and its inn—the old Waterhead, now destroyed—extravagantly dear; "*but*," says John, with his eye for mineral specimens, "it contains several rich coppermines." An interesting touch is the hero-worship with which they went reverently to peep at Southey and Wordsworth in church; too humble to dream of an introduction, and too polite to besiege the poets in their homes, but independent enough to form their own opinions on the personality of the heroes. They did not like the look of Wordsworth at all; Southey they adored. The dominant note of the tour is, however, an ecstatic delight in the mountain scenery; on Skiddaw and Helvellyn all the gamut of admiration is lavished.

On returning home, John began Greek under Dr. Andrews, and was soon versifying Anacreontics in his notebooks. He began to read Byron for himself, with what result we shall see before long; but the most important new departure was the attempt to copy Cruikshank's etchings to Grimm's fairy tales, his real beginning at art. From this practice he learnt the value of the pure, clean line that expresses form. It is a good instance of the authority of these early years over Ruskin's whole life and teaching that in his "Elements of Drawing" he advised young artists to begin with Cruikshank, as he began, and that he wrote appreciatively both of the stories and the etchings so many decades afterwards in the preface to a reprint by J.C. Hotten.

His cousin-sister Mary had been sent to a day-school when Mrs. Ruskin's lessons were superseded by Dr. Andrews, and she had learnt enough drawing to attempt a view of the hotel at Matlock, a thing which John could not do. So, now that he too showed some power of neat draughtsmanship, it was felt that he ought to have her advantages. They got Mr. Runciman the drawing-master, chosen, it may be, as a relative of the well-known Edinburgh artist of the same name, to give him lessons, in the early part of 1831. His teaching was of the kind which preceded the Hardingesque: it aimed at a bold use of the soft pencil, with a certain roundness of composition and richness of texture, a conventional "right way" of drawing anything. This was hardly what John wanted; but, not to be beaten, he facsimiled the master's freehand in a sort of engraver's stipple, which his habitual neatness helped him to do in perfection. Runciman soon put a stop to that, and took pains with a pupil who took such pains with himself—taught him, at any rate, the principles of perspective, and remained his only drawing-master for several years.

A sample of John Ruskin's early lessons in drawing, described by him in letters to his father, may be not without interest. On February 20, 1832, he writes:

"... You saw the two models that were last sent, before you went away. Well, I took my paper, and I fixed my points, and I drew my perspective, and then, as Mr. Runciman told me, I began to invent a scene. You remember the cottage that we saw as we went to Rhaidyr Dhu (*sic*), near Maentwrog, where the old woman lived whose grandson went with us to the fall, so very silently? I thought my model resembled that; so I drew a tree—such a tree, such an enormous fellow—and I sketched the waterfall, with its dark rocks, and its luxuriant wood, and its high mountains; and then I examined one of Mary's pictures to see how the rocks were done, and another to see how the woods were done, and another to see how the mountains were done, and another to see how the cottages were done, and I patched them all together, and I made such a lovely scene—oh, I should get such a scold from Mr. Runciman (that is, if he ever scolded)!"

After the next lesson he wrote, February 27, 1832:

"You know the beautiful model drawing that I gave you an account of in my last. I showed it to Mr. Runciman. He contemplated it for a moment in silence, and then, turning, asked me if I had copied. I told him how I had patched it up; but he said that that was not copying, and although he was not satisfied with the picture, he said there was something in it that would make him totally change the method he had hitherto pursued with me. He then asked Mary for some gray paper, which was produced; then inquired if I had a colour-box; I produced the one you gave me, and he then told me he should begin with a few of the simplest colours, in order to teach me better the effects of light and shade. He should then proceed to teach me water-colour painting, but the latter only as a basis for oil; this last, however, to use his own words, all in due time . . . Oh, if I could paint well before we went to Dover! I should have such sea-pieces . . ."

In March 1834, Runciman was encouraging him in his oil-painting; but a year later he wrote to his father:

"I cannot bear to paint in oil, C. Fielding's tints alone for me! The other costs me double toil, And wants some fifty coats to be Splashed on each spot successively. Faugh, wie es stinckt! I can't bring out, With all, a picture fit to see. My bladders burst; my oils are out—And then, what's all the work about?"

After a few lessons he could rival Mary when they went for their summer excursion. He set to work at once at Sevenoaks to draw cottages; at Dover and Battle he attempted castles. It may be that these first sketches are of the pre-Runciman period; but the Ruskins made the round of Kent in 1831, and though the drawings are by no means in the master's style, they show some practice in using the pencil.

The journey was extended by the old route, conditioned by business as before, round the South Coast to the West of England, and then into Wales. There his powers of drawing failed him; moonlight on Snowdon was too vague a subject for the blacklead point but a hint of it could be conveyed in rhyme:

"Folding like an airy vest,
The very clouds had sunk to rest;
Light gilds the rugged mountain's breast,
Calmly as they lay below;
Every hill seemed topped with snow,
As the flowing tide of light
Broke the slumbers of the night."

Harlech Castle was too sublime for a sketch, but it was painted with the pen:

"So mighty, so majestic, and so lone;
And all thy music, now, the ocean's murmuring."

And the enthusiasm of mountain glory, a sort of ecstacy of uncontrollable passion, strives for articulate deliverance in the climbing song, "I love ye, ye eternal hills."

It was hard to come back to the daily round, the common task, especially when, in this autumn of 1831, to Dr. Andrews' Latin and Greek, the French grammar and Euclid were added, under Mr. Rowbotham. And the new tutor had no funny stories to tell; he was not so engaging a man as the "dear Doctor," and his memory was not sweet to his wayward pupil. But the parents had chosen for the work one who was favourably known by his manuals, and capable of interesting even a budding poet in the mathematics; for our author tells that at Oxford, and ever after, he knew his Euclid without the figures, and that he spent all his spare time in trying to trisect an angle. An old letter from Rowbotham informs Mr. J.J. Ruskin that an eminent mathematician had seen John's attempt, and had said that it was the cleverest he knew. In French, too, he progressed enough to be able to find his way alone in Paris two years later. And however the saucy boy may have satirized his tutor in the droll verses on "Bedtime," Mr. Rowbotham always remembered him with affection, and spoke of him with respect.

In spite of these tedious tutorships, he managed to scribble energetically all this winter, writing with amazing rapidity, as his mother notes: attempts at Waverley novels, which never got beyond the first chapter, imitations of "Childe Harold" and "Don Juan" and scraps in the style of everybody in turn. No wonder his mother sent him to bed at nine punctually, and kept him from school, in vain efforts to quiet his brain. The lack of companions was made up to him in the friendship of Richard Fall, son of a neighbour on "the Hill," a boy without affectation or morbidity of disposition whose complementary character suited him well. An affectionate comradeship sprang up between the two lads, and lasted, until in middle life they drifted apart, in no ill-will, but each going on his own course to his own destiny.

Some real advance was made this winter (1831-32) with his Shelleyan "Sonnet to a Cloud" and his imitations of Byron's "Hebrew Melodies," from which he learnt how to concentrate expression, and to use rich vowel-sounds and liquid consonants with rolling effect. A deeper and more serious turn of thought, that gradually usurped the place of the first boyish effervescence, has been traced by him to the influence of Byron, in whom, while others saw nothing more than wit and passion, Ruskin perceived an earnest mind and a sound judgment.

But the most sincere poem—if sincerity be marked by unstudied phrase and neglected rhyme—the most genuine "lyrical cry" of this period, is that song in which our boy-poet poured forth his longing for the "blue hills" he had loved as a baby, and for those Coniston crags over which, when he became old and sorely stricken, he was still to see the morning break. When he wrote these verses he was nearly fourteen, or just past his birthday. It had been eighteen months since he had been in Wales, and all the weary while he had seen no mountains; but in his regrets he goes back a year farther still, to fix upon the Lakeland hills, less majestic than Snowdon, but more endeared, and he describes his sensations on approaching the beloved objects in the very terms that Dante uses for his first sight of Beatrice:

"I weary for the fountain foaming,
    For shady holm and hill;
My mind is on the mountain roaming,
    My spirit's voice is still.

"The crags are lone on Coniston
    And Glaramara's dell;
And dreary on the mighty one,
    The cloud-enwreathed Sea-fell . . ."

"There is a thrill of strange delight
    That passes quivering o'er me,
When blue hills rise upon the sight,
    Like summer clouds before me."

Judge, then, of the delight with which he turned over the pages of a new book, given him this birthday by the kind Mr. Telford, in whose carriage he had first seen those blue hills—a book in which all his mountain ideals, and more, were caught and kept enshrined—visions still, and of mightier peaks and ampler valleys, romantically "tost" and sublimely "lost," as he had so often written in his favourite rhymes. In the vignettes to Rogers' "Italy," Turner had touched the chord for which John Ruskin had been feeling all these years. No wonder that he took Turner for his leader and master, and fondly tried to copy the wonderful "Alps at Daybreak" to begin with, and then to imitate this new-found magic art with his own subjects and finally to come boldly before the world in passionate defence of a man who had done such great things for him.

This mountain-worship was not inherited from his father, who never was enthusiastic about peaks and clouds and glaciers, though he was interested in all travelling in a general way. So that it was not Rogers' "Italy" that sent the family off to the Alps that summer; but, fortunately for John, his father's eye was caught by the romantic architecture of Prout's "Sketches in Flanders and Germany," when it came out in April, 1853, and his mother proposed to make both of them happy in a tour on the Continent. The business-round was abandoned, but they could see Mr. Domecq on their way back through Paris, and not wholly lose the time.

They waited to keep papa's birthday on May 10, and early next morning drove off—father and mother, John and Mary, Nurse Anne, and the courier Salvador. They crossed to Calais, and posted, as people did in the old times, slowly from point to point; starting betimes, halting at the roadside inns, where John tried to snatch a sketch, reaching their destination early enough to investigate the cathedral or the citadel, monuments of antiquity or achievements of modern civilisation, with impartial eagerness; and before bedtime John would write up his journal and work up his sketches just as if he were at home.

So they went through Flanders and Germany, following Prout's lead by the castles of the Rhine; but at last, at Schaffhausen one Sunday evening—"suddenly—behold—beyond!"—they had seen the Alps. Thenceforward Turner was their guide as they crossed the Splügen, sailed the Italian lakes, wondered at Milan Cathedral, and the Mediterranean at Genoa, and then roamed through the Oberland and back to Chamouni. All this while a great plan shaped itself in the boy's head, no less than to make a Rogers' "Italy" for himself, just as he tried to make a "Harry and Lucy" or a "Dictionary of Minerals." On every place they passed he would write verses and prose sketches, to give respectively the romance and the reality or ridicule; for he saw the comic side of it all, keenly; and he would illustrate the series with Turneresque vignettes, drawn with the finest crowquill pen, to imitate the delicate engravings. By this he learnt more drawing in two or three years than most amateur students do in seven. For the first year he had the "Watchtower of Andernach" and the "Jungfrau from Interlaken" to show, with others of similar style, and thenceforward alternated between Turner and Prout, until he settled into something different from either.

But Turner and Prout were not the only artists he knew; at Paris he found his way into the Louvre, and got leave from the directors, though he was under the age required, to copy. The picture he chose was a Rembrandt.

Between this foreign tour and the next, his amusement was to draw these vignettes, and to write the poems suggested by the scenes he had visited. He had outgrown the evening lessons with Dr. Andrews, and as he was fifteen, it was time to think more seriously of preparing him for Oxford, where his name was put down at Christ Church. His father hoped he would go into the Church, and eventually turn out a combination of a Byron and a bishop—something like Dean Milman, only better. For this, college was a necessary preliminary; for college, some little schooling. So they picked the best day-school in the neighbourhood, that of the Rev. Thomas Dale (afterwards Dean of Rochester), in Grove Lane, Peckham. John Ruskin worked there rather less than two years. In 1835 he was taken from school in consequence of an attack of pleurisy, and lost the rest of that year from regular studies.

More interesting to him than school was the British Museum collection of minerals, where he worked occasionally with his Jamieson's Dictionary. By this time he had a fair student's collection of his own, and he increased it by picking up specimens at Matlock, or Clifton, or in the Alps, wherever he went, for he was not short of pocket-money. He took the greatest pains over his catalogues, and wrote elaborate accounts of the various minerals in a shorthand he invented out of Greek letters and crystal forms.

Grafted on this mineralogy, and stimulated by the Swiss tour, was a new interest in physical geology, which his father so far approved as to give him Saussure's "Voyages dans les Alpes" for his birthday in 1834. In this book he found the complement of Turner's vignettes, something like a key to the "reason why" of all the wonderful forms and marvellous mountain-architecture of the Alps. He soon wrote a short essay on the subject, and had the pleasure of seeing it in print, in Loudon's *Magazine of Natural History* for March, 1834, along with another bit of his writing, asking for information on the cause of the colour of the Rhine-water.

He had already some acquaintance with J.C. Loudon, F.L.S., H.S., etc., and he was on the staff of that versatile editor not long afterwards, and took a lion's share of the writing in the *Magazine of Architecture*. Meanwhile he had been introduced to another editor, and to the publishers with whom he did business for many a year to come. The acquaintance was made in a curious, accidental manner. His cousin Charles Richardson, clerk to Smith, Elder, and Co., had the opportunity of mentioning the young poet's name to Thomas Pringle, editor of the "Friendship's Offering" which John had admired and imitated. Mr. Pringle came out to Herne Hill, and was hospitably entertained as a brother Scot, as not only an editor, but a poet himself—not *only* a poet, but a man of respectability and piety, who had been a missionary in South Africa. In return for this hospitality he gave a good report of John's verses, and, after getting him to re-write two of the best passages in the last tour, carried them off for insertion in his forthcoming number. He did more: he carried John to see the actual Samuel Rogers, whose verses had been adorned by the great Turner's vignettes.

After the pleurisy of April, 1835, his parents took him abroad again, and he made great preparations to use the opportunity to the utmost. He would study geology in the field, and took Saussure in his trunk he would note meteorology: he made a cyanometer—a scale of blue to measure the depth of tone, the colour whether of Rhine-water or of Alpine skies. He would sketch. By now he had abandoned the desire to make MS. albums, after seeing himself in print, and so chose rather to imitate the imitable, and to follow Prout, this time with careful outlines on the spot, than to idealize his notes in mimic Turnerism. He kept a prose journal, chiefly of geology and scenery, as well as a versified description, written in a metre imitated from "Don Juan," but more elaborate, and somewhat of a *tour de force* in rhyming. But that poetical journal was dropped after he had carried it through France, across the Jura, and to Chamouni. The drawing crowded it out, and for the first time he found himself as ready with his pencil as he had been with his pen.

His route is marked by the drawings of that year, from Chamouni to the St. Bernard and Aosta, back to the Oberland and up the St. Gothard; then back again to Lucerne and round by the Stelvio to Venice and Verona, and finally through the Tyrol and Germany homewards. The ascent of the St. Bernard was told in a dramatic sketch of great humour and power of characterization, and a letter to Richard Fall records the night on the Rigi, when he saw the splendid sequence of storm, sunset, moonlight, and daybreak, which forms the subject of one of the most impressive passages of "Modern Painters."

It happened that Pringle had a plate of Salzburg which he wanted to print in order to make up the volume of "Friendship's Offering" for the next Christmas. He seems to have asked John Ruskin to furnish a copy of verses for the picture, and at Salzburg, accordingly, a bit of rhymed description was written and re-written, and sent home to the editor. Early in December the Ruskins returned, and at Christmas there came to Herne Hill a gorgeous gilt morocco volume, "To John Ruskin, from the Publishers." On opening it there were his "Andernach" and "St. Goar," and his "Salzburg" opposite a beautifully-engraved plate, all hills, towers, boats, and figures moving picturesquely under the sunset, in Turner's manner more or less, "Engraved by E. Goodall from a drawing by W. Purser." It was almost like being Mr. Rogers himself.

CHAPTER V

THE GERM OF "MODERN PAINTERS" (1836)

He was now close upon seventeen, and it was time to think seriously of his future. His father went to Oxford early in the year to consult the authorities about matriculation. Meantime they sent him to Mr. Dale for some private lessons, and for the lectures on logic, English literature, and translation, which were given on Tuesdays, Thursdays, and Fridays at King's College, London. John enjoyed his new circumstances heartily. From voluminous letters, it is evident that he was in high spirits and in pleasant company. He was a thorough boy among boys—Matson, Willoughby, Tom Dale and the rest. He joined in their pranks, and contributed to their amusement with his ready good-humour and unflagging drollery.

Mr. Dale told him there was plenty of time before October, and no fear about his passing, if he worked hard. He found the work easy, except epigram-writing, which he thought "excessively stupid and laborious," but helped himself out, when scholarship failed, with native wit. Some of his exercises remain, not very brilliant Latinity; some he saucily evaded, thus:

"Subject: *Non sapere maximum est malum.*

"Non sapere est grave; sed, cum dura epigrammata oportet
    Scribere, tunc sentis præcipue esse malum."

In Switzerland and Italy, during the autumn of 1835, he had made a great many drawings, carefully outlined in pencil or pen on gray paper, and sparsely touched with body colour, in direct imitation of the Prout lithographs. Prout's original coloured sketches he had seen, no doubt, in the exhibition; but he does not seem to have thought of imitating them, for his work in this kind was all intended to be for illustration and not for framing. The "Italy" vignettes likewise, with all their inspiration, suggested to him only pen-etching; he was hardly conscious that somewhere there existed the tiny, coloured pictures that Turner had made for the engraver. Still, now that he could draw really well, his father, who painted in water-colours himself, complied with the demand for better teaching than Runciman's, went straight to the President of the Old Water-Colour Society, and engaged him for the usual course of half a dozen lessons at a guinea a piece. Copley Fielding could draw mountains as nobody else but Turner could, in water-colour; he had enough mystery and poetry to interest the younger Ruskin, and enough resemblance to ordinary views of Nature to please the elder. So they both went to Newman Street to his painting-room, and John worked through the course, and a few extra lessons, but, after all, found Fielding's art was not what he wanted. Some sketches exist, showing the influence of the spongy style; but his characteristic way of work remained for him to devise for himself.

At the Royal Academy Exhibition of 1836 Turner showed the first striking examples of his later style in "Juliet and her Nurse," "Mercury and Argus," and "Rome from Mount Aventine." The strange idealism, the unusualness, the mystery, of these pictures, united with evidence of intense significance and subtle observation, appealed to young Ruskin as it appealed to few other spectators. Public opinion regretted this change in its old favourite, the draughtsman of Oxford colleges, the painter of shipwrecks and castles. And *Blackwood's Magazine*, which the Ruskins, as Edinburgh people and admirers of Christopher North, read with respect, spoke about Turner, in a review of the picture-season, with that freedom of speech which Scotch reviewers claim as a heritage from the days of Jeffrey. Young Ruskin at once dashed off an answer.

The critic had found that Turner was "out of nature"; Ruskin tried to show that the pictures were full of facts, but treated with poetical license. The critic pronounced Turner's colour bad, his execution neglected, and his chiaroscuro childish; in answer to which Ruskin explained that Turner's reasoned system was to represent light and shade by the contrast of warm and cold colour, rather than by the opposition of white and black which other painters used. He denied that his execution was other than his aims necessitated, and maintained that the critic had no right to force his cut-and-dried academic rules of composition on a great genius; at the same time admitting that:

> "The faults of Turner are numerous, and perhaps more egregious than those of any other great existing artist; but if he has greater faults, he has also greater beauties.
>
> "His imagination is Shakespearian in its mightiness. Had the scene of 'Juliet and her Nurse' risen up before the mind of a poet, and been described in 'words that burn,' it had been the admiration of the world... Many-coloured mists are floating above the distant city, but such mists as you might imagine to be ethereal spirits, souls of the mighty dead breathed out of the tombs of Italy into the blue of her bright heaven, and wandering in vague and infinite glory around the earth that they have loved. Instinct with the beauty of uncertain light, they move and mingle among the pale stars, and rise up into the brightness of the illimitable heaven, whose soft, sad blue eye gazes down into the deep waters of the sea for ever—that sea whose motionless and silent transparency is beaming with phosphor light, that emanates out of its sapphire serenity like bright dreams breathed into the spirit of a deep sleep. And the spires of the glorious city rise indistinctly bright into those living mists, like pyramids of pale fire from some vast altar;

and amidst the glory of the dream there is, as it were, the voice of a multitude entering by the eye, arising from the stillness of the city like the summer wind passing over the leaves of the forest, when a murmur is heard amidst their multitudes.

"This, O Maga, is the picture which your critic has pronounced to be 'like models of different parts of Venice, streaked blue and white, and thrown into a flour-tub'!"

Before sending his reply to the editor of *Blackwood*, as had been intended, it was thought only right that Turner should be consulted. The MS. was enclosed to his address in London, with a courteous note from Mr. John James Ruskin, asking his permission to publish. Turner replied, expressing the scorn he felt for anonymous attacks, and jestingly hinting that the art-critics of the old Scotch school found their "meal-tub" in danger from his "flour-tub"; but "he never moved in such matters," so he sent on the MS. to Mr. Munro of Novar, who had bought the picture.

Ten days or so after this episode John Ruskin was matriculated at Oxford (October 18, 1836). He told the story of his first appearance as a gownsman in one of his gossiping letters in verse:

"A night, a day past o'er—the time drew near—
The morning came—I felt a little queer;
Came to the push; paid some tremendous fees;
Past; and was capped and gowned with marvellous ease.
Then went to the Vice-Chancellor to swear
Not to wear boots, nor cut or comb my hair
Fantastically—to shun all such sins
As playing marbles or frequenting inns;
Always to walk with breeches black or brown on;
When I go out, to put my cap and gown on;
With other regulations of the sort, meant
For the just ordering of my comportment.

Which done, in less time than I can rehearse it, I
Found myself member of the University!"

In pursuance of his plan for getting the best of everything, his father had chosen the best college, as far as he knew, that in which social and scholastic advantages were believed to be found in pre-eminent combination, and he had chosen what was thought to be the best position in the college; so that it was as gentleman-commoner of Christ Church that John Ruskin made his entrance into the academic world.

After matriculation, the Ruskins made a fortnight's tour to Southampton and the coast, and returned to Herne Hill. John went back to King's College, and in December was examined in the subjects of his lectures. He wrote to his father on Christmas Eve about the examination in English literature:

> "The students were numerous, and so were the questions; the room was hot, the papers long, the pens bad, the ink pale, and the interrogations difficult. It lasted only three hours. I wrote answers in very magnificent style to all the questions except three or four; gave in my paper and heard no more of the matter: *sic transeunt bore-ia mundi.*"

He went on to mention his "very longitudinal essay," which, since no other essays are reported in his letters about King's College, must be the paper published in 1893, in answer to the question. "Does the perusal of works of fiction act favourably or unfavourably on the moral character?"

At his farewell interview with Mr. Dale he was asked, as he writes to his father, what books he had read, and replied with a pretty long list, including Quintilian and Grotius. Mr. Dale inquired what "light books" he was taking to Oxford: "Saussure, Humboldt, and other works on natural philosophy and geology," he answered. "Then he asked if I ever read any of the modern fashionable novels; on this point I thought he began to look positive, so I gave him a negative, with the exception of Bulwer's, and now and then a laughable one of the Theodore Hook's or Captain Marryat's." And so, with much excellent advice about exercise and sleep, and the way to win the Newdigate, he parted from Mr. Dale.

This Christmas was marked by his first introduction to the scientific world. Mr. Charlesworth, of the British Museum, invited him to a meeting of the Geological Society (January 4, 1837), with promise of introduction to Buckland and Lyell. The meeting, as he wrote, was "amusing and interesting, and very comfortable for frosty weather, as Mr. Murchison got warm and Mr. Greenau *(sic)* witty. The warmth, however, got the better of the wit."

The Meteorological Society also claimed his attention, and in this month he contributed a paper which "Richard [Fall] says will frighten them out of their meteorological wits, containing six close-written folio pages, and having, at its conclusion, a sting in its tail, the very agreeable announcement that it only commences the subject."

CHAPTER VI

A LOVE-STORY (1836-1839)

Early in 1836 the quiet of Herne Hill was fluttered by a long-promised, long-postponed visit. Mr. Domecq at last brought his four younger daughters to make the acquaintance of their English friends. The eldest sister had lately been married to a Count Maison, heir to a peer of France; for Mr. Domecq, thanks in great measure to his partner's energy and talents, was prosperous and wealthy, and moved in the enchanted circles of Parisian society.

To a romantic schoolboy in a London suburb the apparition was dazzling. Any of the sisters would have charmed him, but the eldest of the four, Adèle Clotilde, bewitched him at once with her graceful figure and that oval face which was so admired in those times. She was fair, too—another recommendation. He was on the brink of seventeen, at the ripe moment, and he fell passionately in love with her. She was only fifteen, and did not understand this adoration, unspoken and unexpressed except by intensified shyness; for he was a very shy boy in the drawing-room, though brimming over with life and fun among his schoolfellows. His mother's ideals of education did not include French gallantry; he felt at a loss before these Paris-bred, Paris-dressed young ladies, and encumbered by the very strength of his new-found passion.

And yet he possessed advantages, if he had known how to use them. He was tall and active, light and lithe in gesture, not a clumsy hobbledehoy. He had the face that caught the eye, in Rome a few years later, of Keats'

Severn, no mean judge, surely, of faces and poet's faces. He was undeniably clever; he knew all about minerals and mountains; he was quite an artist, and a printed poet. But these things weigh little with a girl of fifteen who wants to be amused; and so she only laughed at John.

He tried to amuse her, but he tried too seriously. He wrote a story to read her, "Leoni, a Legend of Italy," for of course she understood enough English to be read to, no doubt to be wooed in, seeing her mother was English. The story was of brigands and true lovers, the thing that was popular in the romantic period. The costumery and mannerisms of the little romance are out of date now, and seem ridiculous, though Mr. Pringle and the public were pleased with it then, when it was printed in "Friendship's Offering." But the girl of fifteen only laughed the more.

When they left, he had no interest in his tour-book; even the mountains, for the time, had lost their power, and all his plans of great works were dropped for a new style of verse—the love-poems of 1836.

His father, from whom he kept nothing, approved the verses, and did not disapprove his views on the young lady. Indeed, it is quite plain, from the correspondence of the two gentlemen, that Mr. Domecq intended his friend and partner's son to become his own son-in-law. He had the greatest respect for the Ruskins, and every reason for desiring to link their fortunes still more closely with those of his own family. But to Mrs. Ruskin, with her religious feelings, it was intolerable, unbelievable, that the son whom she had brought up in the nurture and admonition of the strictest Protestantism should fix his heart on an alien in race and creed. The wonder is that their relations were not more strained; there are few young men who would have kept unbroken allegiance to a mother whose sympathy failed them at such a crisis.

As the year went on his passion seemed to grow in the absence of the beloved object. His only plan of winning her was to win his spurs first; but as what? Clearly his forte, it seemed, was in writing. If he could be a successful writer of romances, of songs, of plays, surely she would not refuse him. And so he began another romantic story, "Velasquez, the

Novice," opening with the Monks of St. Bernard, among whom had been, so the tale ran, a mysterious member, whose papers, when discovered, made him out the hero of adventures in Venice. He began a play, which was to be another great work, "Marcolini." He had no playwright's eye for situations, but the conversation is animated, and the characters finely drawn, with more discrimination than one would expect from so young an author.

This work was interrupted at the end of Act III. by pressing calls to other studies. But it was not that he had forgotten Adèle. From time to time he wrote verses to her or about her; and as in 1838 she was sent to school with her sisters at Newhall, near Chelmsford, to "finish" her in English, in that August he saw her again. She had lost some of her first girlish prettiness, but that made no difference. And when the Domecqs came to Herne Hill at Christmas, he was as deeply in love as ever. But she still laughed at him.

His father was fond of her, liked all the sisters, and thought much of them as girls of fine character, but he liked Adèle best. He seems to have been fond of his partner, too, worked very hard in his interests, and behaved very well to his heirs afterwards through many years of responsible and difficult management of their business. And at this time, when he went down to the convent school in Essex, as he often did, he must have had opportunities for seeing how hopeless the case was. Mr. Domecq recognised it, too, but thought, it seems (they manage these things differently in France), that any of his daughters would do as well, and early in 1839 entertained an offer from Baron Duquesne, a rich and handsome young Frenchman. They kept this from John, fearing he would break down at the news, so fully did they recognise the importance of the affair. They even threw other girls in his way. It was not difficult, for by now he had made some mark in magazine literature, and was a steady, rising young man, with considerable expectations. But he could not think of any other girl.

In February or March, 1839, Mr. Domecq died. The Maisons came to England, and the marriage was proposed. Adèle stayed at Chelmsford until September, when he wrote the long poem of "Farewell," dated the eve of their last meeting and parting.

At twenty young men do not die of love; but I find that a fortnight after writing this he was taken seriously ill. During the winter of 1839-40 the negotiations for the marriage in Paris went on. It took place in March. They kept the news from him as long as they could, for he was in the schools next Easter term, and Mr. Brown (his college tutor) had seemed to hope he would get a First, so his mother wrote to her husband. In May he was pronounced consumptive, and had to give up Oxford, and all hope of the distinction for which he had laboured, and with that any plans that might have been entertained for his distinction in the Church. And his parents' letters of the period put it beyond a doubt that this first great calamity of his life was the direct consequence of that unfortunate matchmaking.

For nearly two years he was dragged about from place to place, and from doctor to doctor, in search of health. Thanks partly to wise treatment, more to new faces, and most to a plucky determination to employ himself usefully with his pen and his pencil, he gradually freed himself from the spell, and fifty years afterwards could look back upon the story as a pretty comedy of his youthful days.

CHAPTER VII

"KATA PHUSIN" (1837-1838)

Devoted as she was to her husband, Mrs. Ruskin felt bound to watch over her son at Oxford. It was his health she was always anxious about; doctoring was her forte. He had suffered from pleurisy; caught cold easily; was feared to be weak in the lungs; and nobody but his mother understood him. So taking Mary Richardson, she went up with him (January, 1837), and settled in lodgings at Adams' in the High. Her plan was to make no intrusion on his college life, but to require him to report himself every day to her. She would not be dull; she could drive about and see the country, and to that end took her own carriage to Oxford, the "fly" which had been set up two years before. John had been rather sarcastic about its genteel appearance. "No one," he said, "would sit down to draw the form of it." However, she and Mary drove to Oxford, and reckoned that it would only mean fifteen months' absence from home altogether, great part of which deserted papa would spend in travelling.

John went into residence in Peckwater. At first he spent every evening with his mother and went to bed, as Mr. Dale had told him, at ten. After a few days Professor Powell asked him to a musical evening; he excused himself, and explained why. The Professor asked to be introduced, whereupon says his mother, "I shall return the call, but make no visiting acquaintances."

The "early-to-bed" plan was also impracticable. It was not long before somebody came hammering at his "oak" just as he was getting to sleep, and next morning he told his mother that he really ought to have a glass of wine to give. So she sent him a couple of bottles over, and that very night "Mr. Liddell and Mr. Gaisford" (junior) turned up. "John was glad he had wine to offer, but they would not take any; they had come to see sketches. John says Mr. Liddell looked at them with the eye of a judge and the delight of an artist, and swore they were the best sketches he had ever seen. John accused him of quizzing, but he answered that he really thought them excellent." John said that it was the scenes which made the pictures; Mr. Liddell knew better, and spread the fame of them over the college. Next morning "Lord Emlyn and Lord Ward called to look at the sketches," and when the undergraduates had dropped in one after another, the Dean himself, even the terrible Gaisford, sent for the portfolio, and returned it with august approval.

Liddell, afterwards Dean of Christ Church; Newton, afterwards Sir Charles, of the British Museum; Acland, afterwards Sir Henry, the Professor of Medicine, thus became John Ruskin's friends: the first disputing with him on the burning question of Raphael's art, but from the outset an admirer of "Modern Painters," and always an advocate of its author; the second differing from him on the claims of Greek archæology, but nevertheless a close acquaintance through many long years; and the third for half a century the best of friends and counsellors.

The dons of his college he was less likely to attract. Dr. Buckland, the famous geologist, and still more famous lecturer and talker, took notice of him and employed him in drawing diagrams for lectures. The Rev. Walter Brown, his college tutor, afterwards Rector of Wendlebury, won his goodwill and remained his friend. His private tutor, the Rev. Osborne Gordon, was always regarded with affectionate respect. But the rest seem to have looked upon him as a somewhat desultory and erratic young genius, who might or might not turn out well. For their immediate purpose, the Schools, and Church or State preferment, he seemed hardly the fittest man.

The gentlemen-commoners of Christ Church were a puzzle to Mrs. Ruskin; noblemen of sporting tastes, who rode and betted and drank, and got their impositions written "by men attached to the University for the purpose, at 1s.6d. to 2s.6d., so you have only to reckon how much you will give to avoid chapel." And yet they were very nice fellows. If they began by riding on John's back round the quad, they did not give him the cold shoulder—quite the reverse. He was asked everywhere to wine; he beat them all at chess; and they invaded him at all hours. "It does little good sporting *his* oak," wrote his mother, describing how Lord Desart and Grimston climbed in through his window while he was hard at work. "They say midshipmen and Oxonians have more lives than a cat, and they have need of them if they run such risks."

Once, but once only, he was guilty, as an innocent freshman, of a breach of the laws of his order. He wrote too good an essay. He tells his father:

"OXFORD, *February*, 1837.

"Yesterday (Saturday) forenoon the Sub-dean sent for me, took me up into his study, sat down with me, and read over my essay, pointing out a few verbal alterations and suggesting improvements; I, of course, expressed myself highly grateful for his condescension. Going out, I met Strangeways. 'So you're going to read out to-day, Ruskin. *Do* go it at a good rate, my good fellow. Why do you write such devilish good ones?' Went a little farther and met March. 'Mind you stand on the top of the desk, Ruskin; gentlemen-commoners never stand on the steps.' I asked him whether it would look more dignified to stand head or heels uppermost. He advised heels. Then met Desart. 'We must have a grand supper after this, Ruskin; gentlemen-commoners always have a flare-up after reading their themes.' I told him I supposed he wanted to 'pison my rum-and-water.'"

And though they teased him unmercifully, he seems to have given as good as he got. At a big wine after the event, they asked him whether his essay cost 2s.6d. or 5s. What he answered is not reported; but they proceeded to make a bonfire in Peckwater, while he judiciously escaped to bed.

So for a home-bred boy, thrown into rather difficult surroundings, his first appearance at Christ Church was distinctly a success. "Collections" in March, 1837, went off creditably for him. Hussey, Kynaston and the Dean said he had taken great pains with his work, and had been a pattern of regularity; and he ended his first term very well pleased with his college and with himself.

In his second term he had the honour of being elected to the Christ Church Club, a very small and very exclusive society of the best men in the college: "Simeon, Acland, and Mr. Denison proposed him; Lord Carew and Broadhurst supported." And he had the opportunity of meeting men of mark, as the following letter recounts. He writes on April 22, 1837:

"My Dearest Father,

"When I returned from hall yesterday—where a servitor read, or pretended to read, and Decanus growled at him, 'Speak out!'— I found a note on my table from Dr. Buckland, requesting the pleasure of my company to dinner, at six, to meet two celebrated geologists, Lord Cole and Sir Philip Egerton. I immediately sent a note of thanks and acceptance, dressed, and was there a minute after the last stroke of Tom. Alone for five minutes in Dr. B.'s drawing-room, who soon afterwards came in with Lord Cole, introduced me, and said that as we were both geologists he did not hesitate to leave us together while he did what he certainly very much required—brushed up a little. Lord Cole and I were talking about some fossils newly arrived from India. He remarked in the course of conversation that his friend Dr. B.'s room was cleaner and in better order than he remembered ever to have seen it. There was not a chair fit to sit upon, all covered with dust, broken alabaster candlesticks, withered flower-leaves, frogs cut out of serpentine, broken models of fallen temples, torn papers, old manuscripts, stuffed reptiles, deal boxes, brown paper, wool, tow and cotton, and a considerable variety of other articles. In came Mrs. Buckland, then Sir Philip Egerton and his brother, whom I had seen at Dr. B.'s lecture, though he is not an undergraduate. I was talking to him till dinner-time. While we were sitting over our wine after dinner, in came Dr. Daubeny, one of the most celebrated geologists of the day—a curious little animal, looking through its spectacles with an air very *distinguée*—and Mr. Darwin, whom I had heard read a paper at the Geological Society. He and I got together, and talked all the evening."

The long vacation of 1837 was passed in a tour through the North, during which his advanced knowledge of art was shown in a series of admirable drawings. Their subjects are chiefly architectural, though a few mountain drawings are found in his sketch-book for that summer.

The interest in ancient and picturesque buildings was no new thing, and it seems to have been the branch of art-study which was chiefly encouraged by his father. During this tour among Cumberland cottages and Yorkshire abbeys, a plan was formed for a series of papers on architecture, perhaps in answer to an invitation from his friend Mr. Loudon, who had started an architectural magazine. In the summer he began to write "The Poetry of Architecture; or, The Architecture of the Nations of Europe considered in its Association with Natural Scenery and National Character," and the papers were worked off month by month from Oxford, or wherever he might be, only terminating with the termination of the magazine in January, 1839. They parade a good deal of classical learning and travelled experience; readers of the magazine took their author for some dilettante Don at Oxford. The editor did not wish the illusion to be dispelled, so John Ruskin had to choose a *nom de plume*. He called himself "Kata Phusin" ("according to nature"), for he had begun to read some Aristotle. No phrase would have better expressed his point of view, that of commonsense extended by experience, and confirmed by the appeal to matters of fact, rather than to any authority, or tradition, or committee of taste, or abstract principles.

While these papers were in process of publication "Kata Phusin" plunged into his first controversy, as an opponent of "Parsey's Convergence of Perpendiculars," according to which vertical lines should have a vanishing point, even though they are assumed to be parallel to the plane of the picture.

During this controversy, and just before the summer tour of 1838 to Scotland, John Ruskin was introduced to Miss Charlotte Withers, a young lady who was as fond of music as he was of drawing. They discussed their favourite studies with eagerness, and, to settle the matter, he wrote a long essay on "The Comparative Advantages of the Studies of Music and Painting," in which he set painting as a means of recreation and of education far above music.

Already at nineteen, then, we see him a writer on art, not full-fledged, but attracting some notice. Towards the end of 1838 a question arose as to the best site for the proposed Scott memorial at Edinburgh, and a writer in the *Architectural Magazine* quoted "Kata Phusin" as the authority in such matters, saying that it was obvious, after those papers of his, that design and site should be simultaneously considered; on which the editor "begs the favour of 'Kata Phusin' to let our readers have his opinion on the subject, which we certainly think of considerable importance."

So he discussed the question of monuments in general, and of this one in particular, in a long paper, coming to no very decided opinion, but preferring, on the whole, a statue group with a colossal Scott on a rough pedestal, to be placed on Salisbury Crags, "where the range gets low and broken towards the north at about the height of St. Anthony's Chapel."

His paper did not influence the Edinburgh Committee, but it was not without effect, as the following extract shows.

"BAYSWATER, *November* 30, 1838.

"DEAR SIR,—... Your son is certainly the greatest natural genius that ever it has been my fortune to become acquainted with, and I cannot but feel proud to think that at some future period, when both you and I are under the turf, it will be stated in the literary history of your son's life that the first article of his which was published was in *London's Magazine of Natural History*.—Yours very sincerely,

"J.C. LOUDON"

CHAPTER VIII

SIR ROGER NEWDIGATE'S PRIZE (1837-1839)

Of all the prizes which Oxford could bestow, the Newdigate used to be the most popular. Its fortunate winner was an admitted poet in an age when poetry was read, and he appeared in his glory at Commemoration, speaking what the ladies could understand and admire. The honour was attainable without skill in Greek particles or in logarithms; and yet it had a real value to an intending preacher, for the successful reciter might be felt to have put his foot on the pulpit stairs. John Ruskin was definitely meant for the Church, and he went to Oxford in the avowed hope of getting the Newdigate, if nothing else. His last talk with Mr. Dale was chiefly about ways and means to this end; and before he went up he had begun "The Gipsies" for March, 1837.

The prize was won that year by Arthur Penrhyn Stanley, afterwards Dean of Westminster. Our candidate and his old schoolfellow, Henry Dart, of Exeter College, set to work on the next subject, "The Exile of St. Helena," and after the long vacation read their work to each other, accepting the hints and corrections of a friendly rivalry.

Meantime his old nurse Anne (it is trivial, but a touch of nature), being at Oxford in attendance on the ladies, and keen, as she always was, for Master John's success, heard from the keeper of the Reading-room of criticisms on his published verses. She brought the news to his delighted mother. "He was pleased," she writes, "but says that he forms his own estimate of his poems, and reviews don't alter it; but 'How my father will be delighted! How he will crow!'" Which historiette repeated itself many a time in the family annals.

In Lent term, 1838, he was hard at work on the new poem. He wrote:

> "I must give an immense time every day to the Newdigate, which I must have, if study will get it. I have much to revise. You find many faults, but there are hundreds which have escaped your notice, and many lines must go out altogether which you and I should wish to stay in. The thing must be remodelled, and I must finish it while it has a freshness on it, otherwise it will not be written well. The old lines are hackneyed in my ears, even as a very soft Orleans plum, which your Jewess has wiped and re-wiped with the corner of her apron, till its polish is perfect, and its temperature elevated."

In this March he got through his "Smalls."

> "Nice thing to get over; quite a joke, as everybody says when they've got through with the feathers on. It's a kind of emancipation from freshness—a thing unpleasant in an egg, but dignified in an Oxonian—very. Lowe very kind; Kynaston ditto—nice fellows—urbane. How they *do* frighten people! There was one man all but crying with mere fear. Kynaston had to coax him like a child. Poor fellow! he had some reason to be afraid; did his logic shockingly. People always take up logic because they fancy it doesn't require a good memory, and there is nothing half so productive of pluck; they *never* know it. I was very cool when I got into it; found the degree of excitement agreeable; nibbled the end of my pen and grinned at Kynaston over the table as if *I* had been going to pluck *him*. They always smile when they mean pluck."

The Newdigate for 1838, for all his care and pains, was won by Dart. He was, at any rate, beaten by a friend, and with a poem which his own honourable sympathy and assistance had helped to perfect.

Another trifling incident lets us get a glimpse of the family life of our young poet. The Queen's coronation in June, 1838, was a great event to all the world, and Mr. Ruskin was anxious for his son to see it. Much correspondence ensued between the parents, arranging everything for him, as they always did—which of the available tickets should be accepted, and whether he could stand the fatigue of the long waiting, and so forth. Mrs. Ruskin did not like the notion of her boy sitting perched on rickety scaffolding at dizzy altitudes in the Abbey. Mr. Ruskin, evidently determined to carry his point, went to Westminster, bribed the carpenters, climbed the structure, and reported all safe to stand a century, "though," said he, "the gold and scarlet of the decorations appeared very paltry compared with the Wengern Alp." But he could not find No. 447, and wrote to the Heralds' Office to know if it was a place from which a good view could be got. Blue-mantle replied that it was a very good place, and Lord Brownlow had just taken tickets for his sons close by. Then there was the great question of dress. He went to Owen's and ordered a white satin waistcoat with gold sprigs, and a high dress-coat with bright buttons, and asked his wife to see about white gloves at Oxford—a Court white neckcloth or a black satin would do.

Picture, then, the young Ruskin in those dressy days. A portrait was once sent to Brantwood of a dandy in a green coat of wonderful cut, supposed to represent him in his youth, but suggesting Lord Lytton's "Pelham" rather than the homespun-suited seer of Coniston. "Did you ever wear a coat like that?" I asked. "I'm not so sure that I didn't," said he.

After that, they went to Scotland and the North of England for the summer, and more fine sketches were made, some of which hang now in his drawing-room, and compare not unfavourably with the Prouts beside them. In firmness of line and fulness of insight they are masterly, and mark a rapid progress, all the more astonishing when it is recollected how little time could have been spared for practice. The subjects are chiefly architectural—castles and churches and Gothic details—and one is not surprised to find him soon concerned with the Oxford Society for Promoting the Study of Gothic Architecture. "They were all reverends," says a letter of the time, "and wanted somebody to rouse them."

Science, too, progressed this year. We read of geological excursions to Shotover with Lord Carew and Lord Kildare—one carrying the hammer and another the umbrella—and actual discoveries of saurian remains; and many a merry meeting at Dr. Buckland's, in which, at intervals of scientific talk, John romped with the youngsters of the family. After a while the Dean took the opportunity of a walk through Oxford to the Clarendon to warn him not to spend too much time on science. It did not pay in the Schools nor in the Church, and he had too many irons in the fire.

Drawing, and science, and the prose essays mentioned in the last chapter, and poetry, all these were his by-play. Of the poetry, the Newdigate was but a little part. In "Friendship's Offering" this autumn he published "Remembrance," one of many poems to Adèle, "Christ Church," and the "Scythian Grave." In this last he gave free rein to the morbid imaginations to which his unhappy *affaire de coeur* and the mental excitement of the period predisposed him. Harrison, his literary Mentor, approved these poems, and inserted them in "Friendship's Offering," along with love-songs and other exercises in verse. One had a great success and was freely copied—the sincerest flattery—and the preface to the annual for 1840 publicly thanked the "gifted writer" for his "valuable aid."

At the beginning of 1839 he went into new rooms vacated by Mr. Meux, and set to work finally on "Salsette and Elephanta." He ransacked all sources of information, coached himself in Eastern scenery and mythology, threw in the Aristotelian ingredients of terror and pity, and wound up with an appeal to the orthodoxy of the examiners, of whom Keble was the chief, by prophesying the prompt extermination of Brahminism under the teaching of the missionaries.

This third try won the prize. Keble sent for him, to make the usual emendations before the great work could be given to the world with the seal of Oxford upon it. John Ruskin seems to have been somewhat refractory under Keble's hands, though he would let his fellow-students, or his father, or Harrison, work their will on his MSS. or proofs; being always easier to lead than to drive. Somehow he came to terms with the Professor, and then the Dean, taking an unexpected interest, was at pains to see that his printed copy was flawless, and to coach him for the recitation of it at the great day in the Sheldonian (June 12, 1839).

And now that friends and strangers, publishers in London and professors in Oxford, concurred in their applause, it surely seemed that he had found his vocation, and was well on the high-road to fame as a poet.

CHAPTER IX

THE BROKEN CHAIN (1840-1841)

That 8th of February, 1840, when John Ruskin came of age, it seemed as though all the gifts of fortune had been poured into his lap. What his father's wealth and influence could do for him had been supplemented by a personal charm, which found him friends among the best men of the best ranks. What his mother's care had done in fortifying his health and forming his character, native energy had turned to advantage. He had won a reputation already much wider and more appreciable, as an artist and student of science, and as a writer of prose and verse, than undergraduates are entitled to expect; and, for crowning mercy, his head was not turned. He was reading extremely hard—"in" for his degree examination next Easter term. His college tutor hoped he would get a First. From that it was an easy step to Holy Orders, and with his opportunities preferment was certain.

On his twenty-first birthday, his father, who had sympathized with his admiration for Turner enough to buy two pictures—the "Richmond Bridge" and the "Gosport"—for their Herne Hill drawing-room, now gave him a picture all to himself for his new rooms in St. Aldate's—the "Winchelsea," and settled on him a handsome allowance of pocket-money. The first use he made of his wealth was to buy another Turner. In the Easter vacation he met Mr. Griffith, the dealer, at the private view of the old Water-colour Society, and hearing that the "Harlech Castle" was for sale, he bought it there and then, with the characteristic disregard for money which has always made the vendors of pictures and books and minerals find him extremely pleasant to deal with. But as his love-affair had shown his mother how little he had taken to heart her chiefest care for him, so this first business transaction was a painful awakening to his father, the canny Scotch merchant, who had heaped up riches hoping that his son would gather them.

This "Harlech Castle" transaction, however, was not altogether unlucky. It brought him an introduction to the painter, whom he met when he was next in town, at Mr. Griffith's house. He knew well enough the popular idea of Turner as a morose and niggardly, inexplicable man. As he had seen faults in Turner's painting, so he was ready to acknowledge the faults in his character. But while the rest of the world, with a very few exceptions, dwelt upon the faults, Ruskin had penetration to discern the virtues which they hid. Few passages in his autobiography are more striking than the transcript from his journal of the same evening, recording his first impression:

"'I found in him a somewhat eccentric, keen-mannered, matter-of-fact, English-minded—gentleman; good-natured evidently, bad-tempered evidently, hating humbug of all sorts, shrewd, perhaps a little selfish, highly intellectual, the powers of the mind not brought out with any delight in their manifestation, or intention of display, but flashing out occasionally in a word or a look.' Pretty close that," he adds later, "and full, to be set down at the first glimpse, and set down the same evening."

Turner was not a man to make an intimate of, all at once; the acquaintanceship continued, and it ripened into as close a confidence as the eccentric painter's habits of life permitted. He seems to have been more at home with the father than with the son; but even when the young man took to writing books about him, he did not, as Carlyle is reported to have done in a parallel case, show his exponent to the door.

The occasion of John Ruskin's coming to town this time was not a pleasant one—nothing less than the complete breakdown of his health. It is true that he was working very hard during this spring; but hard reading does not of itself kill people, only when it is combined with real and prolonged mental distress, acting upon a sensitive temperament. The case was thought serious; reading was stopped, and the patient was ordered abroad for the winter.

For that summer there was no hurry to be gone; rest was more needed than change, at first. Late in September the same family-party crossed the sea to Calais. How different a voyage for them all from the merry departures of bygone Maytides! Which way should they turn? Not to Paris, for *there* was the cause of all these ills; so they went straight southwards, through Normandy to the Loire, and saw the châteaux and churches from Orleans to Tours, famous for their Renaissance architecture and for the romance of their chivalric history. Amboise especially made a strong impression upon the languid and unwilling invalid. It stirred him up to write, in easy verse, the tale of love and death that his own situation too readily suggested. In "The Broken Chain" he indulged his gloomy fancy, turning, as it was sure to do, into a morbid nightmare of mysterious horror, not without reminiscence of Coleridge's "Christabel." But through it all he preserved, so to speak, his dramatic incognito; his own disappointment and his own anticipated death were the motives of the tale, but treated in such a manner as not to betray his secret, nor even to wound the feelings of the lady who now was beyond appeal from an honourable lover—taking his punishment like a man.

This poem lasted him, for private writing, all through that journey—a fit emblem of the broken life which it records. A healthier source of distraction was his drawing, in which he had received a fresh impetus from the exhibition of David Roberts' sketches in the East. More delicate than Prout's work, entering into the detail of architectural form more thoroughly, and yet suggesting chiaroscuro with broad washes of quiet tone and touches of light, cleverly introduced—"that marvellous *pop* of light across the foreground," Harding said of the picture of the Great Pyramid—these drawings were a mean between the limited manner of Prout and the inimitable fulness of Turner Ruskin took up the fine pencil and the broad brush, and, with that blessed habit of industry which has helped so many a one through times of trial, made sketch after sketch on the half-imperial board, finished just so far as his strength and time allowed, as they passed from the Loire to the mountains of Auvergne; and to the valley of the Rhone, and thence slowly round the Riviera to Pisa and Florence and Rome.

He was not in a mood to sympathize readily with the enthusiasms of other people. They expected him to be delighted with the scenery, the buildings, the picture-galleries of Italy, and to forget himself in admiration. He did admire Michelangelo; and he was interested in the back-streets and slums of the cities. Something piquant was needed to arouse him; the mild ecstasies of common connoisseurship hardly appeal to a young man between life and death. He met the friends to whom he had brought introductions—Mr. Joseph Severn, who had been Keats' companion, and was afterwards to be the genial Consul at Rome, and the two Messrs. Richmond, then studying art in the regular professional way; one of them to become a celebrated portrait-painter, and the father of men of mark. But his views on art were not theirs; he was already too independent and outspoken in praise of his own heroes, and too sick in mind and body to be patient and to learn.

They had not been a month in Rome before he took the fever. As soon as he was recovered, they went still farther South, and loitered for a couple of months in the neighbourhood of Naples, visiting the various scenes of interest—Sorrento, Amalfi, Salerno. The adventures of this journey are partly told in letters to Mr. Dale, and in the "Letters addressed to a College Friend."

On the way to Naples he had noted and sketched the winter scene at La Riccia, which he afterwards used for a glowing passage in "Modern Painters"; and he had ventured into a village of brigands to draw such a castle as he had once imagined in his "Leoni." From Naples he wrote an account of a landslip near Giagnano, and sent it home to the Ashmolean Society. He seemed better; they turned homewards, when suddenly he was seized with all the old symptoms worse than ever. After another month at Rome, they travelled slowly northwards from town to town; spent ten days of May at Venice, and passed through Milan and Turin, and over the Mont Cenis to Geneva.

At last he was among the mountains again—the Alps that he loved. It was not only that the air of the Alps braced him, but the spirit of mountain-worship stirred him as nothing else could. At last he seemed himself, after more than a year of intense depression; and he records that one day, in church at Geneva, he resolved to *do* something, to *be* something useful. That he could make such a resolve was a sign of returning health; but if, as I find, he had just been reading Carlyle's lately-published lectures on "Heroes," though he did not then accept Carlyle's conclusions nor admire his style, might he not, in spite of his criticism, have been spurred the more into energy by that enthusiastic gospel of action?

They travelled home by Basle and Laon; but London in August, and the premature attempt to be energetic, brought on a recurrence of the symptoms of consumption, as it was called. He wished to try the mountain-cure again, and set out with his friend Richard Fall for a tour in Wales. But his father recalled him to Leamington to try iron and dieting under Dr. Jephson, who, if he was called a quack, was a sensible one, and successful in subduing for several years to come the more serious phases of the disease. The patient was not cured; he suffered from time to time from his chest, and still more from a weakness of the spine, which during all the period of his early manhood gave him trouble, and finished by bending his tall and lithe figure into something that, were it not for his face, would be deformity. In 1847 he was again at Leamington under Jephson, in consequence of a relapse into the consumptive symptoms, after which we hear no more of it. He outgrew the tendency, as so many do. But nevertheless the alarm had been justifiable, and the malady had left traces which, in one way and another, haunted him ever after; for one of the worst effects of illness is to be marked down as an invalid.

At Leamington, then, in September, 1841, he was finding a new life under the doctor's dieting, and new aims in life, which were eventually to resolder for a while the broken chain. Among the Scotch friends of the Ruskins there was a family at Perth whose daughter came to visit at Herne Hill—the Effie Gray whom afterwards he married. She challenged the melancholy John, engrossed in his drawing and geology, to write a fairytale, as the least likely task for him to fulfil. Upon which he produced, at a couple of sittings, "The King of the Golden River," a pretty medley of Grimm's grotesque and Dickens' kindliness and the true Ruskinian ecstasy of the Alps.

CHAPTER X

THE GRADUATE OF OXFORD (1841-1842)

Ready for work again, and in reasonable health of mind and body, John Ruskin sat down in his little study at Herne Hill in November, 1841, with his private tutor, Osborne Gordon. There was eighteen months' leeway to make up, and the dates of ancient history, the details of schematized Aristotelianism, soon slip out of mind when one is sketching in Italy. But he was more serious now about his work, and aware of his deficiencies. To be useful in the world, is it not necessary first to understand all possible Greek constructions? So said the voice of Oxford; but our undergraduate was saved, both now and afterwards, from this vain ambition. "I think it would hardly be worth your while," said Gordon.

He could not now go in for honours, for the lost year had superannuated him. So in April he went up for a pass. In those times, when a pass-man showed unusual powers, they could give him an honorary class; not a high class, because the range of the examination was less than in the honour-school. This candidate wrote a poor Latin prose, it seems; but his divinity, philosophy, and mathematics were so good that they gave him the best they could—an honorary double fourth—upon which he took his B.A. degree, and could describe himself as "A Graduate of Oxford."

The continued weakness of his health kept him from taking steps to enter the Church; and his real interest in art was not crowded out even by the last studies for his examination. While he was working with Gordon, in the autumn of 1841, he was also taking lessons from J.D. Harding; and the famous study of ivy, his first naturalistic sketching, to which we must revert, must have been done a week or two before going up for his examination.

The lessons from Harding were a useful counter-stroke to the excessive and exaggerated Turnerism in which he had been indulging through his illness. The drawings of Amboise, the coast of Genoa, and the Glacier des Bois, though published later, were made before he had exchanged fancy for fact; and they bear, on the face of them, the obvious marks of an unhealthy state of mind. Harding, whose robust common-sense and breezy mannerism endeared him to the British amateur of his generation, was just the man to correct any morbid tendency. He had religious views in sympathy with his pupil, and he soon inoculated Ruskin with his contempt for the minor Dutch school—those bituminous landscapes, so unlike the sparkling freshness that Harding's own water-colour illustrated, and those vulgar tavern scenes, painted, he declared, by sots who disgraced art alike in their works and in their lives.

Until this epoch, John Ruskin had found much that interested him in the Dutch and Flemish painters of the seventeenth century. He had classed them all together as the school of which Rubens, Vandyck and Rembrandt were the chief masters, and those as names to rank with Raphael and Michelangelo and Velasquez. He was a humorist, not without boyish delight in a good Sam-Wellerism, and so could be amused with the "drolls," until Harding appealed to his religion and morality against them. He was a chiaroscurist, and not naturally offended by their violent light and shade, until George Richmond showed him the more excellent way in colour, the glow of Venice, first hinting it at Rome in 1840, and then proving it in London in the spring of 1842 from Samuel Rogers' treasures, of which the chief (now in the National Gallery) was the "Christ appearing to the Magdalen."

Much as the author of "Modern Painters" owed to these friends and teachers, and to the advantages of his varied training, he would never have written his great work without a further inspiration. Harding's especial forte was his method of drawing trees. He looked at Nature with an eye which, for his period, was singularly fresh and unprejudiced; he had a strong feeling for truth of structure as well as for picturesque effect, and he taught his pupils to observe as well as to draw. But in his own practice he rested too much on *having observed*; formed a style, and copied himself if he did not copy the old masters; Hence he held to rules of composition and conscious graces of arrangement; and while he taught naturalism in study, he followed it up with teaching artifice in practice.

Turner, who was not a drawing-master, lay under no necessity to formulate his principles and stick to them. On the contrary, his style developed like a kaleidoscope. He had been in Switzerland and on the Rhine in 1841, "painting his impressions," making water-colour notes from memory of effects that had struck him. From one of these, "Splügen," he had made a finished picture, and now wished to get commissions for more of the same class. Ruskin was greatly interested in this series, because they were not landscapes of the ordinary type, scenes from Nature squeezed into the mould of recognised artistic composition, nor, on the other hand, mere photographic transcripts; but dreams, as it were, of the mountains and sunsets, in which Turner's wealth of detail was suggested, and his knowledge of form expressed, together with the unity which comes of the faithful record of a single impression.

The lesson was soon enforced upon Ruskin's mind by example. One day, while taking his student's constitutional, he noticed a tree-stem with ivy upon it, which seemed not ungraceful, and invited a sketch. As he drew he fell into the spirit of its natural arrangement, and soon perceived how much finer it was as a piece of design than any conventional rearrangement would be. Harding had tried to show him how to generalize foliage; but in this example he saw that not generalization was needed to get its beauty, but truth.

At Fontainebleau soon after, in much the same circumstances, a study of an aspen-tree, idly begun, but carried out with interest and patience, confirmed the principle. At Geneva, once more in the church where he had formed such resolutions the year before, the desire came over him with renewed force; now not only to be definitely employed, but to be employed in the service of a definite mission, which was, in art, exactly what Carlyle had preached in every other sphere of life in that book of "Heroes": the gospel of sincerity.

The design took shape. At Chamouni he studied plants and rocks and clouds, not as an artist to make pictures out of them, nor as a scientist to class them and analyze them; but to learn their aspects and enter into the spirit of their growth and structure. And though on his way home through Switzerland and down the Rhine he made a few drawings in his old style for admiring friends, they were the last of the kind that he attempted. Thenceforward his path was marked out; he had found a new vocation. He was not to be a poet—that was too definitely bound up with the past which he wanted to forget, and with conventionalities which he wished to shake off; not to be an artist, strugging with the rest to please a public which he felt himself called upon to teach; not a man of science, for his botany and geology were to be the means, and not the ends, of his teaching; but the mission was laid upon him to tell the world that Art, no less than other spheres of life, had its Heroes; that the mainspring of their energy was Sincerity, and the burden of their utterance, Truth.

BOOK II

THE ART CRITIC

(1842-1860)

CHAPTER I

"TURNER AND THE ANCIENTS"
(1842-1844)

The neighbour, or the Oxonian friend, who climbed the steps of the Herne Hill house and called upon Mrs. Ruskin, in the autumn and winter of 1842, would learn that Mr. John was hard at work in his own study overhead. Those were its windows, on the second-floor, looking out upon the front-garden; the big dormer-window above was his bedroom, from which he had his grand view of lowland, and far horizon, and unconfined sky, comparatively clear of London smoke. In the study itself, screened from the road by russet foliage and thick evergreens, great things were going on. But Mr. John could be interrupted, would come running lightly downstairs, with both hands out to greet the visitor; would show the pictures, eagerly demonstrating the beauties of the last new Turners, "Ehrenbreitstein" and "Lucerne," just acquired, and anticipating the sunset glories and mountain gloom of the "Goldau" and "Dazio Grande," which the great artist was "realizing" for him from sketches he had chosen at Queen Anne Street. He was very busy—but never too busy to see his friends—writing a book. And, the visitor gone, he would run up to his room and his writing.

In the afternoon his careful mother would turn him out for a tramp round the Norwood lanes; he might look in at the Poussins and Claudes of the Dulwich Gallery, or, for a longer excursion, go over to Mr. Windus, and his roomful of Turner drawings, or sit to George Richmond for the portrait at full length with desk and portfolio, and Mont Blanc in the background. Dinner over, another hour or two's writing, and early to bed, after finishing his chapter with a flourish of eloquence, to be read next morning at breakfast to father and mother and Mary. The vivid descriptions of scenes yet fresh in their memory, or of pictures they treasured, the "thoughts" as they used to be called, allusions to sincere beliefs and cherished hopes, never failed to win the praise that pleased the young writer most, in happy tears of unrestrained emotion. These old-fashioned folk had not learnt the trick of *nil admirari*. Quite honestly they would say, with the German musician, "When I hear good music, then must I always weep."

We can look into the little study and see what this writing was that went on so busily and steadily. It was the long-meditated defence of Turner, provoked by *Blackwood's Magazine* six years before, encouraged by Carlyle's "Heroes," and necessitated by the silence, on this topic, of the more enlightened leaders of thought in an age of connoisseurship and cant.

And as the winter ran out, he was ending his work, happy in the applause of his little domestic circle, and conscious that he was preaching the crusade of Sincerity, the cause of justice for the greatest landscape artist of any age, and justice, at the hands of a heedless public, for the glorious works of the supreme Artist of the universe. Let our young painters, he concluded, go humbly to Nature, "rejecting nothing, selecting nothing, and scorning nothing," in spite of Academic theorists, and in time we should have a school of landscape worthy of the inspiration they would find.

There was his book; the title of it, "Turner and the Ancients." Before publishing, to get more experienced criticism than that of the breakfast-table, he submitted it to his friend, W.H. Harrison. The title, it seemed, was not explicit enough, and after debate they substituted "Modern Painters: their Superiority in the Art of Landscape Painting to all the Ancient Masters proved by Examples of the True, the Beautiful, and the

Intellectual, from the Works of Modern Artists, especially from those of J.M.W. Turner, Esq., R.A." And as the severe tone of many remarks was felt to be hardly supported by the age and standing of so young an author, he was content to sign himself "A Graduate of Oxford." The book was spoken of, but no part of the copy shown, to John Murray, who said he would prefer something about German art. It found immediate acceptance with Messrs. Smith and Elder. Young Ruskin had been doing business for seven years past with that firm; he was well known to them as one of the most "rising" youths of the time, and their own literary editor, Mr. Harrison, was his private Mentor, who revised his proofs and inserted the punctuation, which he usually indicated only by dashes. His dealings with the publishers were generally conducted through his father, who made very fair terms for him, as things went then.

In May, 1843, "Modern Painters," vol. i., was published, and it was soon the talk of the art-world. It was meant to be audacious, and naturally created a storm. The free criticisms of public favourites made an impression, not because they were put into strong language, for the tone of the press was stronger then than it is now, as a whole, but because they were backed up by illustration and argument. It was evident that the author knew something of his subject, even if he were all wrong in his conclusions. He could not be neglected, though he might be protested against, decried, controverted. Artists especially, who do not usually see their works as others see them, and are not accustomed to think of themselves and their school as mere dots and spangles in a perspective of history, could not be entirely content to be classed as Turner's satellites. And while the book contained something that promised to suit every kind of reader everyone found something to shock him. Critics were scandalized at the depreciation of Claude; the religious were outraged at the comparison of Turner, in a passage omitted from later editions, to the Angel of the Sun in the Apocalypse.

But the descriptive passages were such as had never appeared before in prose; and the obvious usefulness of the analyses of natural form and effect made many an artist read on, while he shook his head. Some readily owned their obligation to the new teacher. Holland, for one, wrote to Harrison that he meant to paint the better for the snubbing he had got. Of such as reviewed the book adversely in *Blackwood* and the *Athenæum*, not one undertook to refute it seriously. They merely attacked a detail here and there, which the author discussed in two or three replies, with a patience that showed how confident he was in his position.

He had the good word of some of the best judges of literature. "Modern Painters" lay on Rogers' table; and Tennyson, who a few years before had beaten young Ruskin out of the field of poetry, was so taken with it that he wrote to his publisher to borrow it for him, "as he longed very much to see it," but could not afford to buy it. Sir Henry Taylor wrote to Aubrey de Vere, the poet, begging him to read:

> "A book which seems to me to be far more deeply founded in its criticism of art than any other that I have met with . . . written with great power and eloquence, and a spirit of the most diligent investigation . . . I am told that the author's name is Ruskin, and that he was considered at college as an odd sort of man who would never do anything."

A second edition appeared within 12 months. When the secret of the "Oxford Graduate" leaked out, as it did very soon, through the proud father, Mr. John was lionized. During the winter of 1843 he met celebrities at fashionable dinner-tables; and now that his parents were established in their grander house on Denmark Hill,[1] they could duly return the hospitalities of the great world.

It was one very satisfactory result of the success that the father was more or less converted to Turnerism, and lined his walls with Turner drawings, which became the great attraction of the house, far outshining its seven acres of garden and orchard and shrubbery, and the ampler air of cultured ease. For a gift to his son he bought "The Slave Ship," one of

Turner's latest and most disputed works; and he was all eagerness to see the next volume in preparation.

It was intended to carry on the discussion of "Truth," with further illustrations of mountain-form, trees and skies. And so in May, 1844, they all went away again, that the artist-author might prepare drawings for his plates. He was going to begin with the geology and botany of Chamouni, and work through the Alps, eastward.

At Chamouni they had the good fortune to meet with Joseph Coutet, a superannuated guide, whom they engaged to accompany the eager but inexperienced mountaineer. Coutet was one of those men of natural ability and kindliness whose friendship is worth more than much intercourse with worldly celebrities, and for many years afterwards Ruskin had the advantage of his care—of something more than mere attendance. At any rate, under such guidance, he could climb where he pleased, free from the feeling that people at home were anxious about him.

He was not unadventurous in his scramblings, but with no ambition to get to the top of everything. He wanted to observe the aspects of mountain-form; and his careful outlines, slightly coloured, as his manner then was, and never aiming at picturesque treatment, record the structure of the rocks and the state of the snow with more than photographic accuracy. A photograph often confuses the eye with unnecessary detail; these drawings seized the leading lines, the important features, the interesting points. For example, in his Matterhorn (a drawing of 1849), as Whymper remarks in "Scrambles among the Alps," there are particulars noted which the mere sketcher neglects, but the climber finds out, on closer intercourse, to be the essential facts of the mountain's anatomy. All this is not picture-making, but it is a valuable contribution and preliminary to criticism.

From Chamouni this year they went to Simplon, and met J.D. Forbes, the geologist, whose "viscous theory" of glaciers Ruskin adopted and defended with warmth later on, and to the Bell' Alp, long before it had been made a place of popular resort by Professor

Tyndall's notice. The "Panorama of the Simplon from the Bell' Alp" is to be found in the St. George's (Ruskin) Museum at Sheffield, as a record of his draughtsmanship in this period. Thence to Zermatt with Osborne Gordon; Zermatt, too, unknown to the fashionable tourist, and innocent of hotel luxuries. It is curious that, at first sight, he did not care for the Matterhorn. It was entirely unlike his ideal of mountains. It was not at all like Cumberland. But in a very few years he had come to love the Alps for their own sake, and we find him regretting at Ambleside the colour and light of Switzerland, the mountain glory which our humbler scenery cannot match. And yet he came back to it for a home, not ill-content.

After another visit to Chamouni, he crossed France to Paris, where something awaited him that upset all his plans, and turned his energies into an unexpected channel.

NOTE:

1 To which they removed in October, 1842.

CHAPTER II

CHRISTIAN ART (1845-1847)

At Paris, on the way heme in 1844, he had spent some days in studying Titian and Bellini and Perugino. They were not new to him; but now that he was an art-critic, it behoved him to improve his acquaintance with the old masters. "To admire the works of Pietro Perugino" was one thing; but to understand them was another, a thing which was hardly attempted by "the Landscape Artists of England" to whom the author of "Modern Painters" had so far dedicated his services. He had been extolling modernism, and depreciating "the Ancients" because they could not draw rocks and clouds and trees; and he was fresh from his scientific sketching in the happy hunting-ground of the modern world. A few days in the Louvre made him the devotee of ancient art, and taught him to lay aside his geology for history.

In one way the development was easy. The patient attempt to copy mountain-form had made him sensitive to harmony of line; and in the great composers of Florence and Venice he found a quality of abstract design which tallied with his experience of what was beautiful in Nature. Aiguilles and glaciers, drawn as he drew them, and the figure-subjects of severe Italian draughtsmen, are beautiful by the same laws of composition, however different the associations they suggest.

But *he* had been learning these laws of beauty from Turner and from the Alps; how did the ancients come by them? This could be found only in a thorough study of their lives and times, to begin with, to which he devoted his winter, with Rio and Lord Lindsay and Mrs. Jameson for his authorities. He found that his foes, Caspar Poussin and Canaletto, and the Dutch landscapists, were not the real old masters; that there had been a great age of art before the era of Vandyck and Rubens—even before Michelangelo and Raphael; and that, towards setting up as a critic of the present, he must understand the past out of which it had grown. So he determined to go to Florence and Venice, and to study the religious painters at first hand.

Mountain-study and Turner were not to be dropped. For example, to explain the obvious and notorious licences which Turner took with topography, it was necessary to see in what these licences consisted. Of the later Swiss drawings, one of the wildest and most impressive was the "St. Gothard"; Ruskin wanted to find Turner's point of view, and to see what alterations he had made. He told Turner so, and the artist, who knew that his picture had been realized from a very slight sketch, was naturally rather opposed to this test, as being, from his point of view, merely a waste of time and trouble. He tried to persuade the Ruskins that the Swiss Sonderbund war, then going on, made travelling unsafe, and so forth. But in vain. Mr. John was allowed to go, for the first time alone, without his parents, taking only a servant, and meeting the trustworthy Coutet at Geneva.

With seven months at his own disposal, he did a vast amount of work, especially in drawing. The studies of mountain-form and Italian design, in the year before, had given him a greater interest in the "Liber Studiorum," Turner's early book of Essays in Composition. He found there that use of the pure line, about which he has since said so much, together with a thoughtfully devised scheme of light-and-shade in mezzotint, devoted to the treatment of landscape in the same spirit as that in which the Italian masters treated figure-subjects in their pen-and-bistre studies. And just as he had imitated the Rogers vignettes in his boyhood, now in his youth he tried to emulate the fine abstract flow and searching expressiveness of the etched line, and the studied breadth of shade, by using the quill-pen with washes. At first he kept pretty closely to monochrome. His object was form, and his special talent was for draughtsmanship rather than for colour. But it was this winter's study of the "Liber Studiorum" that started him on his own characteristic course; and while we have no pen-and-wash work of his before 1845 (except a few experiments after Prout), we find him now using the pen continually during the "Modern Painters" period.

On reaching the Lake of Geneva he wrote, or sketched, one of his best-known pieces of verse, "Mont Blanc Revisited," and a few other poems followed, the last of the long series which had once been his chief interest and aim in life. With this lonely journey there came new and deeper feelings; with his increased literary power, fresh resources of diction; and he was never so near being a poet as when he gave up writing verse. Too condensed to be easily understood, too solemn in their movement to be trippingly read, the lines on "The Arve at Cluse," on "Mont Blanc," and "The Glacier," should not be passed over as merely rhetorical. And the reflections on the loungers at Conflans ("Why Stand ye here all the Day Idle?") are full of the spirit in which he was gradually approaching the great problems of his life, to pass through art into the earnest study of human conduct and its final cause.

He was still deeply religious—more deeply so than before, and found the echo of his own thoughts in George Herbert, with whom he "communed in spirit" while he travelled through the Alps. But the forms of outward religion were losing their hold over him in proportion as his inward religion became more real and intense. It was only a few days after writing these lines that he "broke the Sabbath" for the first time in his life, by climbing a hill after church. That was the first shot fired in a war, in one of the strangest and saddest wars between conscience and reason that biography records; strange because the opposing forces were so nearly matched, and sad because the struggle lasted until their field of battle was desolated before either won a victory.

Later on we have to tell how he dwelt in Doubting Castle, and how he escaped. But the pilgrim had not yet met Giant Despair; and his progress was very pleasant in that spring of 1845, the year of fine weather, as he drove round the Riviera, and the cities of Tuscany opened out their treasures to him. There was Lucca, with San Frediano and the glories of Romanesque architecture; Fra Bartolommeo's picture of the Madonna with the Magdalen and St. Catherine of Siena, his initiation into the significance of early religious painting: and, taking hold of his imagination, in her marble sleep, more powerfully than any flesh and blood, the dead lady of St. Martin's Church, Ilaria di Caretto. There was Pisa, with the Campo Santo and the jewel shrine of Sta. Maria della Spina, then undestroyed; the excitement of street sketching among a sympathetic crowd of fraternizing Italians; the Abbé Rosini, Professor of Fine Arts, whom he made friends with, endured as lecturer, and persuaded into scaffold-building in the Campo Santo for study of the frescoes. And there was Florence, with Giotto's campanile and Santa Maria Novella, where the young Protestant frequented monasteries, made hay with monks, sketched with his new-found friends Rudolf Durheim of Berne and Dieudonné the French purist; and spent long days copying Angelico and annotating Ghirlandajo, fevered with the sun of Italy at its strongest, and with the rapture of discovery, "which turns the unaccustomed head like Chianti wine."

Coutet got him away, at last, to the Alps; worn out and in despondent reaction after all this excitement. He spent a month at Macugnaga, reading Shakespeare and trying to draw boulders; drifting gradually back into strength enough to attack the next piece of work, the study of Turner sites on the St. Gothard, where he made the drawings afterwards engraved in "Modern Painters." In August, J.D. Harding was going to Venice, and arranged for a meeting at Baveno, on the Lago Maggiore. Gossip had credited him with a share in "Modern Painters"; now the tables were turned, and Griffith, the picture-dealer, wanted to know if it was true that John Ruskin had helped Harding with his new book, just out. They sketched together, Ruskin perhaps emulating his friend's slap-dash style in the "Sunset" reproduced in his "Poems," and illustrating his own in the "Water-mill." And so they drove together to Verona and thence to Venice.

At Venice they stayed in Danieli's Hotel, on the Riva dei Schiavoni, and began by studying picturesque canal-life. Mr. Boxall, R.A., and Mrs. Jameson, the historian of Sacred and Legendary Art, were their companions. Another old friend, Joseph Severn, had in 1843 gained one of the prizes at the Westminster Hall Cartoons Competition; and a letter from Ruskin, referring to the work there, shows how he still pondered on the subject that had been haunting him in the Alps:

> "With your hopes for the elevation of English art by means of fresco I cannot sympathize ... It is not the material nor the space that can give us thoughts, passions, or power. I see on our Academy walls nothing but what is ignoble in small pictures, and would be disgusting in large ones ... It is not the love of fresco that we want; it is the love of God and His creatures; it is humility, and charity, and self-denial, and fasting, and prayer; it is a total change of character. We want more faith and less reasoning, less strength and more trust. You want neither walls, nor plaster, nor colours—*ça ne fait rien à l'affaire*; it is Giotto, and Ghirlandajo, and Angelico that you want, and that you will and must want until this disgusting nineteenth century has—I can't say breathed, but steamed its last."

So early he had taken up and wrapped round him the mantle of Cassandra.

But he was suddenly to find the sincerity of Ghirlandajo and the religious significance of Angelico united with the matured power of art. Without knowing what they were to meet, Harding and he found themselves one day in the Scuola di S. Rocco, and face to face with Tintoret.

It was the fashion earlier, and it has been the fashion since, to undervalue Tintoret. He is not pious enough for the purists, nor decorative enough for the Pre-Raphaelites. The ruin or the restoration of almost all his pictures makes it impossible for the ordinary amateur to judge them; they need reconstruction in the mind's eye, and that is a dangerous process. Ruskin himself, as he grew older, found more interest in the playful industry of Carpaccio than in the laborious games, the stupendous Titan feats of Tintoret. But at this moment, solemnized before the problems of life, he found these problems hinted in the mystic symbolism of the School of S. Rocco; with eyes now opened to pre-Reformation Christianity, he found its completed outcome in Tintoret's interpretation of the life of Christ and the types of the Old Testament; fresh from the stormy grandeur of the St. Gothard, he found the lurid skies and looming giants of the Visitation, or the Baptism, or the Crucifixion, re-echoing the subjects of Turner as "deep answering to deep"; and, with Harding of the Broad Brush, he recognised the mastery of landscape execution in the Flight into Egypt, and the St. Mary in the Desert.

He devoted the rest of his time chiefly to cataloguing and copying Tintoret. The catalogue appeared in "Stones of Venice," which was suggested by this visit, and begun by some sketches of architectural detail, and the acquisition of daguerreotypes—a new invention which delighted him immensely, as it had delighted Turner, with trustworthy records of detail which sometimes eluded even his industry and accuracy.

At last his friends were gone; and, left alone, he overworked himself, as usual, before leaving Venice with crammed portfolios and closely-written notebooks. At Padua he was stopped by a fever; all through France he was pursued by what, from his account, appears to have been some form of diphtheria, averted only, as he believed, in direct answer to earnest prayer. At last his eventful pilgrimage was ended, and he was restored to his home and his parents. It was not long before he was at work again in his new study, looking out upon the quiet meadow and grazing cows of Denmark Hill, and rapidly throwing into form the fresh impressions of the summer. He was strongly influenced by the sermons of Canon Melvill—the same preacher whom Browning in his youth admired—a good orator and sound analytic expositor, though not a great or independent thinker. Osborne Gordon had recommended him to read Hooker, and he caught the tone and style of the "Ecclesiastical Polity" only too readily, so that much of his work of that winter, the more philosophical part of vol. ii., was damaged by inversions, and Elizabethan quaintness as of ruff and train, long epexegetical sentences, and far-sought pomposity of diction. It was only when he had waded through the chaos which he set himself to survey, that he could lay aside his borrowed stilts, and stand on his own feet in the Tintoret descriptions—rather stiff, yet, from foregone efforts.

This volume, like the first, was completed in the winter, in one long spell of hard work, broken only by a visit to Oxford in January as the guest of Dr. Greswell, Head of Worcester, at a conference for the promotion of art. Smith and Elder accepted the book on Mr. J.J. Ruskin's terms (so his wife wrote), for they had already reported it as called for by the public. The first volume was going into a third edition.

When his book came out he was away again in Italy, trying to show his father all that he had seen in the Campo Santo and Giotto's Tower, and to explain "why it more than startled him." The good man hardly felt the force of it all at once. And there were little passages of arms and some heart-quaking and head-shaking, until Mr. Dale, the old schoolmaster, wrote that he had heard no less a man than Sydney Smith mention the new book in public, in the presence of "distinguished literary characters," as a work of "transcendent talent, presenting the most original views, in the most elegant and powerful language, which would work a complete revolution in the world of taste." When he returned home it was to find a respectful welcome. His word on matters of Art was now really worth something, and before long it was called for. The National Gallery was comparatively in its infancy. It had been established less than twenty-five years, and its manager, Mr. Eastlake (afterwards Sir Charles), had his hands full, what with rascally dealers in forged old masters, and incompetent picture-cleaners; and an economical Government, and a public that neither knew its own mind nor trusted his judgment. A great outcry was set up against him for buying bad works, and spoiling the best by restoration. Ruskin wrote very temperately to *The Times*, pointing out that the damage had been slight compared with what was being done everywhere else, and suggesting that, prevention being better than cure, the pictures should be put under glass, for then they would not need the recurring attentions of the restorer. But he blamed the management for spending large sums on added examples of Guido and Rubens, while they had no Angelico, no Ghirlandajo, no good Perugino, only one Bellini, and, in a word, left his new friends, the early Christian artists, unrepresented. He suggested that pictures might be picked up for next to nothing in Italy; and he begged that the collection might be made historical and educational by being fully representative, and chronologically arranged.

CHAPTER III

"THE SEVEN LAMPS"

"Have you read an Oxford Graduate's letters on art?" wrote Miss Mitford, of "Our Village," on January 27, 1847. "The author, Mr. Ruskin, was here last week, and is certainly the most charming person that I have ever known." The friendship thus begun lasted until her death. She encouraged him in his work; she delighted in his success; and, in the grave reverses which were to befall him, he found her his most faithful supporter and most sympathetic consoler. In return, "his kindness cheered her closing days; he sent her every book that would interest and every delicacy that would strengthen her, attentions which will not surprise those who have heard of his large and thoughtful generosity."[2]

It was natural that a rising man, so closely connected with Scotland, should be welcomed by the leaders of the Scottish school of literature. Sydney Smith, a former Edinburgh professor, had praised the new volume. John Murray, as it seems from letters of the period, made overtures to secure the author as a contributor to his Italian guide-books. Lockhart employed him to write for the *Quarterly Review*.

Lockhart was a person of great interest for young Ruskin, who worshipped Scott; and Lockhart's daughter, even without her personal charm, would have attracted him as the actual grandchild of the great Sir Walter. It was for her sake, he says, rather than for the honour of writing in the famous *Quarterly*, that he undertook to review Lord Lindsay's "Christian Art."

He was known to be a suitor for Miss Lockhart's hand. His father, in view of the success he desired, had been in February looking out for a house in the Lake District; hoping, no doubt, to see him settled there as a sort of successor to Wordsworth and Christopher North. In March, John Ruskin betook himself to the Salutation at Ambleside, with his constant attendant and amanuensis George, for quiet after a tiring winter in London society, and for his new labour of reviewing. But he did not find himself so fond of the Lakes as of old. He wrote to his mother (Sunday, March 28, 1847):

"I finished—and sealed up—and addressed—my last bit of work, last night by ten o'clock—ready to send by to-day's post—so that my father should receive it with this. I could not at all have done it had I stayed at home: for even with all the quiet here, I have had no more time than was necessary. For exercise, I find the rowing very useful, though it makes me melancholy with thinking of 1838,—and the lake, when it is quite calm, is wonderfully sad and quiet:—no bright colours—no snowy peaks. Black water—as still as death;—lonely, rocky islets—leafless woods,—or worse than leafless—the brown oak foliage hanging dead upon them; gray sky;—far-off, wild, dark, dismal moorlands; no sound except the rustling of the boat among the reeds.

"*One o'clock.*—I have your kind note and my father's, and am very thankful that you like what I have written, for I did not at all know myself whether it were good or bad."

In the early summer he went to Oxford, for a meeting of the British Association. He said (June 27, 1847):

"I am not able to write a full account of all I see, to amuse you, for I find it necessary to keep as quiet as I can, and I fear it would only annoy you to be told of all the invitations I refuse, and all the interesting matters in which I take no part. There is nothing for it but throwing one's self into the stream, and going down with one's arms under water, ready to be carried anywhere, or do anything. My friends are all busy, and tired to death. All the members of my section, but especially (Edward) Forbes, Sedgwick, Murchison, and Lord Northampton—and of course Buckland, are as kind to me as men can be; but I am tormented by the perpetual sense of my unmitigated ignorance, for I know no more now than I did when a boy, and I have only one perpetual feeling of being in everybody's way. The recollections of the place, too, and the being in my old rooms, make me very miserable. I have not one moment of profitably spent time to look back to while I was here, and much useless labour and disappointed hope; and I can neither bear the excitement of being in the society where the play of mind is constant, and rolls *over* me like heavy wheels, nor the pain of being alone. I get away in the evenings into the hayfields about Cumnor, and rest; but then my failing sight plagues me. I cannot look at anything as I used to do, and the evening sky is covered with swimming strings and eels. My best time is while I am in the Section room, for though it is hot, and sometimes wearisome, yet I have nothing to *say*,—little to do,—nothing to look at, and as much as I like to hear."

He had to undergo a second disappointment in love; his health broke down again, and he was sent to Leamington to his former doctor, Jephson, once more a "consumptive" patient. Dieted into health, he went to Scotland with a new-found friend, William Macdonald Macdonald of Crossmount. But he had no taste for sport, and could make little use of his opportunities for distraction and relaxation. One battue was enough for him, and the rest of the visit was spent in morbid despondency, digging thistles, and brooding over the significance of the curse of Eden, so strangely now interwoven with his own life—"Thorns a also and Thistles."

At Bower's Well, Perth, where his grandparents had spent their later years, and where his parents had been married, lived Mr. George Gray, a lawyer, and an old acquaintance of the Ruskin family. His daughter Euphemia used to visit at Denmark Hill. It was for her that, some years earlier, "The King of the Golden River" had been written. She had grown up into a perfect Scotch beauty, with every gift of health and spirits which would compensate—the old folk thought—for his retiring and morbid nature. They were anxious, now more than ever, to see him settled. They pressed him, in letters still extant, to propose. We have seen how he was situated, and can understand how he persuaded himself that fortune, after all, was about to smile upon him. Her family had their own reasons for promoting the match, and all united in hastening on the event.

In the Notes to Exhibitions added to a new edition of "Modern Painters," then in the Press, the author mentions a "hurried visit to Scotland in the spring" of 1848. This was the occasion of his marriage at Perth, on April 10. The young couple spent rather more than a fortnight on the way South, among Scotch and English lakes, intending to make a more extended tour in the summer to the cathedrals and abbeys.

The pilgrimage began with Salisbury, where a few days' sketching in the damp and draughts of the cathedral laid the bridegroom low, and brought the tour to an untimely end. In August, the young people were seen safely off to Normandy, where they went by easy stages from town to town, studying the remains of Gothic building. In October they returned and settled in a house of their own, at 31, Park Street, where during the winter he wrote "The Seven Lamps of Architecture," and, as a bit of by-work, a notice of Samuel Prout for the *Art Journal.*

This was Ruskin's first illustrated volume. The plates were engraved by himself in soft-ground etching, such as Prout had used, from drawings he had made in 1846 and 1848. Some are scrappy combinations of various detail, but others, such as the Byzantine capital, the window in Giotto's Campanile, the arches from St. Lo in Normandy, from St. Michele at Lucca, and from the Ca' Foscari at Venice, are effective studies of the actual look of old buildings, seen as they are shown us in Nature, with her light and the shade added to all the facts of form, and her own last touches in the way of weather-softening, and settling-faults, and tufted, nestling plants.

Revisiting the Hôtel de la Cloche at Dijon in later years, Ruskin showed me the room where he had "bitten" the last plate in his wash-hand basin, as a careless makeshift for the regular etcher's bath. He was not dissatisfied with his work himself; the public of the day wanted something more finished. So the second edition appeared with the subjects elaborately popularized in fashionable engraving. More recently they have undergone reduction for a cheap issue. But any book lover knows the value of the original "Seven Lamps" with its San Miniato cover and autograph plates.

As to its reception, or at least the anticipation of it. Charlotte Bronte bears witness in a letter to the publishers.

"I congratulate you on the approaching publication of Mr. Ruskin's new work. If 'The Seven Lamps of Architecture' resemble their predecessor, 'Modern Painters,' they will be no lamps at all, but a new constellation,—seven bright stars, for whose rising the reading world ought to be anxiously agape."

The book was announced for his father's birthday, May 10, 1849, and it appeared while they were among the Alps. The earlier part of this tour is pretty fully described in "Præterita," II. xi., and "Fors," letter xc., and so the visit of Richard Fall, the meeting with Sibylla Dowie, and the death of cousin Mary need not be dwelt on here. From the letters that passed between father and son we find that Mr. John had been given a month's leave from July 26 to explore the Higher Alps, with Coutet his guide and George his valet. The old people stayed at the Hôtel des Bergues, and thought of little else but their son and his affairs, looking eagerly from day to day for the last news, both of him and of his book.

Mr. Ruskin, senior, writes from Geneva on July 29:

> "Miss Tweddale says your book *has made a great sensation.*" On August 4: "The *Spectator*, which Smith sets great value on, has an elaborate favourable notice on 'Seven Lamps,' only ascribing an *infirmity* of temper, quoting railroad passage in proof. Anne was told by American family servant that you were in American Paper, and got it for us, the *New York Tribune* of July 13; first article is your book. They say they are willing to be learners from, rather than critics of, such a book, etc. The *Daily News* (some of the *Punch* people's paper) has a capital notice. It begins: 'This is a masked battery of seven pieces, which blaze away to the total extinction of the small architectural lights we may boast of, etc., etc.'" On August 5: "I have, at a shameful charge of ten francs, got August magazine and Dickens, quite a prohibition for parcels from England. In *British Quarterly*, under æsthetics of Gothic architecture they take four works, you first... As a critic they almost rank you with Goethe and Coleridge, and in style with Jeremy Taylor."

The qualified encouragement of these remarks was further qualified with detailed advice about health; and warnings against the perils of the way, to which Mr. John used to answer on this wise:

> "CORMAYEUR, *Sunday afternoon (July* 29, 1849).

> "MY DEAREST FATHER,

> "(Put the three sheets in order first, 1, 2, 3, then read this, front and *back*, and then 2, and then 3, front and back.) You and

my mother were doubtless very happy when you saw the day clear up as you left St. Martin's. Truly it was impossible that any day could be more perfect towards its close. We reached Nant Bourant at twelve o'clock, or a little before, and Coutet having given his sanction to my wish to get on, we started again soon after one— and reached the top of the Col de Bonhomme about five. You would have been delighted with that view—it is one upon those lovely seas of blue mountain, one behind the other, of which one never tires—this, fortunately, westward—so that all the blue ridges and ranges above Conflans and Beaufort were dark against the afternoon sky, though misty with its light; while eastward a range of snowy crests, of which the most important was the Mont Iseran, caught the sunlight full upon them. The sun was as warm, and the air as mild, on the place where the English travellers sank and perished, as in our garden at Denmark Hill on the summer evenings. There is, however, no small excuse for a man's losing courage on that pass, if the weather were foul. I never saw one so literally pathless—so void of all guide and help from the lie of the ground—so embarrassing from the distance which one has to wind round mere brows of craggy precipice without knowing the direction in which one is moving, while the path is perpetually lost in heaps of shale or among clusters of crags, even when it is free of snow. All, however, when I passed was serene, and even beautiful—owing to the glow which the red rocks had in the sun. We got down to Chapiu about seven—itself one of the most desolately-placed villages I ever saw in the Alps. Scotland is in no place that I have seen, so barren or so lonely. Ever since I passed Shapfells, when a child, I have had an excessive love for this kind of desolation, and I enjoyed my little square chalet window and my chalet supper exceedingly (mutton with garlic)."

He then confesses that he woke in the night with a sore throat, but struggled on next day down the Allée Blanche to Cormayeur.

"I never saw such a mighty heap of stones and dust. The glacier itself is quite invisible from the road (and I had no mind for extra work or scrambling), except just at the bottom, where the ice appears in one or two places, being exactly of the colour of the heaps of waste coal at the Newcastle pits, and admirably adapted therefore to realize one's brightest anticipations of the character and style of the Allée *Blanche*.

"The heap of its moraine conceals, for the two miles of its extent, the entire range of Mont Blanc from the eye. At last you weather the mighty promontory, cross the torrent which issues from its base, and find yourself suddenly at the very foot of the vast slope of torn granite, which from a point not 200 feet lower than the summit of Mont Blanc, sweeps down into the valley of Cormayeur.

"I am quite unable to speak with justice—or think with clearness—of this marvellous view. One is so unused to see a mass like that of Mont Blanc without any snow that all my ideas and modes of estimating size were at fault. I only felt overpowered by it, and that—as with the porch of Rouen Cathedral—look as I would, I could not *see* it. I had not mind enough to grasp it or meet it. I tried in vain to fix some of its main features on my memory; then set the mules to graze again, and took my sketch-book, and marked the outlines—but where is the use of marking contours of a mass of endless—countless—fantastic rock—12,000 feet sheer above the valley? Besides, one cannot have sharp sore-throat for twelve hours without its bringing on some slight feverishness; and the scorching Alpine sun to which we had been exposed without an instant's cessation from the height of the col till now—i.e., from half-past ten to three—had not mended the matter; my pulse was now beginning slightly to quicken and my head slightly to ache—and my impression of the scene is feverish and somewhat painful; I should think like yours of the valley of Sixt."

So he finished his drawing, tramped down the valley after his mule, in dutiful fear of increasing his cold, and found Cormayeur crowded, only an attic *au quatrième* to be had. After trying to doctor himself with gray pill, kali, and senna, Coutet cured his throat with an alum gargle, and they went over the Col Ferret.

The courier Pfister had been sent to meet him at Martigny, and bring latest news and personal report, on the strength of which several days passed without letters, but not without a remonstrance from headquarters. On August 8 he writes from Zermatt:

"I have your three letters, with pleasant accounts of critiques, etc., and painful accounts of your anxieties. I certainly never thought of putting in a letter at Sion, as I arrived there about three hours after Fister left me, it being only two stages from Martigny; and besides, I had enough to do that morning in thinking what I should want at Zermatt, and was engaged at Sion, while we changed horses, in buying wax candles and rice. It was unlucky that I lost post at Visp," etc.

A few days later he says:

"On Friday I had such a day as I have only once or twice had the like of among the Alps. I got up to a promontory projecting from the foot of the Matterhorn, and lay on the rocks and drew it at my ease. I was about three hours at work as quietly as if in my study at Denmark Hill, though on a peak of barren crag above a glacier, and at least 9,000 feet above sea. But the Matterhorn, after all, is not so fine a thing as the aiguille Dru, nor as any one of the aiguilles of Chamouni: for one thing, it is all of secondary rock in horizontal beds, quite rotten and shaly; but there are other causes of difference in impressiveness which I am endeavouring to analyze, but find considerable embarrassment in doing so. There seems no sufficient reason why an isolated obelisk, one-fourth higher than any of them, should not be at least as sublime as they in their dependent grouping; but it assuredly is not. For this reason, as well as because I have not found here the near studies of primitive rock I expected,—for to my great surprise, I find the whole group of mountains, mighty as they are, except the inaccessible Monte Rosa, of secondary limestones or slates,—I should like, if it were possible, to spend a couple of days more on the Montanvert, and at the bases of the Chamouni aiguilles, sleeping at the Montanvert."

And so on, apologetically begging (as other sons beg money) for *time*, to gather the material of "Modern Painters," volume iv.

"I hope you will think whether the objects you are after are worth risks of sore throats or lungs," replied his father, for he had "personified a perpetual influenza" until they got him to Switzerland, and they were very anxious; indeed, Pfister's news from Martigny had scared his mother—not very well herself—into wild plans for recapturing him. However, Osborne Gordon was going to Chamouni with Mr. Pritchard, and so they gave him a little longer; and he made the best use of his time:

"Monday evening (August 20, 1849).

"MY DEAREST FATHER,

"I have to-night a packet of back letters from Viège . . . but I have really hardly time to read them to-night, I had so many notes to secure when I came from the hills. I walk up every day to the base of the aiguilles without the slightest sense of fatigue; work there all day hammering and sketching; and down in the evening. As far as days by myself can be happy they are so, for I love the place with all my heart. I have no over-fatigue or labour, and plenty of time. By-the-by, though in most respects they are incapable of improvement, I recollect that I thought to-day, as I was breaking last night's ice away from the rocks of which I wanted a specimen, with a sharpish wind and small pepper and salt-like sleet beating in my face, that a hot chop and a glass of sherry, if they were to be had round the corner, would make the thing more perfect. There was however nothing to be had round the corner but some Iceland moss, which belonged to the chamois, and an extra allowance of north wind."

This next is scribbled on a tiny scrap of paper:

"GLACIER or GREPPOND, *August* 21.

"MY DEAREST FATHER,

"I am sitting on a gray stone in the middle of the glacier, waiting till the fog goes away. I believe I *may* wait. I write this line in my pocket-book to thank my mother for hers which I did not acknowledge last night. I am glad and sorry that she depends so much on my letters for her comfort. I am sending them now every day by the people who go down, for the diligence is stopped. You may run the chance of missing one or two therefore. I am quite well, and very comfortable—sitting on Joseph's knapsack laid on the stone. The fog is about as thick as that of London in November,—only white; and I see nothing near me but fields of dampish snow with black stones in it."

And then:

> "MONTANVERT, *August* 22.
>
> "I cannot say that on the whole the aiguilles have treated me well. I went up Saturday, Monday and Tuesday to their feet, and never obtained audience until to-day, and then they retired at twelve o'clock; but I have got a most valuable memorandum."

The parental view was put thus:

> GENEVA, *Monday, August* 20, 1849.
>
> "MY DEAREST JOHN,
>
> "I do not know if you have got all my letters, fully explaining to you in what way the want of a *single* letter, on two occasions, did *so* much mischief—made such havoc in our peace. I think my last Thursday's letter entered on it. We are grateful for many letters—that have come. It was merely the accident of the moment when first by illness and then by precipices we were most anxious—being exactly the moment the letters took it into their heads to be not forthcoming. Not writing so often would only keep us more in the dark, with little less anxiety. Please say if you get a letter every day . . ."

Space can hardly be afforded for more than samples of this voluminous correspondence, or interesting quotations might be given about the "ghost-hunt yesterday and a crystal-hunt to-day," and life at the Montanvert, until at last (August 28):

"I have taken my place in diligence for Thursday, and hope to be with you in good time. But I quite feel as if I were leaving home to go on a journey. I shall not be melancholy, however, for I have really had a good spell of it . . . Dearest love to my mother. I don't intend to write again.

"Ever, my dearest father,
"Your most affectionate son,
"J. RUSKIN."

NOTE:

2   "The Friendships of Mary Russell Mitford," edited by the Rev. A.G. L'Estrange.

CHAPTER IV

"STONES OF VENICE" (1849-1851)

A book about Venice had been planned in 1845, during Ruskin's first long working visit. He had made so many notes and sketches both of architecture and painting that the material seemed ready to hand; another visit would fill up the gaps in his information; and two or three months' hard writing would work the subject off, and set him free to continue "Modern Painters." So before leaving home in 1849, he had made up his mind that the next work would be "The Stones of Venice," which, on the appearance of "The Seven Lamps," was announced by the publishers as in preparation.

He left home again early in October; by the end of November he was settled with his wife at Hôtel Danieli, Venice, for the winter. He expected to find without much trouble all the information he wanted as to the dates, styles and history of Venetian buildings; but after consulting and comparing all the native writers, it appeared that the questions he asked of them were just the questions they were unprepared to answer, and that he must go into the whole matter afresh. So he laid himself out that winter for a thorough examination of St. Mark's and the Ducal Palace and the other remains—drawing, and measuring, and comparing their details.

His father had gone back to England in September out of health, and the letters from home did not report improvement. His mother, too, was beginning to fear the loss of her sight; and he could not stay away from them any longer. In February, 1850, he broke off his work in the middle of it, and returned to London. The rest of the year he spent in writing the first volume of "Stones of Venice," and in preparing the illustrations, together with "Examples of the Architecture of Venice," a portfolio of large lithographs and engravings in mezzotint and line, to accompany the work. It was most fortunate for Ruskin that his drawings could be interpreted by such men as Armytage and Cousen, Cuff and Le Keux, Boys and Lupton, and not without advantage to them that their masterpieces should be preserved in his works, and praised as they deserved in his prefaces. But these plates for "Stones of Venice" were in advance of the times. The publisher thought them "caviare to the general," so Mr. J.J. Ruskin told his son; but gave it as his own belief that "some dealers in Ruskins and Turners in 1890 will get great prices for what at present will not sell."

Early in 1850, his father, at his mother's desire, and with the help of W.H. Harrison, collected and printed his poems, with a number of pieces that still remained in MS., the author taking no part in this revival of bygones, which, for the sake of their associations, he was not anxious to recall—though his father still believed that he *might* have been a poet, and *ought* to have been one. This is the volume of "Poems J.R., 1850," so highly valued by collectors.

Another resurrection was "The King of the Golden River," which had lain hidden for the nine years of the Ars Poetica. He allowed it to be published, with woodcuts by the famous "Dicky" Doyle. The little book ran through three editions that year. The first issue must have been torn to rags in the nurseries of the last generation, since copies are so rare as to have brought ten guineas apiece instead of the six shillings at which they were advertised in 1850.

A couple of extracts from letters of 1850 will give some idea of Ruskin's impressions of London society and the Drawing Room:

"MY DEAREST MOTHER,

"Horrible party last night—stiff—large—dull—fidgety—strange,—run-against-everybody-know-nobody sort of party. Naval people. Young lady claims acquaintance with me—I know as much of her as of Queen Pomare—Talk: get away as soon as I can—ask who she is—Lady (—);—as wise as I was before. Introduced to a black man with chin in collar. Black man condescending—I abuse different things to black man: chiefly the House of Lords. Black man says he lives in it—asks where I live—don't want to tell him—obliged—go away and ask who he is—(—); as wise as I was before. Introduced to a young lady—young lady asks if I like drawing—so away and ask who she is—Lady(—). Keep away, with back to wall and look at watch. Get away at last. Very sulky this morning—hope my father better—dearest love to you both."

"PARK STREET, *4 o'clock, (May, 1850)*.

"MY DEAREST FATHER,

"We got through gloriously, though at one place there was the most awkward crush I ever saw in my life—the pit at the Surrey, which I never saw, may perhaps show the like—nothing else. The floor was covered with the ruins of ladies' dresses, torn lace and fallen flowers. But Effie was luckily out of it, and got through unscathed—and heard people saying 'What a beautiful dress!' just as she got up to the Queen. It was fatiguing enough but not so *awkward* as I expected . . .

"The Queen looked much younger and prettier than I expected—very like her pictures, even like those which are thought to flatter most—but I only saw the profile—I could not see the front face as I knelt to her, at least without an upturning of the eyes which I thought would be unseemly—and there were but some two or three seconds allowed for the whole affair . . .

"The Queen gave her hand very graciously: but looked bored; poor thing, well she might be, with about a quarter of a mile square of people to bow to.

"I met two people whom I have not seen for many a day, Kildare and Scott Murray—had a chat with the former and a word with Murray, but nothing of interest . . ."

As one of the chief literary figures of the day, Ruskin could not avoid society, and, as he tells in "Præterita," he was rewarded for the reluctant performance of his duties by meeting with several who became his lifelong friends. Chief among these he mentions Mr. and Mrs. Cowper-Temple, afterwards Lord and Lady Mount Temple. The acquaintance with Samuel Rogers, inauspiciously begun many years before, now ripened into something like friendship; Monckton Milnes (Lord Houghton) and other men of letters were met at Rogers' breakfasts. A little later a visit to the Master of Trinity, Whewell, at Cambridge, brought him into contact with Professer Willis, the authority on Gothic architecture, and other notabilities of the sister University. There also he met Mr. and Mrs. Marshall of Leeds (and Coniston); and he pursued his journey to Lincoln, with Mr. Simpson, whom he had met at Lady Davy's, and to Farnley for a visit to Mr. F.H. Fawkes, the owner of the celebrated collection of Turners (April, 1851).

In London he was acquainted with many of the leading artists and persons interested in art. Of the "teachers" of the day he was known to men so diverse as Carlyle—and Maurice, with whom he corresponded in 1815 about his "Notes on Sheepfolds"—and C.H. Spurgeon, to whom his mother was devoted. He was as yet neither a hermit, nor a heretic: but mixed freely with all sorts and conditions, with one exception, for Puseyites and Romanists were yet as heathen men and publicans to him; and he noted with interest, while writing his review of Venetian history, that the strength of Venice was distinctly Anti-Papal, and her virtues Christian but not Roman. Reflections on this subject were to have formed part of his great work, but the first volume was taken up with the *à priori* development of architectural forms; and the treatment in especial of Venetian matters had to be indefinitely postponed, until another visit had given him the opportunity of gathering his material.

Meanwhile, his wide sympathy had turned his mind toward a subject which then had received little attention, though since then loudly discussed—the reunion of (Protestant) Christians.

He put together his thoughts in a pamphlet on the text "There shall be one fold and one Shepherd," calling it, in allusion to his architectural studies, "Notes on the Construction of Sheepfolds." He proposed a compromise, trying to prove that the pretensions to priesthood on the high Anglican side, and the objections to episcopacy on the Presbyterian, were alike untenable; and hoped that, when once these differences—such little things he thought them—were arranged, a united Church of England might become the nucleus of a world-wide federation of Protestants, a *civitas Dei*, a New Jerusalem.

There were many who agreed with his aspirations: he received shoals of letters from sympathizing readers, most of them praising his aims and criticising his means. Others objected rather to his manner than to his matter; the title savoured of levity, and an art-critic writing on theology was supposed to be wandering out of his province. Tradition says that the "Notes" were freely bought by Border farmers under a rather laughable mistake; but surely it was no new thing for a Scotch reader to find a religious tract under a catching title. There were a few replies; one by Mr. Dyce, who defended the Anglican view with mild persiflage and the usual commonplaces. And there the matter ended, for the public. For Ruskin, it was the beginning of a train of thought which led him far. He gradually learnt that his error was not in asking too much, but in asking too little. He wished for a union of Protestants, forgetting the sheep that are not of *that* fold, and little dreaming of the answer he got, after many days, in "Christ's Folk in the Apennine."

Meanwhile the first volume of "Stones of Venice" had appeared, March, 1851. Its reception was indirectly described in a pamphlet entitled "Something on Ruskinism, with a 'Vestibule' in Rhyme, by an Architect" complaining bitterly of the "ecstasies of rapture" into which the newspapers had been thrown by the new work:

"Your book—since reviewers so swear—may be rational,
Still, 'tis certainly not either loyal or national;"

for it did not join in the chorus of congratulation to Prince Albert and the British public on the Great Exhibition of 1851, the apotheosis of trade and machinery. The "Architect" finds also—what may surprise the modern reader who has not noticed that many an able work has been thought unreadable on its first appearance—that he cannot understand the language and ideas:

"Your style is so soaring—and some it makes sore—
That plain folks can't make out your strange mystical lore."

He will allow the author to be quite right, when he finds something to agree upon; but the moment a sore point is touched, then Ruskin is "insane." In one respect the "Architect" hit the nail on the head: "Readers who are not reviewers by profession can hardly fail to perceive that Ruskinism is violently inimical to *sundry existing interests.*"

The best men, we said, were the first to recognise Ruskin's genius. Let us throw into the opposite scale an opinion of more weight than the "Architect's," in a transcript of the original letter from Carlyle.

"CHELSEA, *March* 9, 1851.

"DEAR RUSKIN,

"I did not know yesterday till your servant was gone that there was any note in the parcel; nor at all what a feat you had done! A loan of the gallant young man's Memoirs was what I expected; and here, in the most chivalrous style, comes a gift of them. This, I think, must be in the style *prior* to the Renaissance! What can I do but accept your kindness with pleasure and gratitude, though it is far beyond my deserts? Perhaps the next man I meet will use me as much below them; and so bring matters straight again! Truly I am much obliged, and return you many hearty thanks.

"I was already deep in the 'Stones'; and clearly purpose to hold on there. A strange, unexpected, and I believe, most true and excellent *Sermon* in Stones—as well as the best piece of schoolmastering in Architectonics; from which I hope to learn much in a great many ways. The spirit and purport of these critical studies of yours are a singular sign of the times to me, and a very gratifying one. Right good speed to you, and victorious arrival on the farther shore! It is a quite new 'Renaissance,' I believe, we are getting into just now: either towards new, *wider* manhood, high again as the eternal stars; or else into final death, and the (marsh?) of Gehenna for evermore! A dreadful process, but a needful and inevitable one; nor do I doubt at all which way the issue will be, though which of the extant nations are to get included in it, and which is to be trampled out and abolished in the process, may be very doubtful. God is great: and sure enough, the changes in the 'Construction of Sheepfolds' as well as in other things, will require to be very considerable.

"We are still labouring under the foul kind of influenza here, I not far from emancipated, my poor wife still deep in the business, though I hope past the deepest. Am I to understand that you too are seized? In a day or two I hope to ascertain that you are well again. Adieu; here is an interruption, here also is the end of the paper.

"With many thanks and regards."

[Signature cut away.]

As soon as the first volume of "Stones of Venice" and the "Notes on the Construction of Sheepfolds" were published, Ruskin took a short Easter holiday at Matlock, and set to work at a new edition of "Modern Painters." This was the fifth reprint of the first volume, and the third of vol. ii. They were carefully and conscientiously revised, and the Postscript indulged in a little triumph at the changed tone of public criticism upon Turner.

But it was too late to have been much service to the great artist himself. In 1845—after saying good-bye and "Why *will* you go to Switzerland? there will be such a *fidge* about you when you're gone"—Turner lost his health, and was never himself again. The last drawings he did for Ruskin (January, 1848), the "Brünig" and the "Descent from the St. Gothard to Airolo," showed his condition unmistakably; and the lonely restlessness of the last, disappointing years were, for all his friends, a melancholy ending to a brilliant career. Ruskin wrote:

"This year (1851) he has no picture on the walls of the Academy; and the *Times* of May 3 says: 'We miss those works of INSPIRATION'!"

"*We* miss! Who misses? The populace of England rolls by to weary itself in the great bazaar of Kensington,³ little thinking that a day will come when those veiled vestals and prancing amazons, and goodly merchandise of precious stones and gold, will all be forgotten as though they had not been; but that the light which has faded from the walls of the Academy is one which a million Koh-i-noors could not rekindle; and that the year 1851 will, in the far future, be remembered less for what it has displayed, than for what it has withdrawn."

NOTE:

3   The Great Exhibition in Hyde Park.

CHAPTER V

PRE-RAPHAELITISM (1851-1853)

The *Times*, in May 1851, missed "those works of inspiration," as Ruskin had at last taught people to call Turner's pictures. But the acknowledged mouthpiece of public opinion found consolation in castigating a school of young artists who had "unfortunately become notorious by addicting themselves to an antiquated style and an affected simplicity in painting . . . We can extend no toleration to a mere servile imitation of the cramped style, false perspective, and crude colour of remote antiquity. We want not to see what Fuseli termed drapery 'snapped instead of folded'; faces bloated into apoplexy, or extenuated into skeletons; colour borrowed from the jars in a druggist's shop, and expression forced into caricature . . . That morbid infatuation which sacrifices truth, beauty, and genuine feeling to mere eccentricity deserves no quarter at the hands of the public."

Ruskin knew nothing personally of these young innovators, and had not at first sight wholly approved of the apparently Puseyite tendency of Rossetti's "Ecce Ancilla Domini," Millais' "Carpenter's Shop," and Holman Hunt's "Early Christian Missionary," exhibited the year before. All these months he had been closely kept to his "Sheepfolds" and "Stones of Venice"; but now he was correcting the proofs of "Modern Painters," vol. i., as thus:

"Chapter the last, section 21: *The duty and after privileges of all students* . . . Go to Nature in all singleness of heart, and walk with her laboriously and trustingly, having no other thoughts but how best to penetrate her meaning, and remember her instruction; rejecting nothing, selecting nothing, and scorning nothing; believing all things to be right and good, and rejoicing always in the truth."

And at Coventry Patmore's request he went to the Academy to look at the pictures in question. Yes; the faces were ugly: Millais' "Mariana" was a piece of idolatrous Papistry, and there was a mistake in the perspective. Collins' "Convent Thoughts"—more Popery; but very careful—"the tadpole too small for its age"; but what studies of plants! And there was his own "Alisma Plantago," which he had been drawing for "Stones of Venice" (vol. i., plate 7) and describing: "The lines through its body, which are of peculiar beauty, mark the different expansions of its fibres, and are, I think, exactly the same as those which would be traced by the currents of a river entering a lake of the shape of the leaf, at the end where the stalk is, and passing out at its point." Curvature was one of the special subjects of Ruskin, the one he found most neglected by ordinary artists. The "Alisma" was a test of observation and draughtsmanship. He had never seen it so thoroughly or so well drawn, and heartily wished the study were his.

Looking again at the other works of the school, he found that the one mistake in the "Mariana" was the only error in perspective in the whole series of pictures; which could not be said of any twelve works, containing architecture, by popular artists in the exhibition; and that, as studies both of drapery and of every other minor detail, there had been nothing in art so earnest or so complete as these pictures since the days of Albert Dürer.

He went home, and wrote his verdict in a letter to *The Times* (May 9, 1851). Next day he asked the price of Hunt's "Two Gentlemen of Verona," and Millais' "Return of the Dove." On the 13th his letter appeared in *The Times*, and on the 26th he wrote again, pointing out beauties, and indications of power in conception, and observation of Nature, and handling, where at first he, like the rest of the public, had been repelled by the wilful ugliness of the faces. Meanwhile the Pre-Raphaelites wrote to tell him that they were neither Papists nor Puseyites. The day after his second letter was published he received an ill-spelt missive, anonymously abusing them. This was the sort of thing to interest his love of poetical justice. He made the acquaintance of several of the Brethren. "Charley" Collins, as his friends affectionately called him, was the son of a respected R.A., and the brother of Wilkie Collins; himself afterwards the author of a delightful book of travel in France, "A Cruise upon Wheels." Millais turned out to be the most gifted, charming and handsome of young artists. Holman Hunt was already a Ruskin-reader, and a seeker after truth, serious and earnest in his religious nature as in his painting.

The Pre-Raphaelites were not, originally, Ruskin's pupils, nor was their movement, directly, of his creation. But it was the outcome of a general tendency which he, more than any man, had helped to set in motion; and it was the fulfilment, though in a way he had not expected, of his wishes.

His attraction to Pre-Raphaelitism was none the less real because it was sudden, and brought about partly by personal influence. And in re-arranging his art-theory to take them in, he had before his mind rather what he hoped they would become than what they were. For a time, his influence over them was great; their first three years were their own; their next three years were practically his; and some of them, the weaker brethren, leaned upon him until they lost the command of their own powers. No artist can afford to use another man's eyes; still less, another man's brain and heart. Ruskin, great as an exponent, was in no sense a master of artists; and if he cheered on the men, who, he believed, were the best of the time, it did not follow that he should be saddled with the responsibility of directing them.

The famous pamphlet on "Pre-Raphaelitism" of August, 1851, showed that the same motives of Sincerity impelled both the Pre-Raphaelite

Brethren and Turner and, in a degree, men so different as Prout, old Hunt, and Lewis. All these were opposed to the Academical School who worked by rule of thumb; and they differed among one another only in differences of physical power and moral aim. Which was all perfectly true, and much truer than the cheap criticism which could not see beyond superficial differences, or the fossil theories of the old school. But Pre-Raphaelitism was an unstable compound, liable to explode upon the experimenter, and its component parts to return to their old antithesis of crude naturalism on the one hand, and affectation of piety or poetry or antiquarianism, on the other. And *that* their new champion did not then foresee. All he knew was that, just when he was sadly leaving the scene, Turner gone and night coming on, new lights arose. It was really far more noteworthy that Millais and Rossetti and Hunt were *men of genius*, than that the "principles" they tried to illustrate were sound, and that Ruskin divined their power, and generously applauded them.

Immediately after finishing the pamphlet on "Pre-Raphaelitism," he left for the Continent with his wife and friends, the Rev. and Mrs. Daniel Moore; spent a fortnight in his beloved Savoy, with the Pritchards; and then crossed the Alps with Charles Newton. On the 1st of September he was at Venice, for a final spell of labour on the palaces and churches. After spending a week with Rawdon Brown he settled at Casa Wetzler, Campo Sta. Maria Zobenigo, and during the autumn and winter not only worked extremely hard at his architecture, but went with his wife into Austrian and Italian society and saw many distinguished visitors. One of them, whom he lectured on the shortcomings of the Renaissance, was Dean Milman. "I am amused at your mode of ciceronizing the Dean of St. Paul's," wrote his father, who kept up the usual close correspondence, and made himself useful in looking up books of reference and consulting authorities like Mr. James Fergusson—for these chapters of easy eloquence were not written without a world of pains. The engravers and the business department of the new publications also required his co-operation, for they were now becoming large ventures. During the three and a half years preceding the summer of 1851 Ruskin seems to have spent £1,680 of profits from his books, making by his writings at this period only about a third of his annual outlay; so that the estimated cost of these great illustrated volumes, some £1,200, was a matter of anxiety to his father, who, together with the publisher, deprecated large plates and technical details, and expressed some impatience to see results from this visit to Venice. He looked eagerly for every new chapter or drawing as it was sent home for criticism. Some passages, such as the description of the Calle San Moise ("Stones of Venice," II. iv,) were unfavourably received by him. Another time he says, "You have a very great difficulty now in writing any more, which is to write up to yourself": or again,—"Smith reports slow sale of 'Stones of Venice' (vol. I.) and 'Pre-Raphaelitism.' The times are sorely against you. The Exhibition has impoverished the country, and literature of a saleable character seems chiefly confined to shilling books in green paper, to be had at railway stations. Smith will have an account against us." He always sent adverse press-notices, on the principle that it was good for John: and every little discouragement or annoyance was discussed in full.

The most serious news, threatening complete interruption of the work rapidly progressing in spite of all, was of Turner's death (December 19, 1851). Old Mr. Ruskin heard of it on the 21st, a "dismal day" to him, spent in sad contemplation of the pictures his son had taught him to love. Soon it came out that John Ruskin was one of the executors named in the will, with a legacy of £20 for a mourning ring:—"Nobody can say you were paid to praise," says his father. It was gossipped that he was expected to write Turner's biography—"five years' work for you," says the old man, full of plans for gathering material. But when one scandal after another reached his ears, he changed his tone, and suggested dropping personal details, and giving a "Life of his Art," in the intended third and final volume of "Modern Painters." Something of the sort was done in the Edinburgh Lectures and at the close of vol. v. of "Modern Painters": and the official life was left to Walter Thornbury, with which

Mr. Ruskin perhaps did not wish to interfere. But he collected a mass of then unpublished material about Turner, which goes far to prove that the kindly view he took of the strange man's morbid and unhappy life was not without justification. At the time, so many legal complications developed that Ruskin was advised to resign his executorship; later on he was able to fulfil its duties as he conceived them, in arranging Turner's sketches for the National Gallery.

Others of his old artist-friends were now passing away. Early in January Mr. J.J. Ruskin called on William Hunt and found him feeble: "I like the little Elshie," he says, nicknaming him after the Black Dwarf, for Hunt was somewhat deformed:

> "He is softened and humanized. There is a gentleness and a greater *bonhomie*—less reserve. I had sent him 'Pre-Raphaelitism.' He had marked it very much with pencil. He greatly likes your notice of people not keeping to their last. So many clever artists, he says, have been ruined by not acting on your principles. I got a piece of advice from Hunt,—never to commission a picture. He could not have done my pigeon so well had he felt he was doing it for anybody."

The pigeon was a drawing he had just bought; in later years at Brantwood.

In February 1852 a dinner-party was given to celebrate in his absence John Ruskin's thirty-third birthday.

> "On Monday, 9th, we had Oldfield (Newton was in Wales), Harrison, George Richmond, Tom, Dr. Grant, and Samuel Prout. The latter I never saw in such spirits, and he went away much satisfied. Yesterday at church we were told that he came home very happy, ascended to his painting-room, and in a quarter of an hour from his leaving our cheerful house was a corpse, from

apoplexy. He never spoke after the fit came on. He had always wished for a sudden death."

Next year, in November, 1853, he tells of a visit paid, by John's request, to W.H. Deverell, the young Pre-Raphaelite, whom he found "in squalor and sickness—with his Bible open—and not long to live—while Howard abuses his picture at Liverpool."

Early in 1852 Charles Newton was going to Greece on a voyage of discovery, and wanted John Ruskin to go with him. But the parents would not hear of his adventuring himself at sea "in those engine-vessels." So Newton went alone, and "dug up loads of Phoenician antiquities." One cannot help regretting that Ruskin lost this opportunity of familiarizing himself with the early Greek art which, twenty years later he tried to expound. For the time he was well enough employed on the "Stones of Venice." He tells the story of this ten months' stay in a letter to his venerable friend Rogers the poet, dated June 23 (1852).

> "I was out of health and out of heart when I first got here. There came much painful news from home, and then such a determined course of bad weather, and every other kind of annoyance, that I never was in a temper fit to write to anyone: the worst of it was that I lost all *feeling* of Venice, and this was the reason both of my not writing to you and of my thinking of you so often. For whenever I found myself getting utterly hard and indifferent I used to read over a little bit of the 'Venice' in the 'Italy' and it put me always into the right tone of thought again, and for this I cannot be enough grateful to you. For though I believe that in the summer, when Venice is indeed lovely, when pomegranate blossoms hang over every garden-wall, and green sunlight shoots through every wave, custom will not destroy, or even weaken, the impression conveyed at first; it is far otherwise in the length and bitterness of the

Venetian winters. Fighting with frosty winds at every turn of the canals takes away all the old feelings of peace and stillness; the protracted cold makes the dash of the water on the walls a sound of simple discomfort, and some wild and dark day in February one starts to find oneself actually balancing in one's mind the relative advantages of land and water carriage, comparing the Canal with Piccadilly, and even hesitating whether for the rest of one's life one would rather have a gondola within call or a hansom."

He then goes on to lament the decay of Venice, the idleness and dissipation of the populace, the lottery gambling; and to forebode the "destruction of old buildings and erection of new" changing the place "into a modern town—a bad imitation of Paris." Better than that he thinks would be utter neglect; St. Mark's Place would again be, what it was in the early ages, a green field, and the front of the Ducal Palace and the marble shafts of St. Mark's would be rooted in wild violets and wreathed with vines:

"She will be beautiful again then, and I could almost wish that the time might come quickly, were it not that so many noble pictures must be destroyed first . . . I love Venetian pictures more and more, and wonder at them every day with greater wonder; compared with all other paintings they are so easy, so instinctive, so natural; everything that the men of other schools did by rule and called composition, done here by instinct and only called truth.

"I don't know when I have envied anybody more than I did the other day the directors and clerks of the Zecca. There they sit at inky deal desks, counting out rolls of money, and curiously weighing the irregular and battered coinage of which Venice boasts; and just over their heads, occupying the place which in a London countinghouse would be occupied by a commercial almanack, a glorious Bonifazio—'Solomon and the Queen of Sheba'; and in a less honourable corner three *old* directors of the Zecca, very mercantile-looking men indeed, counting money also, like the living ones, only a little *more* living, painted by Tintoret; not to speak of the scattered Palma Vecchios, and a lovely Benedetto Diana which no one ever looks at. I wonder when the European mind will again awake to the great fact that a noble picture was not painted to be *hung*, but to be *seen*? I only saw these by accident, having been detained in Venice by soma obliging person who abstracted some [of his wife's jewels] and brought me thereby into various relations with the respectable body of people who live at the wrong end of the Bridge of Sighs—the police, whom, in spite of traditions of terror, I would very willingly have changed for some of those their predecessors whom you have honoured by a note in the 'Italy.' The present police appear to act on exactly contrary principles; yours found the purse and banished the loser; these *don't* find the jewels, and won't let me go away. I am afraid no punishment is appointed in Venetian law for people who steal *time*."

Mr. Ruskin returned to England in July, 1852, and settled next door to his old home on Herne Hill. He said he could not live any more in Park Street, with a dead brick wall opposite his windows. And so, under the roof where he wrote the first volume of "Modern Painters," he finished "Stones of Venice." These latter volumes give an account of St. Mark's and the Ducal Palace and other ancient buildings; a complete catalogue of Tintoret's pictures—the list he had begun in 1845; and a history of the successive styles of architecture, Byzantine, Gothic, and Renaissance, interweaving illustrations of the human life and character that made the art what it was.

The kernel of the work was the chapter on the Nature of Gothic; in which he showed, more distinctly than in the "Seven Lamps," and connected with a wider range of thought, suggested by Pre-Raphaelitism, the doctrine that art cannot be produced except by artists; that architecture, in so far as it is an art, does not mean mechanical execution, by unintelligent workmen, from the vapid working-drawings of an architect's office; and, just as Socrates postponed the day of justice until philosophers should be kings and kings philosophers, so Ruskin postponed the reign of art until workmen should be artists, and artists workmen.

CHAPTER VI

THE EDINBURGH LECTURES (1853-1854)

By the end of June, 1853, "Stones of Venice" was finished, as well as a description of Giotto's works at Padua, written for the Arundel Society. The social duties of the season were over; Ruskin and his wife went north to spend a well-earned holiday. At Wallington in Northumberland, staying with Sir Walter and Lady Trevelyan, he met Dr. John Brown at Edinburgh, author of "Pet Marjorie" and other well-known works, who became his lifelong friend. Ruskin invited Millais, by this time an intimate and heartily-admired friend,[4] to join them at Glenfinlas. Ruskin devoted himself first to foreground studies, and made careful drawings of rock-detail; and then, being asked to give a course of lectures before the Philosophical Society of Edinburgh, he was soon busy writing once more, and preparing the cartoon-sketches, "diagrams" as he called them, to illustrate his subjects. Dr. Acland had joined the party; and he asked Millais to sketch their host as he stood contemplatively on the rocks with the torrent thundering beside him. The picture with additional work in the following winter, became the well-known portrait in the possession of Sir Henry Acland, much the best likeness of this early period.

Another portrait was painted—in words—by one of his audience at Edinburgh on November 1, when he gave the opening lecture of his course, his first appearance on the platform. The account is extracted from the *Edinburgh Guardian* of November 19, 1853:

"Before you can see the lecturer, however, you must get into the hall, and that is not an easy matter, for, long before the doors are opened, the fortunate holders of season tickets begin to assemble, so that the crowd not only fills the passage, but occupies the pavement in front of the entrance and overflows into the road. At length the doors open, and you are carried through the passage into the hall, where you take up, of course, the best available position for seeing and hearing . . . After waiting a weary time . . . the door by the side of the platform opens, and a thin gentleman with light hair, a stiff white cravat, dark overcoat with velvet collar, walking, too with a slight stoop, goes up to the desk, and looking round with a self-possessed and somewhat formal air, proceeds to take off his great-coat, revealing thereby, in addition to the orthodox white cravat, the most orthodox of white waistcoats . . . 'Dark hair, pale face, and massive marble brow—that is my ideal of Mr. Ruskin,' said a young lady near us. This proved to be quite a fancy portrait, as unlike the reality as could well be imagined, Mr. Ruskin has light sand-coloured hair; his face is more red than pale; the mouth well-cut, with a good deal of decision in its curve, though somewhat wanting in sustained dignity and strength; an aquiline nose; his forehead by no means broad or massive, but the brows full and well bound together; the eye we could not see, in consequence of the shadows that fell upon his countenance from the lights overhead, but we are sure it must be soft and luminous, and that the poetry and passion we looked for almost in vain in other features must be concentrated there.[5] After sitting for a moment or two, and glancing round at the sheets on the wall as he takes off his gloves, he rises, and leaning slightly over the desk, with his hands folded across, begins at once,—'You are proud of your good city of Edinburgh,' etc.

"And now for the style of the lecture . . . Properly speaking, there were two styles essentially distinct, and not well blended,—a speaking and a writing style; the former colloquial and spoken offhand; the latter rhetorical and carefully read in quite a different voice,—we had almost said intoned... He has a difficulty in sounding the letter 'r'; [and there is a] peculiar tone in the rising and falling of his voice at measured intervals, in a way scarcely ever heard except in the public lection of the service appointed to be read in churches. These are the two things with which, perhaps you are most surprised,—his dress and manner of speaking—both of which (the white waistcoat notwithstanding) are eminently clerical. You naturally expect, in one so independent, a manner free from conventional restraint, and an utterance, whatever may be the power of voice, at least expressive of a strong individuality; and you find instead a Christ Church man of ten years' standing, who has not yet taken orders; his dress and manner derived from his college tutor, and his elocution from the chapel-reader."

The lectures were a summing up, in popular form, of the chief topics of Ruskin's thought during the last two years. The first (November 1) stated, with more decision and warmth than part of his audience approved, his plea for the Gothic Revival, for the use of Gothic as a domestic style. The next lecture, given three days later, went on to contrast the wealth of ornament in mediæval buildings with the poor survivals of conventionalized patterns which did duty for decoration in nineteenth-century "Greek" architecture; and he raised a laugh by comparing a typical stonemason's lion with a real tiger's head, drawn in the Edinburgh zoological gardens by Mr. Millais.

The last two lectures, on November 15 and 18, were on Painting; briefly reviewing the history of landscape and the life and aims of Turner; and finally, Christian art and Sincerity in imagination, which was now put forth as the guiding principle of Pre-Raphaelitism.

Public opinion was violently divided over these lectures; and they were the cause of much trouble at home. The fact of his lecturing at all aroused strong opposition from his friends and remonstrances from his parents. Before the event his mother wrote: "I cannot reconcile myself to the thought of your bringing yourself personally before the world till you are somewhat older and stronger." Afterwards, his father, while apologizing for the word "degrading," is disgusted at his exposing himself to such an interruption as occurred, and to newspaper comments and personal references. The notion of an "itinerant lecturer" scandalizes him. He hears from Harrison and Holding that John is to lecture even at their very doors—in Camberwell. "I see small bills up," he writes, "with the lecturers' names; among them Mr.—who gets your old clothes!" And he bids him write to the committee that his parents object to his fulfilling the engagement. He postponed his lecture—for ten years; but accepted the Presidency of the Camberwell Institute, which enabled him to appear at their meetings without offence to any.

While staying at Edinburgh, Mr. Ruskin met the various celebrities of modern Athens, some of them at the table of his former fellow-traveller in Venice, Mrs. Jameson. He then returned home to prepare the lectures for printing.

These lectures as published in April, 1854 were fiercely assailed by the old school; but a more serious blow fell on him before that month was out. His wife returned to her parents and instituted a suit against him, to which he made no answer. The marriage was annulled in July. A year later she married Millais.

In May (1854) the Pre-Raphaelites again needed his defence. Mr. Holman Hunt exhibited the "Light of the World" and the "Awakening Conscience." Ruskin made them the theme of two more letters to *The Times*; mentioning, by the way, the "spurious imitations of Pre-Raphaelite work" which were already becoming common. Starting for his summer tour on the Continent, in the Simmenthal he wrote a pamphlet on the opening of the Crystal Palace. There had been much rejoicing over the "new style of architecture" in glass and iron, and its purpose as a palace of art. Ruskin who had declined, in the last chapter of the "Seven Lamps," to join in the cry for a new style, was not at all ready to accept this as any real artistic advance; and took the opportunity to plead again for the great buildings of the past, which were being destroyed or neglected, while the British public was glorifying its gigantic greenhouse. The pamphlet practically suggested the establishment of the Society for the preservation of ancient buildings, which has since come into operation.

This summer of 1854 he projected a study of Swiss history: to tell the tale of six chief towns—Geneva, Fribourg, Basle, Thun, Baden and Schaffhausen, to which in 1858 he added Rheinfelden and Bellinzona. He intended to illustrate the work with pictures of the places described. He began with his drawing of Thun, a large bird's-eye view of the town with its river and bridges, roofs and towers, all exquisitely defined with the pen, and broadly coloured in fluctuating tints that seem to melt always into the same aerial blue; the blue, high up the picture, beyond the plain, deepening into distant mountains.

But his father wanted to see "Modern Painters" completed, and so he began his third volume at Vevey, with the discussion of the grand style, in which he at last broke loose from Reynolds, as was inevitable, after his study of Pre-Raphaelitism, and all the varied experiences of the last ten years. The lesson of the Tulse Hill ivy had been brought home to him in many ways: he had found it to be more and more true that Nature is, after all, the criterion of art, and that the greatest painters were always those whose aim, so far as they were conscious of an aim, was to take fact for their starting-point. Idealism, beauty, imagination, and the rest, though necessary to art, could not, he felt, be made the object of study; they were the gift of heredity, of circumstances, of national aspirations and virtues; not to be produced by the best of rules, or achieved by the best of intentions.

What his own view of his own work was can be gathered from a letter to an Edinburgh student, written on August 6, 1854:

"I am sure I never said anything to dissuade you from trying to excel or to do great things. I only wanted you to be sure that your efforts were made with a substantial basis, so that just in the moment of push your footing might not give way beneath you; and also I wanted you to feel that long and steady effort made in a contented way does more than violent effort made from some strong motive and under some enthusiastic impulse. And I repeat—for of this I am perfectly sure—that the best things are only to be done in this way. It is very difficult thoroughly to understand the difference between indolence and reserve of strength, between apathy and severity, between palsy and patience; but there is all the difference in the world; and nearly as many men are ruined by inconsiderate exertions as by idleness itself. To do as much as you can heartily and happily do each day in a well-determined direction, with a view to far-off results, with present enjoyment of one's work, is the only proper, the only essentially profitable way."

NOTES:

4   "What a beauty of a man he is!" wrote old Mr. Ruskin, "and high in intellect . . . Millais' sketches are 'prodigious'! Millais is the painter of the age." "Capable, it seems to me, of almost everything, if his life and strength be spared," said the younger Ruskin to Miss Mitford.

5   "Mary Russell Mitford found him as a young man 'very eloquent and distinguished-looking, tall, fair, and slender, with a gentle playfulness, and a sort of pretty waywardness that was quite charming.' Sydney Dobell, again, in 1852, discovered an earnestness pervading every feature, giving power to a face that otherwise would be merely lovable for its gentleness. And, finally, one who visited him at Denmark Hill characterized him as emotional and nervous, with a soft, genial eye, a mouth 'thin and severe,' and a voice that, though rich and sweet, yet had a tendency to sink into a plaintive and hopeless tone,"—*Literary World,* May 19, 1893.

CHAPTER VII

THE WORKING MEN'S COLLEGE
(1854-1855)

Philanthropic instincts, and a growing sense of the necessity for social reform, had led Ruskin for some years past towards a group of liberal thinkers with whom he had little otherwise in common. At Venice, in 1852, he had written several articles on education, taxation, and so forth, with which he intended to plunge into active politics. His father, like a cautious man of business who knew his son's powers and thought he knew their limitations, was strongly opposed to this attempt, and used every argument against it. He appealed to his son's sensitiveness, and assured him that he would be "flayed" unless he wrapped himself in the hide of a rhinoceros. He assured him that, without being on the spot to follow the discussions of politicians, it was useless to offer them any opinions whatsoever. And he ended by declaring that it would be the ruin of his business and of his peace of mind if the name of Ruskin were mixed up with Radical electioneering: not that he was unwilling to suffer martyrdom for a cause in which he believed, but he did not believe in the movements afoot—neither the Tailors' Cooperative Society, in which their friend F.J. Furnivall was interested, nor in any outcome of Chartism or Chartist principles. And so for a time the matter dropped.

In 1854, the Rev. F.D. Maurice founded the Working Men's College. Mr. Furnivall sent the circulars to John Ruskin; who thereupon wrote to Maurice, and offered his services. At the opening lecture on October 31,

133

1854, at St. Martin's Hall, Long Acre, Furnivall distributed to all comers a reprint of the chapter "On the Nature of Gothic," which we have already noticed as a statement of the conclusions drawn from the study of art respecting the conditions under which the life of the workman should be regulated. Ruskin thus appeared as contributing, so to say, the manifesto of the movement.

He took charge from the commencement of the drawing-classes—first at 31 Red Lion Square, and afterwards at Great Ormond Street; also super-intending classes taught by Messrs. Jeffery and E. Cooke at the Working Women's (afterwards the Working Men and Women's) College, Queen Square.

In this labour he had two allies; one a friend of Maurice's, Lowes Dickinson, the well-known artist, whose portrait of Maurice was mentioned with honour in the "Notes on the Academy"; his portrait of Kingsley hangs in the hall of the novelist-professor's college at Cambridge. The other helper was new friend.

To people who know him only as the elegant theorist of art, sentimental and egotistic, as they will have it, there must be something strange, almost irreconcilable, in his devotion, week after week and year after year, to these night-classes. Still more must it astonish them to find the mystic author of the "Blessed Damozel," the passionate painter of the "Venus Verticordia," working by Ruskin's side in this rough navvy-labour of philanthropy.

It was early in 1854 that a drawing of D.G. Rossetti was sent to Ruskin by a friend of the painter's. The critic already knew Millais and Hunt personally, but not Rossetti. He wrote kindly, signing himself "yours respectfully," which amused the young painter. He made acquaintance, and in the appendix to his Edinburgh Lectures placed Rossetti's name with those of Millais and Hunt, especially praising their imaginative power, as rivalling that of the greatest of the old masters.

He did more than this. He agreed to buy, up to a certain sum every year, any drawings that Rossetti brought him, at their market price; and his standard of money-value for works of art has never been niggardly. This sort of help, the encouragement to work, is exactly what makes progress possible to a young and independent artist; it is better for him than fortuitous exhibition triumphs—much better than the hack-work which many have to undertake, to eke out their livelihood. And the mere fact of being bought by the eminent art-critic was enough to encourage other patrons.

"He seems in a mood to make my fortune," said Rossetti in the spring of 1854; and early in 1855 Ruskin wrote:

> "It seems to me that, of all the painters I know, you on the whole have the greatest genius; and you appear to me also to be—as far as I can make out—a very good sort of person, I see that you are unhappy, and that you can't bring out your genius as you should. It seems to me then the proper and *necessary* thing, if I can, to make you more happy; and that I shall be more really useful in enabling you to paint properly, and keep your room in order, than in any other way."

He did his best to keep that room in order in every sense. Anxious to promote the painter's marriage with Miss Siddal—"Princess Ida," as Ruskin called her—he offered a similar arrangement to that which he had made with Rossetti; and began in 1855 to give her £150 a year in exchange for drawings up to that value. Rossetti's poems also found a warm admirer and advocate. In 1856, "The Burden of Nineveh" was published anonymously in the *Oxford and Cambridge Magazine*; Ruskin wrote to Rossetti that it was "glorious" and that he wanted to know who was the author,—perhaps not without a suspicion that he was addressing the man who could tell. In 1861 he guaranteed, or advanced, the cost of "The Early Italian Poets," up to £100, with Smith and Elder; and endeavoured, but unsuccessfully, to induce Thackeray to find a place for other poems in *The Cornhill Magazine*.

Mr. W.M. Rossetti, in his book on his brother "as Designer and Writer" and in his "Family Letters," draws a pleasant picture of the intimacy between the artist and the critic. "At one time," he says, "I am sure they even loved one another." But in 1865 Rossetti, never very tolerant of criticism and patronage, took in bad part his friend's remonstrances about the details of "Venus Verticordia." Eighteen months later, Ruskin tried to renew the old acquaintance. Rossetti did not return his call; and further efforts on Ruskin's part, up to 1870, met with little response. But the lecture on Rossetti in "The Art of England" shows that on one side at least "their parting," as Mr. W.M. Rossetti says, "was not in anger;" and the portrait of 1861, now in the Oxford University Galleries, will remain as a memorial of the ten years' friendship of the two famous men.

At Red Lion Square, during Lent term, 1855, the three teachers worked together every Thursday evening. With the beginning of the third term, March 29, the increase of the class made it more convenient to divide their forces. Rossetti thenceforward taught the figure on another night of the week; while the elementary and landscape class continued to meet on Thursdays under Ruskin and Lowes Dickinson. In 1856 the elementary and landscape class was further divided, Mr. Dickinson taking Tuesday evenings, and Ruskin continuing the Thursday class, with the help of William Ward as under-master. Later on, G. Allen, J. Bunney, and W. Jeffrey were teachers. Burne-Jones, met in 1856 at Rossetti's studio, was also pressed into the service for a time.

There were four terms in the Working Men's College year, the only vacation, except for the fortnight at Christmas, being from the beginning of August to the end of October. Ruskin did not always attend throughout the summer term, though sometimes his class came down to him into the country to sketch. He kept up the work without other intermission until May, 1858, after which the completion of "Modern Painters" and many lecture-engagements took him away for a time. In the spring of 1860 he was back at his old post for a term; but after that he discontinued regular attendance, and went to the

Working Men's College only at intervals, to give addresses or informal lectures to students and friends. On such occasions the "drawing-room" or first floor of the house in which the College was held would be always crowded, with an audience who heard the lecturer at his best; speaking freely among friends out of a full treasure-house "things new and old"—accounts of recent travel, lately-discovered glories of art, and the growing burden of the prophecy that in those years was beginning to take more definite shape in his mind.

As a teacher, Ruskin spared no pains to make the work interesting. He provided—Mr. E. Cooke informs me that he was the first to provide—casts from natural leaves and fruit in place of the ordinary conventional ornament; and he sent a tree to be fixed in a corner of the class-room for light and shade studies. Mr. W. Ward in the preface to the volume of letters already quoted says that he used to bring his minerals and shells, and rare engravings and drawings, to show them.

"His delightful way of talking about these things afforded us most valuable lessons. To give an example: he one evening took for his subject a cap, and with pen and ink showed us how Rembrandt would have etched, and Albert Dürer engraved it. This at once explained to us the different ideas and methods of the two masters. On another evening he would take a subject from Turner's 'Liber Studiorum,' and with a large sheet of paper and some charcoal, gradually block in the subject, explaining at the same time the value and effect of the lines and masses."

And for sketching from nature he would take his class out into the country, and wind up with tea and talk. "It was a treat to hear and see him with his men," writes Dr. Furnivall.

His object in the work, as he said before the Royal Commission on National Institutions, was *not to make artists*, but to make the workmen better men, to develop their powers and feelings,—to educate them, in short. He always has urged young people intending to study art as a profession to enter the Academy Schools, as Turner and the Pre-Raphaelites did, or to take up whatever other serious course of practical discipline was open to them. But he held very strongly that everybody could learn drawing, that their eyes could be brightened and their hands steadied, and that they could be taught to appreciate the great works of nature and of art, without wanting to make pictures or to exhibit and sell them.

It was with this intention that he wrote the "Elements of Drawing" in 1856, supplemented by the "Elements of Perspective" in 1859; the illustrations for the book were characteristic sketches by the author, beautifully cut by his pupil, W.H. Hooper, who was one of a band of engravers and copyists formed by these classes at the Working Men's College. In spite of the intention not to make artists by his teaching, Ruskin could not prevent some of his pupils from taking up art as a profession; and those who did so became, in their way, first-rate men. George Allen as a mezzotint engraver, Arthur Burgess as a draughtsman and woodcutter, John Bunney as a painter of architectural detail, W. Jeffery as an artistic photographer, E. Cooke as a teacher, William Ward as a facsimile copyist, have all done work whose value deserves acknowledgment, all the more because it was not aimed at popular effect, but at the severe standard of the greater schools. But these men were only the side issue of the Working Men's College enterprise. Its real result was in the proof that the labouring classes could be interested in Art; and that the capacity shown by the Gothic workman had not entirely died out of the nation, in spite of the interregnum, for a full century, of manufacture. And the experience led Ruskin forward to wider views on the nature of the arts, and on the duties of philanthropic effort and social economy.

CHAPTER VIII

"MODERN PAINTERS" CONTINUED
(1855-1856)

It was in the year 1855 that Ruskin first published "Notes on the Royal Academy and other Exhibitions." He had been so often called upon to write his opinion of Pre-Raphaelite pictures, either privately or to the newspapers, or to mark his friends' catalogues, that he found at last less trouble in printing his notes once for all. The new plan was immediately popular; three editions of the pamphlet were called for between June 1 and July 1. Next year he repeated the "Notes" and six editions were sold.

In spite of a dissentient voice here and there, he was really by that time recognised as the leading authority upon taste in painting. He was trusted by a great section of the public, who had not failed to notice how completely he and his friends were winning the day. The proof of it was in the fact that they were being imitated on all sides; Ruskinism in writing and Pre-Raphaelitism in painting were becoming fashionable.

But at the same time the movement gave rise to the Naturalist-landscape school, a group of painters who threw overboard the traditions of Turner and Prout, Constable and Harding, and the rest, just as the Pre-Raphaelite Brethren threw over the Academical masters. For such men their study was their picture; they devised tents and huts in wild glens and upon waste moors, and spent weeks in elaborating their details directly from nature, instead of painting at home from sketches on the spot.

This was the fulfilment of his advice to young artists; and so far as young artists worked in this way, for purposes of study, he encouraged them. But he did not fail to point out that this was not all that could be required of them. Even such a work as Brett's "Val d'Aosta," marvellous as it was in observation and finish, was only the beginning of a new era, not its consummation. It was not the painting of detail that could make a great artist; but the knowledge of it, and the masterly use of such knowledge. A great landscapist would know the facts and effects of nature, just as Tintoret knew the form of the human figure; and he would treat them with the same freedom, as the means of expressing great ideas, of affording by the imagination noble grounds for noble emotion, which, as Ruskin had been writing at Vevey in 1854, was poetry. Meanwhile the public and the critic ought to become familiar with the aspects of nature, in order to recognise the difference between the true poetry of painting, and the mere empty sentimentalism which was only the rant and bombast of landscape art.

With such feelings as these he wrote the third and fourth volumes of "Modern Painters," (published respectively January 15 and April 14, 1856). The work was afterwards interrupted only by a recurrence of his old cough, in the exceptionally cold summer of 1855. He went down to Tunbridge Wells, where his cousin, William Richardson of Perth, was practising as a doctor; it was not long before the cough gave way to treatment, and he was as busy as ever. About October of that year he wrote to Mrs. Carlyle as follows, in a letter printed by Professor C.E. Norton, conveniently summing up his year:

"Not that I have not been busy—and very busy, too. I have written, since May, good six hundred pages, had them rewritten, cut up, corrected, and got fairly ready for press—and am going to press with the first of them on Gunpowder Plot day, with a great hope of disturbing the Public Peace in various directions. Also, I have prepared above thirty drawings for engravers this year, retouched the engravings (generally the worst part of the business), and etched some on steel myself. In the course of the six hundred pages I have had to make various remarks on German Metaphysics, on Poetry, Political Economy, Cookery, Music, Geology, Dress, Agriculture, Horticulture, and Navigation,[6] all of which subjects I have had to 'read up' accordingly, and this takes time. Moreover, I have had my class of workmen out sketching every week in the fields during the summer; and have been studying Spanish proverbs with my father's partner, who came over from Spain to see the Great Exhibition. I have also designed and drawn a window for the Museum at Oxford; and have every now and then had to look over a parcel of five or six new designs for fronts and backs to the said Museum.

"During my above-mentioned studies of horti2culture, I became dissatisfied with the Linnæan, Jussieuan, and Everybody-elseian arrangement of plants, and have accordingly arranged a system of my own; and unbound my botanical book, and rebound it in brighter green, with all the pages through-other, and backside foremost—so as to cut off all the old paging numerals; and am now printing my new arrangement in a legible manner, on interleaved foolscap. I consider this arrangement one of my great achievements of the year. My studies of political economy have induced me to think also that nobody knows anything about that; and I am at present engaged in an investigation, on independent principles, of the natures of money, rent, and taxes, in an abstract form, which sometimes keeps me awake all night. My studies of German metaphysics have also induced me to think that the Germans don't know anything about *them*; and to engage in a serious enquiry into the meaning of Bunsen's great sentence in the beginning of the second volume of the 'Hippolytus,' about the Finite realization of Infinity; which has given me some trouble.

"The course of my studies of Navigation necessitated my going to Deal to look at the Deal boats; and those of geology to rearrange all my minerals (and wash a good many, which, I am sorry to say, I found wanted it). I have also several pupils, far and near, in the art of illumination; an American young lady to direct in the study of landscape painting, and a Yorkshire young lady to direct in the purchase of Turners,—and various little bye things besides. But I am coming to see you."

The tone of humorous exaggeration of his discoveries and occupations was very characteristic. But he was then growing into the habit of leaving the matter in hand, as he often did afterwards, to follow side issues, and to take up new studies with a hasty and divided attention; the result of which was seen in his sub-title for the third volume of "Modern Painters"—"Of Many Things"; which amused his readers not a little. But that he still had time for his friends is seen in the account of a visit to Denmark Hill, written this year by James Smetham.

"I walked there through the wintry weather, and got in about dusk. One or two gossiping details will interest you before I give you what I care for; and so I will tell you that he has a large house with a lodge, and a valet and footman and coachman, and grand rooms glittering with pictures, chiefly Turner's, and that his father and mother live with him, or he with them . . . His father is a fine old gentleman, who has a lot of bushy gray hair, and eyebrows sticking up all rough and knowing, with a comfortable way of coming up to you with his hands in his pockets, and making *you* comfortable, and saying, in answer to your remark, that 'John's' prose works are pretty good. His mother is a ruddy, dignified, richly dressed old gentlewoman of seventy-five, who knows Chamonix better than Camberwell; evidently a *good* old lady, with the 'Christian Treasury' tossing about on the table. She puts 'John' down, and holds her own opinions, and flatly contradicts him; and he receives all her opinions with a soft reverence and gentleness that is pleasant to witness . . .

"I wish I could reproduce a good impression of 'John' for you, to give you the notion of his 'perfect gentleness and lowlihood.' He certainly bursts out with a remark, and in a contradictious way, but only because he believes it, with no air of dogmatism or conceit. He is different at home from that which he is in a lecture before a mixed audience, and there is a spiritual sweetness in the half-timid expression of his eyes; and in bowing to you, as in taking wine, with (if I heard aright) 'I drink to thee,' he had a look that has followed me, a look bordering on tearful.

"He spent some time in this way. Unhanging a Turner from the wall of a distant room, he brought it to the table and put it in my hands; then we talked; then he went up into his study to fetch down some illustrative print or drawing; in one case, a literal view which he had travelled fifty miles to make, in order to compare with the picture. And so he kept on gliding all over the house, hanging and unhanging, and stopping a few minutes to talk."

And yet there were many with whom he had to deal who did not look at things in his light; who took his criticism as personal attack, and resented it with bitterness. There is a story told (but not by himself) about one of the "Notes on the Academy," which he was then publishing—how he wrote to an artist therein mentioned that he regretted he could not speak more favourably of his picture, but he hoped it would make no difference in their friendship. The artist replied (so they say) in these terms: "Dear Ruskin,—Next time I meet you, I shall knock you down; but I hope it will make no difference in our friendship." "Damn the fellow! why doesn't he stand up for his friends?" said another disappointed acquaintance. Perhaps Ruskin, secure in his "house with a lodge, and a valet and footman and coachman," hardly realized that a cold word from his pen sometimes meant the failure of an important Academy picture, and serious loss of income—that there was bitter truth underlying *Punch's* complaint of the Academician:

> "I paints and paints.
> Hears no complaints,
>   And sells before I'm dry;
> Till savage Ruskin
> Sticks his tusk in,
>   And nobody will buy."

Against these incidents should be set such an anecdote as the following, told by Mr. J.J. Ruskin in a letter of June 3, 1858:

> "Vokins wished me to name to you that Carrick, when he read your criticism on 'Weary Life,' came to him with the cheque Vokins had given, and said your remarks were all right, and that he could not take the price paid by Vokins the buyer; he would alter the picture. Vokins took back the money, only agreeing to see the picture when it was done."

John Ruskin in reply said he did not see why Carrick should have returned the cheque.

A letter from Mrs. Browning describes a visit to Denmark Hill, and ends,—"I like Mr. Ruskin very much, and so does Robert; very gentle, yet earnest—refined and truthful. I like him very much. We count him one among the valuable acquaintances made this year in England." This has been dated 1855; but Ruskin, writing to Miss Mitford from Glenfinlas, 17th August, 1853, says, "I had the pleasure this spring, of being made acquainted with your dear Elizabeth Browning, as well as with her husband. I was of course prepared to like *her*, but I did not expect to like *him* as much as I did. I think he is really a very fine fellow, and *she* is the only sensible woman I have yet met with on the subject of Italian politics. Evidently a noble creature in all things." In June, 1850, he had met Robert Browning, on the invitation of Coventry Patmore, and said: "He is the only person whom I have ever heard talk ration-ally about the Italians, though on the Liberal side."

In these volumes of "Modern Painters" he had to discuss the Mediæval and Renaissance spirit in its relation to art, and to illustrate from Browning's poetry, "unerring in every sentence he writes of the Middle Ages, always vital and right and profound; so that in the matter of art there is hardly a principle connected with the mediæval temper that he has not struck upon in those seemingly careless and too rugged lines of his." This was written twenty-five years before the Browning Society was heard of, and at a time when the style of Browning was an offence to most people. To Ruskin, also, it had been some, thing of a puzzle; and he wrote to the poet, asking him to explain himself; which the poet accordingly did.

That Ruskin was open to conviction and conversion could be shown from the difference in his tone of thought about poetry before and after this period; that he was the best of friends with the man who took him to task for narrowness, may be seen from the following letter, written on the next Christmas Eve:

"MY DEAR MR. RUSKIN,

"Your note having just arrived, Robert deputes me to write for him while he dresses to go out on an engagement. It is the evening. All the hours are wasted, since the morning, through our not being found at the Rue de Grenelle, but here—and our instinct of self-preservation or self-satisfaction insists on our not losing a moment more by our own fault.

"Thank you, thank you for sending us your book, and also for writing my husband's name in it. It will be the same thing as if you had written mine—except for the pleasure, as you say, which is greater so. How good and kind you are!

"And not well. That is worst. Surely you would be better if you had the summer in winter we have here. But I was to write only a word—Let it say how affectionately we regard you.

"ELIZABETH BARRETT BROWNING

"3, RUE DU COLYSÉE,
"*Thursday Evening, 24th" (December,* 1855).

NOTE:

6   Most of these subjects will be easily recognised in "Modern Painters," Vols. III. and IV. The "Navigation" refers to the "Harbours of England."

CHAPTER IX

"THE POLITICAL ECONOMY OF ART"
(1857-1858)

The humble work of the drawing-classes at Great Ormond Street was teaching Ruskin even more than he taught his pupils. It was showing him how far his plans were practicable; how they should be modified; how they might be improved; and especially what more, beside drawing-classes, was needed to realize his ideal. He was anxiously willing to co-operate with every movement, to join hands with any kind of man, to go anywhere, do anything that might promote the cause he had at heart.

Already at the end of 1854 he had given three lectures, his second course, at the Architectural Museum, specially addressed to workmen in the decorative trades. His subjects were design and colour, and his illustrations were chiefly drawn from mediæval illumination, which he had long been studying. These were informal, quasi-private affairs, which nevertheless attracted notice owing to the celebrity of the speaker. It would have been better if his addresses had been carefully prepared and authentically published; for a chance word here and there raised replies about matters of detail in which his critics thought they had gained a technical advantage, adding weight to his father's desire not to see him "expose himself" in this way. There were no more lectures until the beginning of 1857.

On January 23rd, 1857, he spoke before the Architectural Association upon "The Influence of Imagination in Architecture," repeating and amplifying what he had said at Edinburgh about the subordinate value of proportion, and the importance of sculptured ornament based on natural forms. This of course would involve the creation of a class of stone-carvers who could be trusted with the execution of such work. Once grant the value of it, and public demand would encourage the supply, and the workmen would raise themselves in the effort.

A louder note was sounded in an address at the St. Martin's School of Art, Castle Street, Long Acre (April 3rd, 1857), where, speaking after George Cruikshank, his old friend—practically his first master—and an enthusiastic philanthropist and temperance advocate, Ruskin gave his audience a wider view of art than they had known before: "the kind of painting they most wanted in London was painting cheeks red with health." This was anticipating the standpoint of the Oxford Lectures, and showed how the inquiry was beginning to take a much broader aspect.

Another work in a similar spirit, the North London School of Design, had been prosperously started by a circle of men under Pre-Raphaelite influence, and led by Thomas Seddon. He had given up historical and poetic painting for naturalistic landscape, and had returned from the East with the most valuable studies completed, only to break down and die prematurely. His friends, among them Holman Hunt, were collecting money to buy from the widow his picture of Jerusalem from the Mount of Olives, to present it to the National Gallery as a memorial of him; and at a meeting for the purpose, Ruskin spoke warmly of his labours in the cause of the working classes.

In the summer of 1857 the Art Treasures Exhibition was held at Manchester, and Ruskin was invited to lecture. The theme he chose was "The Political Economy of Art." He had been studying political economy for some time back, but, as we saw from his letter to Carlyle, he had found no answer in the ordinary text-books for the questions he tried to put. He wanted to know what Bentham and Ricardo and Mill, the great authorities, would advise him as to the best way of employing artists, of educating workmen, of elevating public taste, of regulating patronage;

but these subjects were not in their programme. And so he put together his own thoughts into two lectures upon Art considered as Wealth: first, how to get it; next, how to use it.[7]

There were very few points in these lectures that were not vigorously contested at the moment, and conceded in the sequel—in some form or other. The paternal function of government, the right of the state to interfere in matters beyond its traditional range, its duty with regard to education—all this was quite contrary to the prevailing habits of thought of the time, especially at Manchester, the headquarters of the *laissez faire* school; but to Ruskin, who, curiously enough, had just then been referring sarcastically to German philosophy, knowing it only at second-hand, and unaware of Hegel's political work—to him this Platonic conception of the state was the only possible one, as it is to most people nowadays. In the same way, his practical advice has been accepted, perhaps unwittingly, by our times. We do now understand the difference between artistic decoration and machine-made wares; we do now try to preserve ancient monuments, and to use art as a means of education. And we are in a fair way, it seems, of lowering the price of modern pictures, as he bids us, to "not more than £500 for an oil picture and £100 for a water-colour."

After a visit to the Trevelyans at Wallington he went with his parents to Scotland; for his mother, now beginning to grow old, wanted to revisit the scenes of her youth. They went to the Highlands and as far north as the Bay of Cromarty, and then returned by way of the Abbeys of the Lowlands, to look up Turner sites, as he had done in 1845 on the St. Gothard. From the enjoyment of this holiday he was recalled to London by a letter from Mr. Wornum saying that he could arrange the Turner drawings at the National Gallery.

His first letter on the National Gallery, in 1847, has been noticed. He had written again to *The Times* (December 29th, 1852), pressing the same point—namely, that if the pictures were put under glass no cleaning nor restoring would be needed; and that the Gallery ought not to be considered as a grand hall, decorated with pictures, but as a convenient museum, with a chronological sequence of the best works of all schools,—every picture hung on the line and accompanied by studies for it, if procurable, and engravings from it.

Now—in 1857—question was raised of removing the National Gallery from Trafalgar Square. The South Kensington Museum was being formed, and the whole business of arranging the national art treasures was gone into by a Royal Commission, consisting of Lord Broughton (in the chair), Dean Milman, Prof. Faraday, Prof. Cockerell, and George Richmond. Ruskin was examined before them on April 6th, and re-stated the opinions he had written to *The Times*, adding that he would like to see two National Galleries—one of popular interest, containing such works as would catch the public eye and enlist the sympathy of the untaught; and another containing only the cream of the collections, in pictures, sculpture and the decorative crafts, arranged for purposes of study. This was suggested as an ideal; of course, it would involve more outlay, and less display, than any Parliamentary vote would sanction, or party leader risk.

Another question of importance was the disposal of the pictures and sketches which Turner had left to the nation. Ruskin was one of the executors under the will; but, on finding that, though Turner's intention was plain, there were technical informalities which would make the administration anything but easy, he declined to act. It was not until 1856 that the litigation was concluded, and Turner's pictures and sketches were handed to the Trustees of the National Gallery. Ruskin, whose want of legal knowledge had made his services useless before, now felt that he could carry out the spirit of Turner's will by offering to arrange the sketches; which were in such a state of confusion that only some person with knowledge of the artist's habits of work and subjects could, so to speak, *edit* them; and the editor would need no ordinary skill, patience and judgment, into the bargain.

Meanwhile, for that winter (1856-7) a preliminary exhibition was held of Turner's oil-paintings, with a few water-colours, at Marlborough

House, then the headquarters of the Department of Science and Art, soon afterwards removed to South Kensington. Ruskin wrote a catalogue, with analysis of Turner's periods of development and characteristics; which made the collection intelligible and interesting to curious sight-seers. They showed their appreciation by taking up five editions in rapid succession.

Just before lecturing at Manchester, he wrote again on the subject to *The Times*; and in September his friend R.N. Wornum, Director of the National Gallery in succession to Eastlake and Uwins, wrote—as we saw—that he might arrange the sketches as he pleased. He returned from Scotland, and set to work on October 7th.

It was strange employment for a man of his powers; almost as removed from the Epicurean Olympus of "cultured ease" popularly assigned to him, as night-school teaching and lecturing to workmen. But, beside that it was the carrying out of Turner's wishes, he always had a certain love for experimenting in manual toil; and this was work in which his extreme neatness and deftness of hand was needed, no less than his knowledge and judgment. During the winter for full six months, he and his two assistants worked, all day and every day, among the masses of precious rubbish that had been removed from Queen Anne Street to the National Gallery.

Mr. J.J. Ruskin wrote, on February 19 and 21, 1852:

"I have just been through Turner's house with Griffith. His labour is more astonishing than his genius. There are £80,000 of oil pictures done and undone—Boxes half as big as your Study Table, filled with Drawings and Sketches. There are Copies of Liber Studiorum to fill all your Drawers and more, and House Walls of proof plates in Reams—they may go at 1/-each . . .

"Nothing since Pompeii so impressed me as the interior of Turner's house; the accumulated dust of 40 years partially cleared off; Daylight for the first time admitted by opening a window on the finest productions of art buried for 40 years. The Drawing Room has, it is reckoned, £25,000 worth of proofs, and sketches, and Drawings, and Prints. It is amusing to hear Dealers saying there can be no Liber Studiorums—when I saw neatly packed and well labelled as many Bundles of Liber Studiorum as would fill your entire Bookcase, and England and Wales proofs in packed and labelled Bundles like Reams of paper, as I told you, piled nearly to Ceiling . . .

"The house must be dry as a Bone—the parcels were apparently quite uninjured. The very large pictures were spotted, but not much. They stood leaning against another in the large low Rooms. Some *finished* go to Nation, many unfinished *not*: no frames. Two are given unconditional of Gallery Building—*very fine*: if (and this is a condition) *placed beside Claude*. The style much like the laying on in Windmill Lock in Dealer's hands, which, now it is cleaned, comes out a real Beauty. I believe Turner loved it. The will desires all to be framed and repaired and put into the best showing state; as if he could not release his money to do this till he was dead. The Top of his Gallery is one ruin of Glass and patches of paper, now only just made weather-proof . . .

"I saw in Turner's Rooms, *Geo. Morlands* and *Wilsons* and *Claudes* and *portraits* in various stiles *all by Turner*. He copied every man, was every man first, and took up his own style, casting all others away. It seems to me you may keep your money and revel for ever and for nothing among Turner's Works."

Among the quantities so recklessly thrown aside for dust, damp, soot, mice and worms to destroy—some 15,000 Ruskin reckoned at first, 19,000 later on—there were many fine drawings, which had been used by the engravers, and vast numbers of interesting and valuable studies in colour and in pencil. Four hundred of these were extricated from the chaos, and with infinite pains cleaned, flattened, mounted, dated and described, and placed in sliding frames in cabinets devised by Ruskin, or else in swivel frames, to let both sides of the paper be seen. The first results of the work were shown in an Exhibition at Marlborough House during the winter, for which he wrote another catalogue. Of the whole collection he began a more complete account, which was too elaborate to be finished in that form; but in 1881 he published a "Catalogue of the Drawings and Sketches of J M.W. Turner, R.A., at present exhibited in the National Gallery," so that his plan was practically fulfilled.

During 1858 Ruskin continued to lecture at various places on subjects connected with his Manchester addresses—the relation of art to manufacture, and especially the dependence of all great architectural design upon sculpture or painting of organic form. The first of the series was given at the opening of the Architectural Museum at South Kensington, January 13th, 1858, entitled "The Deteriorative Power of Conventional Art over Nations;" in which he showed that naturalism, as opposed to meaningless pattern-making, was always a sign of life. For example, the strength of the Greek, Florentine and Venetian art arose out of the search for truth, not, as it is often supposed, out of striving after an ideal of beauty; and as soon as nature was superseded by recipe, the greatest schools hastened to their fall. From which he concluded that modern design should always be founded on natural form, rather than upon the traditional patterns of the east or of the mediævals.

On February 16th he spoke on "The Work of Iron, in Nature, Art and Policy," at Tunbridge Wells; a subject similar to that of his address to the St. Martin's School of the year before, but amplified into a plea for the use of wrought-iron ornament, as in the new Oxford Museum, then building, and on April 25th he again addressed St. Martin's School.

The Oxford Museum was an experiment in the true Gothic revival. The architects, Sir Thomas Deane and Benjamin Woodward, had allowed their workmen to design parts of the detail, such as capitals and spandrils, quite in the spirit of Ruskin's teaching, and the work was accordingly of deep interest to him. So far back as April, 1856, he had given an address to the men employed at the Museum, whom he met, on Dr. Acland's invitation, at the Workmen's Reading Rooms. He said that his object was not to give some labouring men the chance of becoming masters of other labouring men, and to help the few at the expense of the many, but to lead them to those sources of pleasure, and power over their own minds and hands, that more educated people possess. He did not sympathize with the socialism that had been creeping into vogue since 1848. He thought existing social arrangements good, and he agreed with his friends, the Carlyles, who had found that it was only the incapable who could not get work. But it was the fault of the wealthy and educated that working people were not better trained; it was not the working-men's fault, at bottom. The modern architect used his workman as a mere tool; while the Gothic spirit set him free as an original designer, to gain—not more wages and higher social rank, but pleasure and instruction, the true happiness that lies in good work well done.

To explain the design of the Oxford Museum and to enlist support, he wrote two letters to Dr. Acland (May 25th, 1858, and January 20th, 1859), which formed part of a small book, reporting its aims and progress, illustrated with an engraving of one of the workmen's capitals. Ruskin himself contributed both time and money to the work, and his assistance was not unrecognised. In 1858 "Honorary Studentships" (i.e., fellowships) were created at Christ Church by the Commissioners' ordinances. At the first election held, December 6th, 1858, there were chosen for the compliment Ruskin, Gladstone, Sir G. Cornewall Lewis, Dr. (Sir) H.W. Acland, and Sir F.H. Gore Ouseley. At the second, December 15th, 1858, were elected Henry Hallam, the Earl of Stanhope, the Earl of Elgin, the Marquis of Dalhousie and Viscount Canning.

Parallel with this movement for educating the "working-class," there was the scheme for the improvement of middle-class education, which was then going on at Oxford—the beginning of University Extension—supported by the Rev. F. Temple (later Archbishop of Canterbury), and Mr. (afterwards Sir) Thomas Dyke Acland. Ruskin was heartily for them;

and in a letter on the subject, he tried to show how the teaching of Art might be made to work in with the scheme. He did not think that in this plan, any more than at the Working Men's College, there need be an attempt to teach drawing with a view to forming artists; but there were three objects they might hold in view: the first, to give every student the advantage of the happiness and knowledge which the study of Art conveys; the next, to enforce some knowledge of Art amongst those who were likely to become patrons or critics; and the last, *to leave no Giotto lost among hill shepherds.*

NOTE:

7   July 10 and 13, 1857. He went to Manchester from Oxford, where he had been staying with the Liddells, writing enthusiastically of the beauty of their children and the charm of their domestic life.

CHAPTER X

"MODERN PAINTERS" CONCLUDED
(1838-1860)

Oxford and old friends did not monopolise Ruskin's attention: he was soon seen at Cambridge—on the same platform with Richard Redgrave, R.A., the representative of Academicism and officialism—at the opening of the School of Art for workmen on October 29th, 1858. His Inaugural Address struck a deeper note, a wider chord, than previous essays; it was the forecast of the last volume of "Modern Painters," and it sketched the train of thought into which he had been led during his tour abroad, that summer.

The battles between faith and criticism, between the historical and the scientific attitudes, which had been going on in his mind, were taking a new form. At the outset, we saw, naturalism overpowered respect for tradition—in the first volume of "Modern Painters;" then the historical tendency won the day, in the second volume. Since that time, the critical side had been gathering strength, by his alliance with liberal movements and by his gradual detachment from associations that held him to the older order of thought. As in his lonely journey of 1845 he first took independent ground upon questions of religion and social life, so in 1858, once more travelling alone, he was led by his meditations,—freed from the restraining presence of his parents—to conclusions which he had been all these years evading, yet finding at last inevitable.

He went abroad for a third attempt to write and illustrate his History of Swiss Towns. He spent part of May on the Upper Rhine between Basle and Schaffhausen, June and half of July on the St. Gothard route and at Bellinzona. In reflecting over the sources of Swiss character, as connected with the question of the nature of art and its origin in morality, he was struck with the fact that all the virtues of the Swiss did not make them artistic. Compared with most nations they were as children in painting, music and poetry. And, indeed, they ranked with the early phases of many great nations—the period of pristine simplicity "uncorrupted by the arts."

From Bellinzona he went to Turin on his way to the Vaudois Valleys, where he meant to compare the Waldensian Protestants with the Swiss. Accidentally he saw Paul Veronese's "Queen of Sheba" and other Venetian pictures; and so fell to comparing a period of fully ripened art with one of artlessness; discovering that the mature art, while it appeared at the same time with decay in morals, did not spring from that decay, but was rooted in the virtues of the earlier age. He grasped a clue to the puzzle, in the generalisation that Art is the product of human happiness; it is contrary to asceticism; it is the expression of pleasure. But when the turning point of national progress is once reached, and art is regarded as the laborious incitement to pleasure,—no longer the spontaneous blossom and fruit of it,—the decay sets in for art as for morality. Art, in short, is created *by* pleasure, not *for* pleasure. The standard of thought, the attitude of mind, of the Waldensians, he now perceived to be quite impossible for himself. He could not look upon every one outside their fold as heathens and publicans; he could not believe that the pictures of Paul Veronese were works of iniquity, nor that the motives of great deeds in earlier ages were lying superstitions. He took courage to own to himself and others that it was no longer any use trying to identify his point of view with that of Protestantism. He saw both Protestants and Roman Catholics, in the perspective of history, converging into a primitive, far distant, ideal unity of Christianity, in which he still believed; but he could take neither side, after this.

The first statement of the new point of view was, as we said, the Inaugural Lecture of the Cambridge School of Art. The next important utterance was at Manchester, February 22nd, 1859, where he spoke on the "Unity of Art," by which he meant—not the fraternity of handicrafts with painting, as the term is used nowadays—but that, in whatever branch of Art, the spirit of Truth or Sincerity is the same. In this lecture there is a very important passage showing how he had at last got upon firm ground in the question of art and morality: "*I do* NOT *say in the least that in order to be a good painter you must be a good man*; but I do say that in order to be a good natural painter there must be strong elements of good in the mind, however warped by other parts of the character." So emphatic a statement deserves more attention than it has received from readers and writers who assume to judge Ruskin's views after a slight acquaintance with his earlier works. He was well aware himself that his mind had been gradually enlarging, and his thoughts changing; and he soon saw as great a difference between himself at forty and at twenty-five, as he had formerly seen between the Boy poet and the Art critic. He became as anxious to forget his earlier books, as he had been to forget his verse-writing; and when he came to collect his "Works," these lectures, under the title of "The Two Paths," were (with "The Political Economy of Art") the earliest admitted into the library.

After this Manchester lecture he took a driving tour in Yorkshire—posting in the old-fashioned way—halting at Bradford for the lecture on "Modern Manufacture and Design" (March 1st), and ending with a visit to the school at Winnington, of which more in a later chapter.

In 1859 the last Academy Notes, for the time being, were published. The Pre-Raphaelite cause had been fully successful, and the new school of naturalist landscape was rapidly asserting itself. Old friends were failing, such as Stanfield, Lewis, and Roberts: but new men were growing up, among whom Ruskin welcomed G.D. Leslie, F. Goodall, J.C. Hook,—who had come out of his "Pre-Raphaelite measles" into the healthy naturalism of "Luff Boy!"—Clarence Whaite, Henry Holiday, and John Brett, who showed the "Val d'Aosta." Millais' "Vale of Rest" was the picture which attracted most notice: something of the old rancour against the school was revived in the *Morning Herald*, which called his works "impertinences," "contemptible," "indelible disgrace," and so on. It was the beginning of a transition from the delicacy of the Pre-Raphaelite Millais to his later style; and as such the preacher of "All great art is delicate" could not entirely defend it. But the serious strength of the imagination and the power of the execution he praised with unexpected warmth.

He then started on the last tour abroad with his parents. He had been asked, rather pointedly, by the National Gallery Commission, whether he had seen the great German museums, and had been obliged to reply that he had not. Perhaps it occurred to him or to his father that he ought to see the pictures at Berlin and Dresden and Munich, even though he heartily disliked the Germans with their art and their language and everything that belonged to them,—except Holbein and Dürer. By the end of July the travellers were in North Switzerland; and they spent September in Savoy, returning home by October 7th.

Old Mr. Ruskin was now in his seventy-fifth year and his desire was to see the great work finished before he died. There had been some attempt to write this last volume of "Modern Painters" in the previous winter, but it had been put off until after the visit to Germany had completed a study of the great Venetian painters—especially Titian and Veronese. Now at last, in the autumn of 1859, he finally set to work on the writing.

The assertion of Turner's genius had been necessary in 1843, but Turner was long since dead; his fame was thoroughly vindicated; his bequest to the nation dealt with, so far as possible. Early Christian Art was recognised—almost beyond its claims. The Pre-Raphaelites and naturalistic landscapists no longer needed the hand which "Modern Painters" had held out to them by the way. Of the great triad of Venice,

Tintoret had been expounded, Veronese and Titian were now taken up and treated with tardy, but ample recognition.

And now, after twenty years of labour, Ruskin had established himself as the recognised leader of criticism and the exponent of painting and architecture. He had created a department of literature all his own. He had enriched the art of England with examples of a new and beautiful draughtsmanship, and the language with passages of poetic description and eloquent declamation, quite, in their way, unrivalled. He had built up a theory of art, so far uncontested; and thrown new light on the Middle Ages and Renaissance, illustrating, in a way then novel, their chronicles by their remains. He had beaten down opposition, risen above detraction, and won the prize of honour—only to realise, as he received it, that the fight had been but a pastime tournament, after all; and to hear, through the applause, the enemy's trumpet sounding to battle. For now, without the camp, there were realities to face; as to Art—"the best in this kind are but shadows."

BOOK III

HERMIT AND HERETIC

(1860-1870)

CHAPTER I

"UNTO THIS LAST" (1860-1861)

At forty years of age Ruskin finished "Modern Painters." From that time art was sometimes his text, rarely his theme. He used it as the opportunity, the vehicle, so to say, for teachings of wider range and deeper import; teachings about life as a whole, conclusions in ethics and economics and religion, to which he sought to lead others, as he was led, by the way of art.

During the time when he was preaching his later doctrines, he wished to suppress the interfering evidences of the earlier. He let his works on art run out of print, not for the benefit of second-hand booksellers, but in the hope that he could fix his audience upon the burden of his prophecy for the time being. But the youthful works were still read; high prices were paid for them, or they were smuggled in from America. And when the epoch of "Fors" had passed, he agreed to the reprinting of all that early material. He called it obsolete and trivial; others find it interestingly biographical—perhaps even classical.

This year, then, 1860, the year of the Italian Kingdom, of Garibaldi, and of the beginning of the American war, marks his turning point, from the early work, summed up in the old "Selections," to the later work.

Until he was forty, Mr. Ruskin was a writer on art; after that his art was secondary to ethics. Until he was forty he was a believer in English Protestantism; afterwards he could not reconcile current beliefs with the facts of life as he saw them, and had to reconstruct his creed from the foundations. Until he was forty he was a philanthropist, working heartily with others in a definite cause, and hoping for the amendment of wrongs, without a social upheaval. Even in the beginning of 1860, in his evidence before the House of Commons Select Committee on Public Institutions, he was ready with plans for amusing and instructing the labouring classes, and noting in them a "thirsty desire" for improvement. But while his readiness to make any personal sacrifice, in the way of social and philanthropic experiment, and his interest in the question were increasing, he became less and less sanguine about the value of such efforts as the Working Men's College, and less and less ready to co-operate with others in their schemes. He began to see that no tinkering at social breakages was really worth while; that far more extensive repairs were needed to make the old ship seaworthy.

So he set himself, by himself, to sketch the plans for the repairs. Naturally sociable, and accustomed to the friendly give-and-take of a wide acquaintance, he withdrew from the busy world into a busier solitude. During the next few years he lived much alone among the Alps, or at home, thinking out the problem; sometimes feeling, far more acutely than was good for clear thought, the burden of the mission that was laid upon him. In March, 1863, he wrote from his retreat at Mornex to Norton:

> "The loneliness is very great, and the peace in which I am at present is only as if I had buried myself in a tuft of grass on a battlefield wet with blood—for the cry of the earth about me is in my ears continually, if I do not lay my head to the very ground."

And a few months later:

> "I am still very unwell, and tormented between the longing for rest and lovely life, and the sense of this terrific call of human crime for resistance and of human misery for help, though it

seems to me as the voice of a river of blood which can but sweep me down in the midst of its black clots, helpless."

Sentences like these, passages here and there in the last volume of "Modern Painters," and still more, certain passages omitted from that volume, show that about 1860 something of a cloud had been settling over him,—a sense of the evil of the world, a horror of great darkness. In his earlier years, his intense emotion and vivid imagination had enabled him to read into pictures of Tintoret or Turner, into scenes of nature and sayings of great books, a meaning or a moral which he so vividly communicated to the reader as to make it thenceforward part and parcel of the subject, however it came there to begin with. It is useless to wonder whether Turner, for instance, consciously meant what Ruskin found in his works. A great painter does not paint without thought, and such thought is apt to show itself whether he will or no. But it needs imaginative sympathy to detect and describe the thought. And when that sympathy was given to suffering, to widespread misery, to crying wrongs; joined also with an intense passion for justice, which had already shown itself in the defence of slighted genius and neglected art; and to the Celtic temperament of some highstrung seer and trance-prophesying bard; it was no wonder that Ruskin became like one of the hermits of old, who retreated from the world to return upon it with stormy messages of awakening and flashes of truth more impressive, more illuminating than the logic of schoolmen and the state-craft of the wise.

And then he began to take up an attitude of antagonism to the world, he who had been the kindly helper and minister of delightful art. He began to call upon those who had ears to hear to come out and be separate from the ease and hypocrisy of Vanity Fair. Its respectabilities, its orthodoxies, he could no longer abide. Orthodox religion, orthodox morals and politics, orthodox art and science, alike he rejected; and was rejected by each of them as a brawler, a babbler, a fanatic, a heretic. And even when kindly Oxford gave him a quasi-academical position, it did not bring him, as it brings many a heretic, back to the fold.

In this period of storm and stress he stood alone. The old friends of his youth were one by one passing away, if not from intercourse, still from full sympathy with him in his new mood. His parents were no longer the guides and companions they had been; they did not understand the business he was about. And so he was left to new associates, for he could not live without some one to love,—that was the nature of the man, however lonely in his work and wanderings.

The new friends of this period were, at first, Americans; as the chief new friends of his latest period (the Alexanders) were American, too. Charles Eliot Norton, after being introduced to him in London in 1855, met him again by accident on the Lake of Geneva—the story is prettily told in "Præterita." Ruskin adds:

> "Norton saw all my weaknesses, measured all my narrownesses, and, from the first, took serenely, and as it seemed of necessity, a kind of paternal authority over me, and a right of guidance ... I was entirely conscious of his rectorial power, and affectionately submissive to it, so that he might have done anything with me, but for the unhappy difference in our innate, and unchangeable, political faiths."

So, after all, he stood alone.

Another friend about this time was Mrs. H. Beecher Stowe, to whom he wrote on June 18th, 1860, from Geneva:

> "It takes a great deal, when I am at Geneva, to make me wish myself anywhere else, and, of all places else, in London; nevertheless, I very heartily wish at this moment that I were looking out on the Norwood Hills, and were expecting you and the children to breakfast to-morrow.

"I had very serious thoughts, when I received your note, of running home; but I expected that very day an American friend, Mr. Stillman, who, I thought, would miss me more here than you in London, so I stayed.

"What a dreadful thing it is that people should have to go to America again, after coming to Europe! It seems to me an inversion of the order of nature. I think America is a sort of 'United' States of Probation, out of which all wise people, being once delivered, and having obtained entrance into this better world, should never be expected to return (sentence irremediably ungrammatical), particularly when they have been making themselves cruelly pleasant to friends here. My friend Norton, whom I met first on this very blue lake water, had no business to go back to Boston again, any more than you . . .

"So you have been seeing the Pope and all his Easter performances! I congratulate you, for I suppose it is something like 'Positively the last appearance on any stage.' What was the use of thinking about *him*? You should have had your own thoughts about what was to come after him. I don't mean that Roman Catholicism will die out so quickly. It will last pretty nearly as long as Protestantism, which keeps it up; but I wonder what is to come next. That is the main question just now for everybody."

W.J. Stillman had been a correspondent about 1851,—"involved in mystical speculations, partly growing out of the second volume of 'Modern Painters,'" as he said of himself in an article on "John Ruskin" in the *Century* Magazine (January, 1888). With him Ruskin spent July and August of 1860 at Chamouni. He did but little drawing, and in the few sketches that remain of that summer there is evidence that his mind was far away from its old love of mountains and of streamlets. His lonely walks in the pinewoods of the Arveron were given to meditation on a great problem which had been set, as it seemed, for him to solve, ever since he had written that chapter on "The Nature of Gothic." Now at last, in the solitude of the Alps, he could grapple with the questions he had raised; and the outcome of the struggle was "Unto this Last."

The year before, from Thun and Bonneville and Lausanne (August and September, 1859) he had written letters to E.S. Dallas, suggested by the strikes in the London building trade. In these he appears to have sketched the outline of a new conception of social science, which he was now elaborating with more attempt at system and brevity than he had been accustomed to use.

These new papers, painfully thought out and carefully set down in his room at the Hôtel de l'Union, he used—as long before he read his daily chapter to the breakfast party at Herne Hill—to read to Stillman: and he sent them to the *Cornhill Magazine*, started the year before by Smith and Elder. Ruskin had already contributed to it a paper on "Sir Joshua and Holbein," a stray chapter from Vol. V., "Modern Painters." His reputation as a writer and philanthropist, together with the friendliness of editor and publisher, secured the insertion of the first three,—from August to October. The editor then wrote to say that they were so unanimously condemned and disliked, that, with all apologies, he could only admit one more. The series was brought hastily to a conclusion in November: and the author, beaten back as he had never been beaten before, dropped the subject, and "sulked," so he called it, all the winter.

It is pleasant to notice that neither Thackeray, the editor nor Smith, the publisher quarrelled with the author who had laid them open to the censure of their public,—nor he with them. On December 21st, he wrote to Thackeray, in answer apparently, to a letter about lecturing for a charitable purpose: and continued:

> "The mode in which you direct your charity puts me in mind of a matter that has lain long on my mind, though I never have had the time or face to talk to you of it. In somebody's drawing-room, ages ago, you were speaking accidentally of M. de Marvy.[8]

I expressed my great obligation to him; on which you said that I could prove my gratitude, if I chose, to his widow,—which choice I then not accepting, have ever since remembered the circumstance as one peculiarly likely to add, so far as it went, to the general impression on your mind of the hollowness of people's sayings and hardness of their hearts. The fact is, I give what I give almost in an opposite way to yours. I think there are many people who will relieve hopeless distress for one who will help at a hopeful pinch; and when I have the choice I nearly always give where I think the money will be fruitful rather than merely helpful. I would lecture for a school when I would *not* for a distressed author; and would have helped De Marvy to perfect his invention, but not—unless I had no other object—his widow after he was gone. In a word, I like to prop the falling more than to feed the fallen."

The winter passed without any great undertaking. G.F. Watts proposed to add Ruskin's portrait to his gallery of celebrities; but he was in no mood to sit. Rossetti did, however, sketch him this year. In March he presented eighty-three Turner drawings to Oxford, and twenty-five to Cambridge. The address of thanks with the great seal of Oxford University is dated March 23rd, 1861; the Catalogue of the Cambridge collection is dated May 28th.

On April 2nd he addressed the St. George's Mission Working Men's Institute, and shortly afterwards, though at this time in a much enfeebled state of health, gave a lecture before "a most brilliant audience," as the *London Review* reported, at the Royal Institution (April 19th, 1861). Carlyle wrote to his brother John:

"Friday last I was persuaded—in fact had inwardly compelled myself as it were—to a lecture of Ruskin's at the Institution, Albemarle Street, Lecture on Tree Leaves as physiological, pictorial, moral, symbolical objects. A crammed house, but tolerable even to me in the gallery. The lecture was thought to 'break down,' and indeed it quite did '*as a lecture*'; but only did from *embarras de richesses*—a rare case. Ruskin did blow asunder as by gunpowder explosions his leaf notions, which were manifold, curious, genial; and in fact, I do not recollect to have heard in that place any neatest thing I liked so well as this chaotic one."

Papers on "Illuminated Manuscripts" (read before the Society of Antiquaries on June 6th) and on "The Preservation of Ancient Buildings" (read to the Ecclesiological Society a fortnight later) show that old interests were not wholly forgotten, even in the stress of new pursuits, by this man of many-sided activity.

During May, 1861, he paid a visit to the school girls at Winnington, in June and July he took a holiday at Boulogne with the fisher folk, in August he went to Ireland as guest of the Latouches of Harristown, County Kildare, and in September he returned to the Alps, spending the rest of the year at Bonneville and Lucerne.

NOTE:

8   Louis Marvy, an engraver, and political refugee after the French Revolution of 1848. He produced the plates, and Thackeray the text, of "Landscape Painters of England, in a series of steel engravings, with short Notices."

CHAPTER II

"MUNERA PULVERIS" (1862)

After an autumn among the Alps, hearing that the Turner drawings in the National Gallery had been mildewed, he ran home to see about them in January 1862; and was kept until the end of May. He found that his political economy work was not such a total failure as it had seemed. Froude, then editor of *Fraser's Magazine*, thought there was something in it, and would give him another chance. So, by way of a fresh start, he had his four *Cornhill* articles published in book form; and almost simultaneously, in June 1862 the first of the new series appeared.

The author had then returned to Lucerne with Mr. and Mrs. Burne-Jones, with whom he crossed the St. Gothard to Milan, where he tried to forget the harrowing of hell in a close study of Luini, and in copying the "St. Catherine" now at Oxford. Ruskin has never said so much about Luini as, perhaps, he intended. A short notice in the "Cestus of Aglaia," and occasional references scattered up and down his later works, hardly give the prominence in his writings that the painter held in his thoughts. It was about this time that he was made an Hon. Member of the Florentine Academy.

He re-crossed the Alps, and settled to his work on political economy at Mornex, where he spent the winter except for a short run home, which gave him the opportunity of addressing the Working Men's College on November 29.

His retreat is described in one of his letters home:

"MORNEX, *August* 31 (1862).

"MY DEAREST MOTHER,

"This ought to arrive on the evening before your birthday: it is not possible to reach you in the morning, not even by telegraph as I once did from Mont Cenis, for—(may Heaven be devoutly thanked therefore)—there are yet on Mont Salève neither rails nor wires . . .

"The place I have got to is at the end of all carriage-roads, and I am not yet strong enough to get farther, on foot, than a five or six miles' circle, within which is assuredly no house to my mind. I cast, at first, somewhat longing eyes on a true Savoyard château—notable for its lovely garden and orchard—and its unspoiled, unrestored, arched gateway between two round turrets, and Gothic-windowed keep. But on examination of the interior—finding the walls, though six feet thick, rent to the foundation—and as cold as rocks, and the floors all sodden through with walnut oil and rotten-apple juice—heaps of the farm stores having been left to decay in the ci-devant drawing room, I gave up all medieval ideas, for which the long-legged black pigs who lived like gentlemen at ease in the passage, and the bats and spiders who divided between them the corners of the turret-stair, have reason—if they knew it—to be thankful.

"The worst of it is that I never had the gift, nor have I now the energy, to *make* anything of a place; so that I shall have to put up with almost anything I can find that is healthily habitable in a good situation. Meantime, the air here being delicious and the rooms good enough for use and comfort, I am not troubling myself much, but trying to put myself into better health and humour; in which I have already a little succeeded."

After describing the flowers of the Salève he continues:

"My Father would be quite wild at the 'view' from the garden terrace—but he would be disgusted at the shut in feeling of the house, which is in fact as much shut in as our old Herne Hill one; only to get the 'view' I have but to go as far down the garden as to our old 'mulberry tree.' By the way there's a magnificent mulberry tree, as big as a common walnut, covered with black and red fruit on the other side of the road. Coutet and Allen are very anxious to do all they can now that Crawley is away; and I don't think I shall manage very badly," etc.

A little later he took in addition a cottage in which the Empress of Russia had once stayed: it commanded a finer view than the larger house, which has since been turned into a hotel (Hôtel et Pension des Glycines). This place was for some time the hermitage in which he wrote his political economy. Of his lonely rambles he wrote later on:

"If I have a definite point to reach, and common work to do at it—I take people—anybody—with me; but all my best *mental* work is necessarily done alone; whenever I wanted to think, in Savoy, I used to leave Coutet at home. Constantly I have been alone on the Glacier des Bois—and far among the loneliest aiguille recesses. I found the path up the Brezon above Bonneville in a lonely walk one Sunday; I saw the grandest view of the Alps of Savoy I ever gained, on the 2nd of January, 1862, alone among the snow wreaths on the summit of the Salève. You need not fear for me on 'Langdale Pikes' after that."

In September the second article appeared in *Fraser*. "Only a genius like Mr. Ruskin could have produced such hopeless rubbish," says a newspaper of the period. Far worse than any newspaper criticism was the condemnation of Denmark Hill. His father, whose eyes had glistened over early poems and prose eloquence, strongly disapproved of this heretical economy. It was a bitter thing that his son should become prodigal of a hardly earned reputation, and be pointed at for a fool. And it was intensely painful for a son "who had never given his father a pang that could be avoided," as old Mr. Ruskin had once written, to find his father, with one foot in the grave, turning against him. In December the third paper appeared. History repeated itself, and with the fourth paper the heretic was gagged. A year after, his father died; and these *Fraser* articles were laid aside until the end of 1871, when they were taken up again, and published on New Year's Day 1872, as "Munera Pulveris."

From the outset, however, he was not without supporters. Carlyle wrote on June 30, 1862:

> "I have read, a month ago, your *First* in *Fraser*, and ever since have had a wish to say to it and you, *Euge macte nova virtute*. I approved in every particular; calm, definite, clear; rising into the sphere of *Plato* (our almost best), wh'h in exchange for the sphere of *Macculloch, Mill and Co.* is a mighty improvement! Since that, I have seen the little *green* book, too; reprint of your *Cornhill* operations,—about 2/3 of wh'h was read to me (*known* only from what the contradict'n of sinners had told me of it);—in every part of wh'h I find a high and noble sort of truth, not one doctrine that I can intrinsically dissent from, or count other than salutary in the extreme, and pressingly needed in Engl'd above all."

Erskine of Linlathen wrote to Carlyle, August 7th, 1862:

"I am thankful for any unveiling of the so-called science of political economy, according to which, avowed selfishness is the Rule of the World. It is indeed most important preaching—to preach that there is not one God for religion and another God for human fellowship—and another God for buying and selling—that pestilent polytheism has been largely and confidently preached in our time, and blessed are those who can detect its mendacities, and help to disenchant the brethren of their power . . ."

J.A. Froude, then editor of *Fraser*, and to his dying day Mr. Ruskin's intimate and affectionate friend, wrote to him on October 24 (1862?):

"The world talks of the article in its usual way. I was at Carlyle's last night . . . He said that in writing to your father as to subject he had told him that when Solomon's temple was building it was credibly reported that at least 10,000 sparrows sitting on the trees round declared that it was entirely wrong—quite contrary to received opinion—hopelessly condemned by public opinion, etc. Nevertheless it got finished and the sparrows flew away and began to chirp in the same note about something else."

CHAPTER III

THE LIMESTONE ALPS (1863)

Our hermit among the Alps of Savoy differed in one respect from his predecessors. They, for the most part, saw nothing in the rocks and stones around them except the prison walls of their seclusion; he could not be within constant sight of the mountains without thinking over the wonders of their scenery and structure. And it was well for him that it could be so. The terrible depression of mind which his social and philanthropic work had brought on, found a relief in the renewal of his old mountain-worship. After sending off the last of his *Fraser* papers, in which, when the verdict had twice gone against him, he tried to show cause why sentence should not be passed, the strain was at its severest. He felt, as few others not directly interested felt, the sufferings of the outcast in English slums and Savoyard hovels; and heard the cry of the oppressed in Poland and in Italy: and he had been silenced. What could he do but, as he said in the letters to Norton, "lay his head to the very ground," and try to forget it all among the stones and the snows?

He wandered about geologizing, and spent a while at Talloires on the Lake of Annecy, where the old Abbey had been turned into an inn, and one slept in a monk's cell and meditated in the cloister of the monastery, St. Bernard of Menthon's memory haunting the place, and St. Germain's cave close by in the rocks above. At the end of May he came back to England, and was invited to lecture again at the Royal Institution. The subject he chose was "The Stratified Alps of Savoy."

At that time many distinguished foreign geologists were working at the Alps; but little of conclusive importance had been published, except in papers embedded in Transactions of various societies. Professor Alphonse Favre's great work did not appear until 1867, and the "Mechanismus der Gebirgsbildung" of Professor Heim not till 1878; so that for an English public the subject was a fresh one. To Ruskin it was familiar: he had been elected a Fellow of the Geological Society in 1840, at the age of twenty-one; he had worked through Savoy with his Saussure in hand nearly thirty years before, and, many a time since that, had spent the intervals of literary business in rambling and climbing with the hammer and note-book. In the field he had compared Studer's meagre sections, and consulted the available authorities on physical geology, though he had never entered upon the more popular sister-science of palaeontology. He left the determination of strata to specialists: his interest was fixed on the structure of mountains—the relation of geology to scenery; a question upon which he had some right to be heard, as knowing more about scenery than most geologists, and more about geology than most artists.

As examples of Savoy mountains this lecture described in detail the Salève, on which he had been living for two winters, and the Brezon, the top of which he had tried to buy from the commune of Bonneville—one of his many plans for settling among the Alps. The commune thought he had found a gold-mine up there, and raised the price out of all reason. Other attempts to make a home in the châteaux or chalets of Savoy were foiled, or abandoned, like his earlier idea to live in Venice. But his scrambles on the Salève led him to hesitate in accepting the explanation given by Alphonse Favre of the curious north-west face of steeply inclined vertical slabs, which he suspected to be created by cleavage, on the analogy of other Jurassic precipices. The Brezon—*brisant*, breaking wave—he took as type of the billowy form of limestone Alps in general, and his analysis of it was serviceable and substantially correct.

This lecture was followed in 1864 by desultory correspondence with Mr. Jukes and others in *The Reader*, in which he merely restated his conclusions, too slightly to convince. Had he devoted himself to a thorough examination of the subject—but this is in the region of what might have been. He was more seriously engaged in other pursuits, of more immediate importance. Three days after his lecture he was being examined before the Royal Academy Commission, and after a short summer visit to various friends in the north of England, he set out again for the Alps, partly to study the geology of Chamouni and North Switzerland, partly to continue his drawings of Swiss towns at Baden and Lauffenburg, with his pupil John Bunney. But even there the burden of his real mission could not be shaken off, and though again seeking health and a quiet mind, he could not quite keep silence, but wrote letters to English newspapers on the depreciation of gold (repeating his theory of currency), and on the wrongs of Poland and Italy; and he put together more papers, not then published, in continuation of his "Munera Pulveris."

Since about 1850, Carlyle had been gradually becoming more and more friendly with John Ruskin; and now that this social and economical work had been taken up, he began to have a real esteem for him, though always with a patronizing tone, which the younger man's open and confessed discipleship accepted and encouraged. This letter especially shows both men in an unaccustomed light: Ruskin, hating tobacco, sends his "master" cigars; Carlyle, hating cant, replies rather in the tone of the temperance advocate, taking a little wine for his stomach's sake:

"CHELSEA, 22 *Feby*, 1865

"DEAR RUSKIN,

"You have sent me a munificent Box of Cigars; for wh'h what can I say in ans'r? It makes me both sad and glad. *Ay de mi*.

"We are such stuff,
Gone with a puff—Then
think, and smoke Tobacco!'

"The Wife also has had her Flowers; and a letter wh'h has charmed the female mind. You forgot only the first chapter of 'Aglaia';—don't forget; and be a good boy for the future.

"The Geology Book wasn't *Jukes*; I found it again in the Magazine,—reviewed there: 'Phillips,'[9] is there such a name? It has ag'n escaped me. I have a notion to come out actually some day soon; and take a serious Lecture from you on what you really know, and can give me some intelligible outline of, ab't the Rocks,—*bones* of our poor old Mother; wh'h have always been venerable and strange to me. Next to nothing of rational could I ever learn of the subject . . .

"Yours ever,
"T. CARLYLE."

NOTE:

[9] "Jukes,"—Mr. J.B. Jukes, F.R.S., with whom Ruskin had been discussing in *The Reader*. "Phillips," the Oxford Professor of Geology, and a friend of Ruskin's.

CHAPTER IV

"SESAME AND LILIES" (1864)

Wider aims and weaker health had not put an end to Ruskin's connection with the Working Men's College, though he did not now teach a drawing-class regularly. He had, as he said, "the satisfaction of knowing that they had very good masters in Messrs. Lowes Dickinson, Jeffery and Cave Thomas," and his work was elsewhere. He was to have lectured there on December 19th, 1863; but he did not reach home until about Christmas; better than he had been; and ready to give the promised address on January 30th, 1864. Beside which he used to visit the place occasionally of an evening to take note of progress, and some of his pupils were now more directly under his care.

It was from one of these visits to the College, on February 27th, that he returned, past midnight, and found his father waiting up for him, to read some letters he had written. Next morning the old man, close upon seventy-nine years of age, was struck with his last illness; and died on March 3rd. He was buried at Shirley Church, near Addington, in Surrey, not far from Croydon; and the legend on his tomb records: "He was an entirely honest merchant, and his memory is, to all who keep it, dear and helpful. His son, whom he loved to the uttermost, and taught to speak truth, says this of him."

Mr. John James Ruskin, like many other of our successful merchants, had been an open-handed patron of art, and a cheerful giver, not only to needy friends and relatives, but also to various charities. For example, as a kind of personal tribute to Osborne Gordon, his son's tutor, he gave £5,000 toward the augmentation of poor Christ-Church livings. His son's open-handed way with dependants and servants was learned from the old merchant, who, unlike many hard-working money-makers, was always ready to give, though he could not bear to lose. In spite of which he left a considerable fortune behind him,—considerable when it is understood to be the earnings of his single-handed industry and steady sagacity in legitimate business, without indulgence in speculation. He left £120,000 with various other property, to his son. To his wife he left his house and £37,000, and a void which it seemed at first nothing could fill. For of late years the son had drifted out of their horizon, with ideas on religion and the ordering of life so very different from theirs; and had been much away from home—he sometimes said, selfishly, but not without the greatest of all excuses, necessity. And so the two old people had been brought closer than ever together; and she had lived entirely for her husband. But, as Browning said,—"Put a stick in anywhere, and she will run up it"—so the brave old lady did not faint under the blow, and fade away, but transferred her affections and interests to her son. Before his father's death the difference of feeling between them, arising out of the heretical economy, had been healed. Old Mr. Ruskin's will treated his son with all confidence in spite of his unorthodox views and unbusiness-like ways. And for nearly eight years longer his mother lived on, to see him pass through his probation-period into such recognition as an Oxford Professorship implied, and to find in her last years his later books "becoming more and more what they always ought to have been" to her.

At the same time, her failing sight and strength needed a constant household companion. Her son, though he did not leave home yet awhile for any long journeys, could not be always with her. Only six weeks after the funeral he was called away for a time to fulfil a lecture-engagement at Bradford. Before going he brought his pretty young Scotch cousin. Miss Joanna Ruskin Agnew, to Denmark Hill for a week's visit.

She recommended herself at once to the old lady, and to Carlyle, who happened to call, by her frank good-nature and unquenchable spirits; and her visit lasted seven years, until she was married to Arthur Severn, son of the Ruskins' old friend, Joseph Severn, British Consul at Rome. Even then she was not allowed far out of their sight, but settled in the old house at Herne Hill: "nor virtually," said Ruskin in the last chapter of "Præterita," "have she and I ever parted since."

All through that year he remained at home, except for short necessary visits, and frequent evenings with Carlyle. And when, in December, he gave those lectures in Manchester which afterwards, as "Sesame and Lilies," became his most popular work, we can trace his better health of mind and body in the brighter tone of his thought. We can hear the echo of Carlyle's talk in the heroic, aristocratic, Stoic ideals, and in the insistence on the value of books and free public libraries,[10]—Carlyle being the founder of the London Library. And we may suspect that his thoughts on women's influence and education had been not a little directed by those months in the company of "the dear old lady and ditto young" to whom Carlyle used to send his love.

In 1864 a new series of papers on Art was begun, the only published work upon Art of all these ten years. The papers ran in *The Art Journal* from January to July, 1865, and from January to April. 1866, under the title of "The Cestus of Aglaia," by which was meant the Girdle, or restraining law, of Beauty, as personified in the wife of Hephaestus, "the Lord of Labour." Their intention was to suggest, and to evoke by correspondence, "some laws for present practice of art in our schools, which may be admitted, if not with absolute, at least with a sufficient consent, by leading artists." As a first step the author asked for the elementary rules of drawing. For his own contribution he showed the value of the "pure line," such as he had used in his own early drawings. Later on, he had adopted a looser and more picturesque style of handling the point; and in the "Elements of Drawing" he had taught his readers to take Rembrandt's etchings as exemplary. But now he felt that this "evasive" manner, as he called it, had its dangers. And so these papers attempted to supersede the amateurish object lesson of the earlier work by stricter rules for a severer style; prematurely, as it proved, for the chapters came to an end before the promised code was formulated. The same work was taken up again in "The Laws of Fésole"; but the use of the pure line, which Ruskin's precepts failed to enforce, was, in the end, taught to the public by the charming practice of Mr. Walter Crane and Miss Greenaway.

A lecture at the Camberwell Working Men's Institute on "Work and Play" was given on January 24th, 1865; which, as it was printed in "The Crown of Wild Olive," we will notice further on. Various letters and papers on political and social economy and other subjects hardly call for separate notice: with the exception of one very important address to the Royal Institution of British Architects, given May 15th, "On the Study of Architecture in our Schools."

NOTE:

10 The first lecture, "Of Kings' Treasuries," was given, December 6th, 1864, at Rusholme Town Hall, Manchester, in aid of a library fund for the Rusholme Institute. The second, "Queens' Gardens," was given December 14th, at the Town Hall, King Street, now the Free Reference Library, Manchester, in aid of schools for Ancoats.

CHAPTER V

"ETHICS OF THE DUST" (1865)

Writing to his father from Manchester about the lecture of February 22, 1859—"The Unity of Art"—Ruskin mentions, among various people of interest whom he was meeting, such as Sir Elkanah Armitage and Mrs. Gaskell, how "Miss Bell and four young ladies came from Chester to hear me, and I promised to pay them a visit on my way home, to their apparent great contentment."

The visit was paid on his way back from Yorkshire. He wrote:

"WINNINGTON, NORTHWICH, CHESHIRE.
"12 *March*, 1859.

"This is such a nice place that I am going to stay till Monday: an enormous old-fashioned house—full of galleries and up and down stairs—but with magnificently large rooms where wanted: the drawing-room is a huge octagon—I suppose at least forty feet high—like the tower of a castle (hung half way up all round with large and beautiful Turner and Raphael engravings) and with a baronial fireplace:—and in the evening, brightly lighted, with the groups of girls scattered round it, it is a quite beautiful scene in its way. Their morning chapel, too, is very interesting:—though only a large room, it is nicely fitted with reading desk and seats like a college chapel, and two pretty and rich stained-glass windows—

and well-toned organ. They have morning prayers with only one of the lessons—and without the psalms: but singing the Te Deum or the other hymn—and other choral parts: and as out of the thirty-five or forty girls perhaps twenty-five or thirty have really available voices, well trained and divided, it was infinitely more beautiful than any ordinary church service—like the Trinita di Monte Convent service more than anything else, and must be very good for them, quite different in its effect on their minds from our wretched penance of college chapel.

"The house stands in a superb park, full of old trees and sloping down to the river; with a steep bank of trees on the other side; just the kind of thing Mrs. Sherwood likes to describe;—and the girls look all healthy and happy as can be, down to the little six-years-old ones, who I find know me by the fairy tale as the others do by my large books:—so I am quite at home.

"They have my portrait in the library with three others—Maurice, the Bp. of Oxford, and Archdeacon Hare,—so that I can't but stay with them over the Sunday."

The principles of Winnington were advanced; the theology—Bishop Colenso's daughter was among the pupils; the Bishop of Oxford had introduced Ruskin to the managers, who were pleased to invite the celebrated art-critic to visit whenever he travelled that way, whether to lecture at provincial towns, or to see his friends in the north, as he often used. And so between March 1859 and May 1868, after which the school was removed, he was a frequent visitor; and not only he, but other lions whom the ladies entrapped:—mention has been made in print (in "The Queen of the Air") of Charles Halle, whom Ruskin met there in 1863, and greatly admired.

"I like Mr. and Mrs. Halle so very much," he wrote home, "and am entirely glad to know so great a musician and evidently so good and wise a man. He was very happy yesterday evening, and actually sat down and played quadrilles for us to dance to—which is, in its way, something like Titian sketching patterns for ball-dresses. But afterwards he played Home, sweet Home, with three variations—*quite* the most wonderful thing I have ever heard in music. Though I was close to the piano, the motion of the fingers was entirely invisible—a mere *mist* of rapidity; the *hands* moving slowly and softly, and the variation, in the ear, like a murmur of a light fountain, far away. It was beautiful too to see the girls' faces round, the eyes all wet with feeling, and the little coral mouths fixed into little half open gaps with utter intensity of astonishment."

Ruskin could not be idle on his visits; and as he was never so happy as when he was teaching somebody, he improved the opportunity by experiments in education permitted there for his sake. Among other things, he devised singing dances for a select dozen of the girls, with verses of his own writing; one, a maze to the theme of "Twist ye, twine ye," based upon the song in "Guy Mannering," but going far beyond the original motive in its variations weighted with allegoric thought. Deep as the feeling of this little poem is, there is a nobler chord struck in the Song of Peace, the battle-cry of the good time coming; in the faith—who else has found it?—that looks forward to no selfish victory of narrow aims, but to the full reconciliation of hostile interests and the blind internecine struggle of this perverse world, in the clearer light of the millennial morning.

Ruskin's method of teaching, as illustrated in "Ethics of the Dust," has been variously pooh-poohed by his critics. It has seemed to some absurd to mix up Theology, and Crystallography, and Political Economy, and Mythology, and Moral Philosophy, with the chatter of school-girls and the romps of the playground. But it should be understood, before reading this book, which is practically the report of these Wilmington talks, that it is printed as an illustration of a method. It showed that play-lessons need not want either depth or accuracy; and that the requirement was simply capacity on the part of the teacher.

The following letter from Carlyle was written in acknowledgment of an early copy of the book, of which the preface is dated Christmas, 1865.

"CHELSEA,
"*20 Decr, 1865.*

"The 'Ethics of the Dust,' wh'h I devoured with't pause, and intend to look at ag'n, is a most shining Performance! Not for a long while have I read anything tenth-part so radiant with talent, ingenuity, lambent fire (sheet—and *other* lightnings) of all commendable kinds! Never was such a lecture on *Crystallography* before, had there been nothing else in it,—and there are all manner of things. In power of *expression* I pronounce it to be supreme; never did anybody who had *such* things to explain explain them better. And the bit of Egypt'n mythology, the cunning *Dreams* ab't Pthah, Neith, etc., apart from their elucidative quality, wh'h is exquisite, have in them a *poetry* that might fill any Tennyson with despair. You are very dramatic too; nothing wanting in the stage-direct'ns, in the pretty little indicat'ns: a very pretty stage and *dramatis personæ* altogeth'r. Such is my first feeling ab't y'r Book, dear R.—Come soon, and I will tell you all the *faults* of it, if I gradually discover a great many. In fact, *come* at any rate!

"Y'rs ever,
"T. CARLYLE."

The Real Little Housewives, to whom the book was dedicated, were not quite delighted—at least, they said they were not—at the portraits drawn of them, in their pinafores, so to speak, with some little hints at failings and faults which they recognised through the mask of *dramatis personæ*. Miss "Kathleen" disclaimed the singing of "Vilikins and his Dinah," and so on. It is difficult to please everybody. The public did not care about the book; the publisher hoped Mr. Ruskin would write no more dialogues: and so it remained, little noticed, for twelve years. In 1877 it was republished and found to be interesting, and in 1905 the 31st thousand (authorised English edition) had been issued. At that time, however, Sesame and Lilies had run to 160,000 copies.

Winnington Hall, the scene of these pastimes, is now, I understand, used by Messrs. Brunner, Mond & Co. as a commonroom or clubhouse for the staff in their great scientific industry.

CHAPTER VI

"THE CROWN OF WILD OLIVE"
(1865-1866)

Mention has been made of an address to working men at the Camberwell Institute, January 24th, 1865. This lecture was published in 1866, together with two others,[11] under the title of "The Crown of Wild Olive"—that is to say, the reward of human work, a reward "which should have been of gold, had not Jupiter been so poor," as Aristophanes said.

True work, he said, meant the production (taking the word production in a broad sense) of the means of life; every one ought to take some share in it, according to his powers: some working with the head, some with the hands; but all acknowledging idleness and slavery to be alike immoral. And, as to the remuneration, he said, as he had said before in "Unto this Last," Justice demands that equal energy expended should bring equal reward. He did not consider it justice to cry out for the equalization of incomes, for some are sure to be more diligent and saving than others; some work involves a great preliminary expenditure of energy in qualifying the worker, as contrasted with unskilled labour. But he did not allow that the possession of capital entitled a man to unearned increment; and he thought that, in a community where a truly civilized morality was highly developed, the general sense of society would recognise an average standard of work and an average standard of pay for each class.

In the next two lectures he spoke of the two great forms of Play, the great Games of Money-making and War. He had been invited to lecture at

Bradford, in the hope that he would give some useful advice towards the design of a new Exchange which was to be built; in curious forgetfulness, it would appear, of his work during the past ten years and more. Indeed, the picture he drew them of an ideal "Temple to the Goddess of Getting-on" was as daring a sermon as ever prophet preached. But when he came to tell them that the employers of labour might be true captains and kings, the leaders and the helpers of their fellow-men, and that the function of commerce was not to prey upon society but to provide for it, there were many of his hearers whose hearts told them that he was right, and whose lives have shown, in some measure, that he did not speak in vain.

Still stranger, to hearers who had not noted the conclusion of his third volume of "Modern Painters," was his view of war, in the address to the Royal Military Academy at Woolwich, in December 1865. The common view of war as destroyer of arts and enemy of morality, the easy acceptance of the doctrine that peace is an unqualified blessing, the obvious evils of battle and rapine and the waste of resources and life throughout so many ages, have blinded less clear-sighted and less widely-experienced thinkers to another side of the teaching of history, which Ruskin dwelt upon with unexpected emphasis.

But modern war, horrible, not from its scale, but from the spirit in which the upper classes set the lower to fight like gladiators in the arena, he denounced; and called upon the women of England, with whom, he said, the real power of life and death lay, to mend it into some semblance of antique chivalry, or to end it in the name of religion and humanity.

In the *New Review* for March 1892, there appeared a series of "Letters of John Ruskin to his Secretary," which, as the anonymous contributor remarked, illustrate "Ruskin the worker, as he acts away from the eyes of the world; Ruskin the epistolographer, when the eventuality of the printing-press is not for the moment before him Ruskin the good Samaritan, ever gentle and open-handed when true need and a good cause make appeal to his tender heart; Ruskin the employer, considerate, generous—an ideal master."

Charles Augustus Howell became known to Ruskin (in 1864 or 1865) through the circle of the Pre-Raphaelites; and, as the editor of the letters puts it, "by his talents and assiduity" became the too-trusted friend and *protégé* of Ruskin, Rossetti and others of their acquaintance. It was he who proposed and carried out the exhumation, reluctantly consented to, of Rossetti's manuscript poems from his wife's grave, in October, 1869; for which curious service to literature let him have the thanks of posterity. But he was hardly the man to carry out Ruskin's secret charities, and long before he had lost Rossetti's confidence[12] he had ceased to act as Ruskin's secretary.

From these letters, however, several interesting traits and incidents may be gleaned, such as anecdotes about the canary which was anonymously bought at the Crystal Palace Bird Show (February 1866) for the owner's benefit: about the shopboy whom Ruskin was going to train as an artist; and about the kindly proposal to employ the aged and impoverished Cruikshank upon a new book of fairy tales, and the struggle between admiration for the man and admission of his loss of power, ending in the free gift of the hundred pounds promised.

In April, 1866, after writing the Preface to "The Crown of Wild Olive," and preparing the book for publication, Ruskin was carried off to the Continent for a holiday with Sir Walter and Lady Trevelyan, her niece Miss Constance Hilliard (Mrs. Churchill), and Miss Agnew (Mrs. Severn), for a thorough rest and change after three years of unintermitting work in England. They intended to spend a couple of months in Italy. On the day of starting, Ruskin called at Cheyne Walk with the usual bouquet for Mrs. Carlyle, to learn that she had just met with her death, in trying to save her little dog, the gift of Lady Trevelyan. He rejoined his friends, and they crossed the Channel gaily, in spite of what they thought was rather a cloud over him. At Paris they read the news. "Yes," he said, "I knew. But there was no reason why I should spoil your pleasure by telling you."

On his arrival at Dijon he wrote to Carlyle, who in answer after giving way to his grief—"my life all laid in ruins, and the one light of it as if gone out,"—continued:—"Come and see me when you get home; come oftener and see me, and speak *more* frankly to me (for I am very true to y'r highest interests and you) while I still remain here. You can do nothing for me in Italy; except come home improved."

But before this letter reached Ruskin, he too had been in the presence of death, and had lost one of his most valued friends. Their journey to Italy had been undertaken chiefly for the sake of Lady Trevelyan's health, as the following extracts indicate:

"PARIS, *2nd May, 1866.*

"Lady Trevelyan is much better to-day, but it is not safe to move her yet—till to-morrow. So I'm going to take the children to look at Chartres cathedral—we can get three hours there, and be back to seven o'clock dinner. We drove round by St. Cloud and Sèvres yesterday; the blossomed trees being glorious by the Seine,—the children in high spirits. It reminds me always too much of Turner—every bend of these rivers is haunted by him."

"DIJON, *Sunday, 6th May, 1866.*

"Lady Trevelyan is *much* better, and we hope all to get on to Neufchatel to-morrow. The weather is quite fine again though not warm; and yesterday I took the children for a drive up the little valley which we used to drive through on leaving Dijon for Paris. There are wooded hills on each side, and we got into a sweet valley, as full of nightingales as our garden is of thrushes, and with slopes of broken rocky ground above, covered with the lovely blue milk-wort, and purple columbines, and geranium, and wild strawberry-flowers. The children were intensely delighted, and I took great care that Constance should not run about so as to heat herself, and we got up a considerable bit of hill quite nicely, and with greatly increased appetite for tea, and general mischief. They have such appetites that I generally call them 'my two little pigs.' There is a delightful French waiting-maid at dinner here—who says they are both 'charmantes,' but highly approves of my title for them nevertheless."

"NEUFCHATEL, *10th May*, 1866.

"Lady Trevelyan is still too weak to move. We had (the children and I) a delightful day yesterday at the Pierre à Bot, gathering vetches and lilies of the valley in the woods, and picnic afterwards on the lovely mossy grass, in view of all the Alps—Jungfrau, Eiger, Blumlis Alp, Altels, and the rest, with intermediate lake and farmsteads and apple-blossom—very heavenly."

Here, within a few days, Lady Trevelyan died. Throughout her illness she had been following the progress of the new notes on wild-flowers (afterwards to be "Proserpina") with keen interest, and Sir Walter lent the help of botanical science to Ruskin's more poetical and artistic observations. For the sake of this work, and for the "children," and with a wise purpose of bearing up under the heavy blow that had fallen, the two friends continued their journey for a while among the mountains.

From Thun they went to Interlachen and the Giessbach. Ruskin occupied himself closely in tracing Studer's sections across the great lake-furrow of central Switzerland—"something craggy for his mind to break upon," as Byron said when he was in trouble. At the Giessbach there was not only geology and divine scenery, enjoyable in lovely weather, but an interesting figure in the foreground, the widowed daughter of the hotel landlord, beautiful and consumptive, but brave as a Swiss girl should be. They all seem to have fallen in love with her, so to speak the young English girls as much as the impressionable art-critic: and the new human interest in her Alpine tragedy relieved, as such interests do, the painfulness of the circumstances through which they had been passing. Her sister Marie was like an Allegra to this Penserosa; bright and brilliant in native genius. She played piano-duets with the young ladies; taught Alpine botany to the savants; guided them to the secret dells and unknown points of view; and with a sympathy unexpected in a stranger, beguiled them out of their grief, and won their admiration and gratitude. Marie of the Giessbach was often referred to in letters of the time, and for many years after, with warmly affectionate remembrances.

A few bits from his letters to his mother, which I have been permitted to copy, will indicate the impressions of this summer's tour.

"HÔTEL DU GIESBACH, *6th June, 1866,*

"MY DEAREST MOTHER,

"Can you at all fancy walking out in the morning in a garden full of lilacs just in rich bloom, and pink hawthorn in masses; and along a little terrace with lovely pinks coming into cluster of colour all over the low wall beside it; and a sloping bank of green sward from it—and below that, the Giesbach! Fancy having a real Alpine waterfall in one's garden,—seven hundred feet high. You see, we are just in time for the spring, here, and the strawberries are ripening on the rocks. Joan and Constance have been just scrambling about and gathering them for me. Then there's the blue-green lake below, and Interlaken and the lake of Thun in the distance. I think I never saw anything so beautiful. Joan will write to you about the people, whom she has made great friends with, already."

"*7th June, 1866.*

"I cannot tell you how much I am struck with the beauty of this fall: it is different from everything I have ever seen in torrents. There are so many places where one gets near it without being wet, for one thing; for the falls are, mostly, not vertical so as to fly into mere spray, but over broken rock, which crushes the water into a kind of sugar-candy-like foam, white as snow, yet glittering; and composed, not of bubbles, but of broken-up water. Then I had forgotten that it plunged straight into the lake; I got down to the lake shore on the other side of it yesterday, and to see it plunge clear into the blue water, with the lovely mossy rocks for its flank, and for the lake edge, was an unbelievable kind of thing; it is all as one would fancy cascades in fairyland. I do not often endure with patience any cockneyisms or showings off at these lovely places. But they do one thing here so interesting that I can forgive it. One of the chief cascades (about midway up the hill) falls over a projecting rock, so that one can walk under the torrent as it comes over. It leaps so clear that one is hardly splashed, except at one place. Well, when it gets dark, they burn, for five minutes, one of the strongest steady fireworks of a crimson colour, behind the fall. The red light shines right through, turning the whole waterfall into a torrent of fire."

"*11th June, 1866.*

"We leave, according to our programme, for Interlachen to-day,—with great regret, for the peace and sweetness of this place are wonderful and the people are good; and though there is much drinking and quarrelling among the younger men, there appears to be neither distressful poverty, nor deliberate crime: so that there is more of the sense I need, and long for, of fellowship with human creatures, than in any place I have been at for years. I believe they don't so much as lock the house-doors at night; and the faces of the older peasantry are really very beautiful. I have done a good deal of botany, and find that wild-flower botany is more or less inexhaustible, but the cultivated flowers are infinite in their caprice. The forget-me-nots and milkworts are singularly beautiful here, but there is quite as much variety in English fields as in these, as long as one does not climb much—and I'm very lazy, compared to what I used to be,"

"*LAUTERBRUNNEN, 13th June, 1866.*

"We had a lovely evening here yesterday, and the children enjoyed and understood it better than anything they have yet seen among the Alps. Constance was in great glory in a little walk I took her in the twilight through the upper meadows: the Staubbach seen only as a grey veil suspended from its rock, and the great Alps pale above on the dark sky. She condescended nevertheless to gather a great bunch of the white catchfly,—to make 'pops' with,—her friend Marie at the Giesbach having shown her how a startling detonation may be obtained, by skilful management, out of its globular calyx.

"This morning is not so promising,—one of the provoking ones which will neither let you stay at home with resignation, nor go anywhere with pleasure. I'm going to take the children for a little quiet exploration of the Wengern path, to see how they like it, and if the weather betters—we may go on. At all events I hope to find an Alpine rose or two."

In June, 1866, the Professorship of Poetry at Oxford was vacant; and Ruskin's friends were anxious to see him take the post. He, however, felt no especial fitness or inclination for it, and did not stand. Three years later he was elected to a Professorship that at this time had not been founded.

After spending June in the Oberland, he went homewards through Berne, Vevey and Geneva, to find his private secretary with a bundle of begging letters, and his friend Carlyle busy with the defence of Governor Eyre.

In 1865 an insurrection of negroes at Morant Bay, Jamaica, had threatened to take the most serious shape, when it was stamped out by the high-handed measures of Mr. Eyre. After the first congratulations were over another side to the question called for a hearing. The Baptist missionaries declared that among the negroes who were shot and hanged *in terrorem* were peaceable subjects, respectable members of their own native congregations, for whose character they could vouch; they added that the gravity of the situation had been exaggerated by private enmity and jealousy of their work and creed. A strong committee was formed under Liberal auspices, supported by such men as John Stuart Mill and Thomas Hughes, the author of "Tom Brown's Schooldays"—men whose motive was above suspicion—to bring Mr. Eyre to account.

Carlyle, who admired the strong hand, and had no interest in Baptist missionaries, accepted Mr. Eyre as the saviour of society in his West Indian sphere; and there were many, both in Jamaica and at home, who believed that, but for his prompt action, the white population would have been massacred with all the horrors of a savage rebellion. Ruskin had been for many years the ally of the Broad Church and Liberal party. But he was now coming more and more under the personal influence of Carlyle; and when it came to the point of choosing sides, declared himself, in a letter to the *Daily Telegraph* (December 20th, 1865), a Conservative and a supporter of order; and joined the Eyre Defence Committee with a subscription of £100. The prominent part he took, for example, in the meeting of September, 1866, was no doubt forced upon him by his desire to save Carlyle, whose recent loss and shaken nerves made such business especially trying to him. Letters of this period remain, in which Carlyle begs Ruskin to "be diligent, I bid you!"—and so on, adding, "I must absolutely *shut up* in that direction, to save my sanity." And so it fell to the younger man to work through piles of pamphlets and newspaper correspondence, to interview politicians and men of business, and—what was so very foreign to his habits—to take a leading share in a party agitation.

But in all this he was true to his Jacobite instincts. He had been brought up a Tory; and though he had drifted into an alliance with the Broad Church and philosophical Liberals, he was never one of them. Now that his father was gone, perhaps he felt a sort of duty to own himself his father's son; and the failure of liberal philanthropy to realise his ideals, and of liberal philosophy to rise to his economic standards, combined with Carlyle to induce him to label himself Conservative. But his conservatism could not be accepted by the party so called. Fortunately, he did not need or ask their recognition. He took no interest in party politics, and never in his life voted at a Parliamentary election. He only meant to state in the shortest terms that he stood for loyalty and order.

NOTES:

11 Republished in 1873, with a fourth lecture added, and a Preface and notes on the political growth of Prussia, from Carlyle's "Frederick."
12 In the manner described by Mr. W.M. Rossetti at p. 351, Vol. I., of "D.G. Rossetti, his family letters," to which the reader is referred.

CHAPTER VII

"TIME AND TIDE" (1867)

The series of letters published as "Time and Tide by Weare and Tyne" were addressed[13] to Thomas Dixon, a working cork-cutter of Sunderland, whose portrait by Professor Legros is familiar to visitors at the South Kensington Museum. He was one of those thoughtful, self-educated working men in whom, as a class, Ruskin had been taking a deep interest for the past twelve years, an interest which had purchased him a practical insight into their various capacities and aims, and the right to speak without fear or favour. At this time there was an agitation for Parliamentary reform, and the better representation of the working classes; and it was on this topic that the letters were begun, though the writer went on to criticise the various social ideals then popular, and to propose his own. He had already done something of the sort in "Unto this Last"; but "Time and Tide" is much more complete, and the result of seven years' further thought and experience. His "Fors Clavigera" is a continuation of these letters, but written at a time when other work and ill health broke in upon his strength. "Time and Tide" is not only the statement of his social scheme as he saw it in his central period, but, written as these letters were—at a stroke, so to speak—condensed in exposition and simple in language, they deserve the most careful reading by the student of Ruskin.

Before this work was ended, Carlyle had come back from Mentone to Chelsea, and was begging his friend, in the warmest terms, to come and see him. Shortly afterward, a passage which Ruskin would not retract gave offence to Carlyle. But the difference was healed, and later years reveal the sage of Chelsea as kindly and affectionate as ever. This friendship between the two greatest writers of their age, between two men of vigorous individuality, outspoken opinions, and widely different tastes and sympathies, is a fine episode in the history of both.

In May, Ruskin was invited to Cambridge to receive the honorary degree of LL.D., and to deliver the Rede Lecture. The *Cambridge Chronicle* of May 24th, 1867, says: "The body of the Senate House was quite filled with M.A.'s and ladies, principally the latter, whilst there was a large attendance of undergraduates in the galleries, who gave the lecturer a most enthusiastic reception." A brief report of the lecture was printed in the newspaper; but it was not otherwise published, and the manuscript seems to have been mislaid for thirty years. I take the liberty of copying the opening sentences as a specimen of that Academical oratory which Mr. Ruskin then adopted, and used habitually in his earlier lectures at Oxford.

The title of the discourse was "The Relation of National Ethics to National Arts."

> "In entering on the duty to-day entrusted to me, I should hold it little respectful to my audience if I disturbed them by expression of the diffidence which they know that I must feel in first speaking in this Senate House; diffidence which might well have prevented me from accepting such duty, but ought not to interfere with my endeavour simply to fulfil it. Nevertheless, lest the direction which I have been led to give to my discourse, and the narrow limits within which I am compelled to confine the treatment of its subject may seem in anywise inconsistent with the purpose of the founder of this Lecture—or with the expectations of those by whose authority I am appointed to deliver it, let me at once say that I obeyed their command, not thinking myself able to teach any dogma in the philosophy of the arts, which could be of any

new interest to the members of this University: but only that I might obtain the sanction of their audience, for the enforcement upon other minds of the truth, which—after thirty years spent in the study of art, not dishonestly, however feebly—is manifest to me as the clearest of all that I have learned, and urged upon me as the most vital of all I have to declare."

He then distinguished between true and false art, the true depending upon sincerity, whether in literature, music or the formative arts: he reinforced his old doctrine of the dignity of true imagination as the attribute of healthy and earnest minds; and energetically attacked the commercial art-world of the day, and the notion that drawing-schools were to be supported for the sake of the gain they would bring to our manufacturers.

In this lecture we see the germ of the ideas, as well as the beginning of the style, of the Oxford Inaugural course, and the "Eagle's Nest"; something quite different in type from the style and teaching of the addresses to working men, or to mixed popular audiences at Edinburgh or Manchester, or even at the Royal Institution. At this latter place, on June 4th, Sir Henry Holland in the chair, he lectured on "The Present State of Modern Art, with reference to advisable arrangement of the National Gallery," repeating much of what he had said in "Time and Tide" about the taste for the horrible and absence of true feeling for pure and dignified art in the theatrical shows of the day, and in the admiration for Gustave Doré, then a new fashion. Mr. Ruskin could never endure that the man who had illustrated Balzac's "Contes Drôlatiques" should be chosen by the religious public of England as the exponent of their sacred ideals.

In July after a short visit to Huntly Burn near Abbotsford, he went to Keswick for a few weeks, from whence he wrote the rhymed letters to his cousin at home, quoted (with the date wrongly given as 1857) in "Præterita" to illustrate his "heraldic character" of "Little Pigs" and to shock exoteric admirers. Like, for example, Rossetti and Carlyle, Ruskin was fond of playful nicknames and grotesque terms of endearment. He never stood upon his dignity with intimates; and was ready to allow the liberties he took, much to the surprise of strangers.

He reached Keswick by July 4, and spent his time chiefly in walks upon the hills, staying at the Derwentwater Hotel. He wrote:

"Keswick, *19th July, '67, Afternoon, 1/2 past 3*.

"My dearest Mother,

"As this is the last post before Sunday I send one more line to say I've had a delightful forenoon's walk—since 1/2 past ten—by St. John's Vale, and had pleasant thoughts, and found one of the most variedly beautiful torrent beds I ever saw in my life; and I feel that I gain strength, slowly but certainly, every day. The great good of the place is that I can be content without going on great excursions which fatigue and do me harm (or else worry me with problems;)—I am *content* here with the roadside hedges and streams; and this contentment is the great thing for health,—and there is hardly anything to annoy me of absurd or calamitous human doing; but still this ancient cottage life—very rude and miserable enough in its torpor—but clean, and calm, not a vile cholera and plague of bestirred pollution, like back streets in London. There is also much more real and deep beauty than I expected to find, in some of the minor pieces of scenery, and in the cloud effects."

"*July 16*.

"I have the secret of extracting sadness from all things, instead of joy, which is no enviable talisman. Forgive me if I ever write in a way that may pain you. It is best that you should know, when

I write cheerfully, it is no pretended cheerfulness; so when I am sad—I think it right to confess it."

"*30th July.*

"Downes[14] arrived yesterday quite comfortably and in fine weather. It is not bad this morning, and I hope to take him for a walk up Saddleback, which, after all, is the finest, to my mind, of all the Cumberland hills—though that is not saying much; for they are much lower in effect, in proportion to their real height, than I had expected. The beauty of the country is in its quiet roadside bits, and rusticity of cottage life and shepherd labour. Its mountains are sorrowfully melted away from my old dreams of them."

Next day he "went straight up the steep front of Saddleback by the central ridge to the summit. It is the finest thing I've yet seen, there being several bits of real crag-work, and a fine view at the top over the great plains of Penrith on one side, and the Cumberland hills, as a chain, on the other. Fine fresh wind blowing, and plenty of crows. Do you remember poor papa's favourite story about the Quaker whom the crows ate on Saddleback? There were some of the biggest and hoarsest-voiced ones about the cliff that I've ever had sympathetic croaks from;—and one on the top, or near it, so big that Downes and Crawley, having Austrian tendencies in politics, took it for a 'black eagle.' Downes went up capitally, though I couldn't get him down again, because he *would* stop to gather ferns. However, we did it all and came down to Threlkeld—of the Bridal of Triermain,

"'The King his way pursued
By lonely Threlkeld's waste and wood,'

"in good time for me to dress and, for a wonder, go out to dinner with Acland's friends the Butlers."

As an episode in this visit to Keswick, ten days were given to the neighbourhood of Ambleside, "to show Downes Windermere."

> "Waterhead, Windermere,
> "*10th August, 1867, Evening.*

"I was at Coniston to-day. Our old Waterhead Inn, where I was so happy playing in the boats, *exists* no more.—Its place is grown over with smooth Park grass—the very site of it forgotten! and, a quarter of a mile down the lake, a vast hotel built in the railroad station style—making up, I suppose, its fifty or eighty beds, with coffee-room—smoking-room—and every pestilent and devilish Yankeeism that money can buy, or speculation plan.

"The depression, whatever its cause, does not affect my strength. I walked up a long hill on the road to Coniston to-day (gathering wild raspberries)—then from this new Inn, two miles to the foot of Coniston Old Man; up it; down again—(necessarily!)—and back to dinner, without so much as warming myself—not that there was much danger of doing that at the top; for a keen west wind was blowing drifts of cloud by at a great pace, and one was glad of the shelter of the pile of stones, the largest and *oldest* I ever saw on a mountain top. I suppose the whole mountain is named from it. It is of the shape of a beehive, strongly built, about 15 feet high (so that I made Downes follow me up it before I would allow he had been at the top of the Old Man) and covered with lichen and short moss. Lancaster sands and the Irish sea were very beautiful, and so also the two lakes of Coniston and Windermere, lying in the vastest space of sweet cultivated country I have ever looked over,—a great part of the view from the Rigi being merely over black pine forest, even on the plains. Well, after dinner, the evening was very beautiful, and I walked up the long hill on the road back from Coniston—and kept ahead of the carriage for two miles: I was sadly vexed when I had to get in: and now—I don't feel as if I had been walking at all—and shall probably lie awake for an hour or two—and feeling as if I had not had exercise enough to send me to sleep."

"LANGDALE, *13th August, Evening.*

"It is perfectly calm to-night, not painfully hot—and the full moon shining over the mountains, opposite my window, which are the scene of Wordsworth's 'Excursion.' It was terribly hot in the earlier day, and I did not leave the house till five o'clock. Then I went out, and in the heart of Langdale Pikes found the loveliest rock-scenery, chased with silver waterfalls, that I ever set foot or heart upon. The Swiss torrent-beds are always more or less savage, and ruinous, with a terrible sense of overpowering strength and danger, lulled. But here, the sweet heather and ferns and star mosses nestled in close to the dashing of the narrow streams;—while every cranny of crag held its own little placid lake of amber, trembling with falling drops—but quietly trembling—not troubled into ridgy wave or foam—the rocks themselves, *ideal* rock, as hard as iron—no—not quite that, but *so* hard that after breaking some of it, breaking solid white quartz seemed like smashing brittle loaf sugar, in comparison—and cloven into the most noble masses; not grotesque, but majestic and full of harmony with the larger mountain mass of which they formed a part. Fancy what a place! for a hot afternoon after five, with no wind—and absolute solitude; no creature—except a lamb or two—to mix any ruder sound or voice with the plash of the innumerable streamlets."

It was during this tour that he looked at a site on the hill above Bowness-on-Windermere, where Mr. T. Richmond, the owner, proposed building him a house. He liked the view, but found it too near the railway station.

After spending September with his mother at Norwood under the care of Dr. Powell, he was able to return home, prepare "Time and Tide" for publication, and write the preface on Dec. 14th. On the 19th the book was out, and immediately bought up. A month later the second edition was issued.

NOTES:

13   During February, March and April, 1867, and published in the *Manchester Examiner* and *Leeds Mercury*.
14   The gardener at Denmark Hill.

CHAPTER VIII

AGATES, AND ABBEVILLE (1868)

Of less interest to the general reader, though too important a part of Ruskin's life and work to be passed over without mention, are his studies in Mineralogy. We have heard of his early interest in spars and ores; of his juvenile dictionary in forgotten hieroglyphics; and of his studies in the field and at the British Museum. He had made a splendid collection, and knew the various museums of Europe as familiarly as he knew the picture-galleries. In the "Ethics of the Dust" he had chosen Crystallography as the subject in which to exemplify his method of education; and in 1867, after finishing the letters to Thomas Dixon, he took refuge, as before, among the stones, from the stress of more agitating problems.

In the lecture on the Savoy Alps in 1863 he had referred to a hint of Saussure's that the contorted beds of the limestones might possibly be due to some sort of internal action, resembling on a large scale that separation into concentric or curved bands which is seen in calcareous deposits. The contortions of gneiss were similarly analogous, it was suggested, to those of the various forms of silica. Ruskin did not adopt the theory, but put it by for examination in contrast with the usual explanation of these phenomena, as the simple mechanical thrust of the contracting surface of the earth.

In 1863 and 1866 he had been among the Nagelflüh of Northern Switzerland, studying the puddingstones and breccias. He saw that the difference between these formations, in their structural aspect, and the hand-specimens in his collection of pisolitic and brecciated minerals was chiefly a matter of size; and that the resemblances in form were very close. And so he concluded that if the structure of the minerals could be fully understood a clue might be found to the very puzzling question of the origin of mountain structure.

Hence his attempt to analyze the structure of agates and similar banded and brecciated minerals, in the series of papers in the *Geological Magazine*;[15] an attempt which though it was never properly completed, and fails to come to any general conclusion, is extremely interesting as an account of beautiful and curious natural forms till then little noticed by mineralogists.

A characteristic anecdote of this period is preserved in "Arrows of the Chace."

> "The *Daily Telegraph* of January 21st, 1868, contained a leading article upon the following facts. It appeared that a girl, named Matilda Griggs, had been nearly murdered by her seducer, who, after stabbing her in no less than thirteen places, had then left her for dead. She had, however, still strength enough to crawl into a field close by, and there swooned. The assistance she met with in this plight was of a rare kind. Two calves came up to her, and disposing themselves on either side of her bleeding body, thus kept her warm and partly sheltered from cold and rain. Temporarily preserved, the girl eventually recovered, and entered into recognizances, under a sum of forty pounds, to prosecute her murderous lover. But 'she loved much,' and failing to prosecute, forfeited her recognizances, and was imprisoned by the Chancellor of the Exchequer for her debt. 'Pity the poor debtor,' wrote the *Daily Telegraph*, and in the next day's issue appeared the following letter, probably not intended for the publication accorded to it. 'Sir,—Except in 'Gil Blas,' I never read of anything Astræan on the earth so perfect as the story in your fourth article to-day. I

send you a cheque for the Chancellor. If forty, in legal terms, means four hundred, you must explain the farther requirements to your impulsive public.

"'I am, Sir, your faithful servant, 'J. RUSKIN.'"

The writer of letters like this naturally had a large correspondence, beside that which a circle of private friends and numberless admirers and readers elicited. About this time it grew to such a pitch that he was obliged to print a form excusing him from letter-writing on the ground of stress of work. And indeed, this year, though he did not publish his annual volume, as usual, he was fully occupied with frequent letters to newspapers, several lectures and addresses, a preface to the reprint of his old friend Cruikshank's "Grimm," and the beginning of a new botanical work, "Proserpina," in addition to the mineralogy, and a renewed interest in classical studies. Of the public addresses the most important was that on "The Mystery of Life and its Arts," delivered in the theatre of the Royal College of Science, Dublin (May 13th), and printed in "Sesame and Lilies."

After this visit to Ireland he spent a few days at Winnington; and late in August crossed the Channel, for rest and change at Abbeville. For the past five years he had found too little time for drawing; it was twenty years since his last sketching of French Gothic, except for a study (now at Oxford), of the porch at Amiens, in 1856. He took up the old work where he had left it, after writing the "Seven Lamps," with fresh interest and more advanced powers of draughtsmanship as shown in the pencil study of the Place Amiral Courbet, now in the drawing school at Oxford.

The following are extracts from the usual budget of home letters; readers of "Fors" will need no further introduction to their old acquaintance, the tallow-chandler.

"ABBEVILLE, *Friday, 18th Sept.*, 1868.

"You seem to have a most uncomfortable time of it, with the disturbance of the house. However, I can only leave you to manage these things as you think best—or feel pleasantest to yourself. I am saddened by another kind of disorder, France is in everything so fallen back, so desolate and comfortless, compared to what it was twenty years ago—the people so much rougher, clumsier, more uncivil—everything they do, vulgar and base. Remnants of the old nature come out when they begin to know you. I am drawing at a nice tallow-chandler's door, and to-day, for the first time had to go inside for rain. He was very courteous and nice, and warned me against running against the candle-ends—or bottoms, as they were piled on the shelves, saying—'You must take care, you see, not to steal any of my candles'—or 'steal *from* my candles,' meaning not to rub them off on my coat. He has a beautiful family of cats—papa and mamma and two superb kittens—half Angora."

"*22nd Sept.*

"I am going to my cats and tallow-chandler . . . I was very much struck by the superiority of manner both in him and in his two daughters who serve at the counter, to persons of the same class in England. When the girls have weighed out their candles, or written down the orders that are sent in, they instantly sit down to their needlework behind the counter, and are always busy, yet always quiet; and their father, though of course there may be vulgar idioms in his language which I do not recognize, has entirely the manners of a gentleman."

30th Sept.

"I have the advantage here I had not counted on. I see by the papers that the weather in England is very stormy and bad. Now, though it is showery here, and breezy, it has always allowed me at some time of the day to draw. The air is tender and soft, invariably—even when blowing with force; and to-day, I have seen quite the loveliest sunset I ever yet saw,—one at Boulogne in '61 was richer; but for delicacy and loveliness nothing of past sight ever came near this."

Earlier on the same day he had written:

"I am well satisfied with the work I am doing, and even with my own power of doing it, if only I can keep myself from avariciously trying to do too much, and working hurriedly. But I can do *very* little quite *well*, each day: with that however it is my bounden duty to be content.

"And now I have a little piece of news for you. Our old Herne Hill house being now tenantless, and requiring some repairs before I can get a tenant, I have resolved to keep it for myself, for my rougher mineral work and mass of collection; keeping only my finest specimens at Denmark Hill. My first reason for this, is affection for the old house:—my second, want of room;—my third, the incompatibility of hammering, washing, and experimenting on stones with cleanliness in my stores of drawings. And my fourth is the power I shall have, when I want to do anything very quietly, of going up the hill and thinking it out in the old garden, where your greenhouse still stands, and the aviary—without fear of interruption from callers.

"It may perhaps amuse you, in hours which otherwise would be listless, to think over what may be done with the old house. I have ordered it at once to be put in proper repair by Mr. Snell; but for the furnishing, I can give no directions at present: it is to be very simple, at all events, and calculated chiefly for museum work and for stores of stones and books: and you really must not set your heart on having it furnished like Buckingham Palace.

"I have bought to-day, for five pounds, the front of the porch of the Church of St. James. It was going to be entirely destroyed. It is worn away, and has little of its old beauty; but as a remnant of the Gothic of Abbeville—as I happen to be here—and as the church was dedicated to my father's patron saint (as distinct from mine) I'm glad to have got it. It is a low arch—with tracery and niches, which ivy, and the Erba della Madonna, will grow over beautifully, wherever I rebuild it."

At Abbeville he had with him as usual his valet Crawley; and as before he sent for Downes the gardener, to give him a holiday, and to enjoy his raptures over every new sight. C.E. Norton came on a short visit, and Ruskin followed him to Paris, where he met the poet Longfellow (October 7). At last on Monday, 19th October, he wrote:

"Only a line to-day, for I am getting things together, and am a little tired, but very well, and glad to come home, though much mortified at having failed in half my plans, and done nothing compared to what I expected. But it is better than if I were displeased with all I *had* done. It isn't Turner—and it isn't Correggio—it isn't even Prout—but it isn't bad."

Returning home, he gave an account of his autumn's work in the lecture at the Royal Institution, January 29th, 1869, on the "Flamboyant Architecture of the Valley of the Somme." This lecture was not then published in full: but part of the original text is printed in the third chapter of the work we have next to notice, "The Queen of the Air."

NOTE:

15 August and November, 1867, January, April and May, 1868, December, 1869, and January, 1870, illustrated with very fine mezzotint plates and woodcuts.

CHAPTER IX

"THE QUEEN OF THE AIR" (1869)

In spite of a "classical education" and the influence of Aristotle upon the immature art-theories of his earlier works, Ruskin was known, in his younger days, as a Goth, and the enemy of the Greeks. When he began life, his sense of justice made him take the side of Modern Painters against classical tradition. Later on, when considering the great questions of education and the aims of life, he entirely set aside the common routine of Greek and Latin grammar as the all-in-all of culture. But this was not because he shared Carlyle's contempt for classical studies.

In "Modern Painters," Vol. III., he had followed out the indications of nature-worship, and tried to analyse in general terms the attitude of the Greek spirit towards landscape scenery, as betrayed in Homer and Aristophanes and the poets usually read. Since that time his interest in Greek literature had been gradually increasing. He had made efforts to improve his knowledge of the language; and he had spent many days in sketching and studying the terra-cottas and vases and coins at the British Museum. He had also taken up some study of Egyptology, through Champollion, Bunsen and Birch, in the hope of tracing the origin of Greek decorative art. Comparative mythology, at that time, was a department of philology, introduced to the English public chiefly by Max Müller. Under his influence Ruskin entered step by step upon an inquiry which afterwards became of singular importance in his life and thought.

In 1865 he had told his hearers at Bradford that Greek Religion was not, as commonly supposed, the worship of Beauty, but of Wisdom and Power. They did not, in their great age, worship "Venus," but Apollo and Athena. And he regarded their mythology as a sincere tradition, effective in forming a high moral type, and a great school of art. In the "Ethics of the Dust" he had explained the myth of Athena as parallel to that of Neith in Egypt; and in his fable of Neith and St. Barbara he had hinted at a comparison, on equal terms, of Ancient and Mediæval mythology. He ended by saying that, though he would not have his young hearers believe "that the Greeks were better than we, and that their gods were real angels," yet their art and morals were in some respects greater, and their beliefs were worth respectful and sympathetic study. The "Queen of the Air" is his contribution to this study.

On March 9th, 1869, his lecture at University College, London, on "Greek Myths of Cloud and Storm," began with an attempt to explain in popular terms how a myth differs from mere fiction on the one hand and from allegory on the other, being "not conceived didactically, but didactic in its essence, as all good art is." He showed that Greek poetry dealt with the series of Nature-myths with which were interwoven ethical suggestions; that these were connected with Egyptian beliefs, but that the full force of them was only developed in the central period of Greek history, and their interpretation was to be read in a sympathetic analysis of the spirit of men like Pindar and Æschylus. "The great question," he said, "in reading a story is, always, not what wild hunter dreamed, or what childish race first dreaded it; but what wise man first perfectly told, and what strong people first perfectly lived by it. And the real meaning of any myth is that which it has at the noblest age of the nation among whom it was current."

In the next chapter he worked out, as a sequel to his lecture, two groups of Animal-myths; those connected with birds, and especially the dove, as type of Spirit, and those connected with the serpent in its various significances. These two studies were continued, more or less, in "Love's

Meinie" and in the lecture printed in "Deucalion," as the third group, that of Plant-myths, was carried on in "Proserpina." The volume contained also extracts from the lecture on the Architecture of the Valley of the Somme, and two numbers of the "Cestus of Aglaia," and closed with a paper on The Hercules of Camarina, read to the South Lambeth Art School on March 15th. This study of a Greek coin had already formed the subject of an address at the Working Men's College, and anticipated the second course of Oxford Lectures. For the rest, "The Queen of the Air" is marked by its statement, more clearly than before in Ruskin's writing, of the dependence of moral upon physical life, and of physical upon moral science. He speaks with respect of the work of Darwin and Tyndall; but as formerly in the Rede Lecture, and afterwards in the "Eagle's Nest," he claims that natural science should not be pursued as an end in itself, paramount to all other conclusions and considerations; but as a department of study subordinate to ethics, with a view to utility and instruction.

Before this book was quite ready for publication, and after a sale of some of his less treasured pictures at Christie's he left home for a journey to Italy, to revisit the subjects of "Stones of Venice," as in 1868 he had revisited those of the "Seven Lamps." At Vevey, on the way, he wrote his preface (May 1st).

By quiet stages he passed the Simplon, writing from Domo d'Ossola, 5th May, 1869:

> "I never yet had so beautiful a day for the Simplon as this has been; though the skin of my face is burning now all over—to keep me well in mind of its sunshine. I left Brieg at 6 exactly—light clouds breaking away into perfect calm of blue. Heavy snow on the col—about a league—with the wreaths in many places higher than the carriage. Then, white crocus all over the fields, with Soldanelle and Primula farinosa. I walked about three miles up, and seven down, with great contentment; the waterfalls being

all in rainbows, and one beyond anything I ever yet saw; for it fell in a pillar of spray against shadow behind, and became rainbow altogether. I was just near enough to get the belt broad, and the down part of the arch: and the whole fall became orange and violet against deep shade. To-morrow I hope to get news of you all, at Baveno."

"BAVENO, *Thursday, 6th May,* 1869.

"It is wet this morning, and very dismal, for we are in a ghastly new Inn, the old one being shut up; and there is always a re-action after a strong excitement like the beauty of the Simplon yesterday, which leaves one very dull. But it is of no use growling or mewing. I hope to be at Milan to-morrow—at Verona for Sunday. I have been reading Dean Swift's life, and 'Gulliver's Travels' again. Putting the delight in dirt, which is a mere disease, aside, Swift is very like me, in most things:—in opinions exactly the same."

At Milan, next day, he went to see the St. Catherine of Luini which he had copied, and found it wantonly damaged by the carelessness of masons who put their ladders up against it, just as if it were a bit of common whitewashed wall.

On the 8th he reached Verona after seventeen years' absence, and on the 10th he was in Venice. There, looking at the works of the old painters with a fresh eye, and with feelings and thoughts far different from those with which he had viewed them as a young man, in 1845, he saw beauties he had passed over before, in the works of a painter till then little regarded by connoisseurs, and entirely neglected by the public. Historians of art like Crowe and Cavalcaselle[16] had indeed examined Carpaccio's works and investigated his life, along with the lives and works of many another obscure master: artists like Hook and Burne-Jones had admired his pictures; Ruskin had mentioned his backgrounds twice or thrice in "Stones of Venice." But no writer had noticed his extraordinary interest as an exponent of the mythology of the Middle Ages, as the illustrator of poetical folk-lore derived from those antique myths of Greece, and newly presented by the genius of Christianity.

This was a discovery for which Ruskin was now ripe, He saw at once that he had found a treasure-house of things new and old. He fell in love with St. Ursula as, twenty-four years earlier, he had fallen in love with the statue of Ilaria at Lucca; and she became, as time after time he revisited Venice for her sake, a personality, a spiritual presence, a living ideal, exactly as the Queen of the Air might have been to the sincere Athenian in the pagan age of faith. The story of her life and death became an example, the conception of her character, as read in Carpaccio's picture, became a standard for his own life and action in many a time of distress and discouragement. The thought of "What would St. Ursula say?" led him—not always, but far more often than his correspondents knew—to burn the letter of sharp retort upon stupidity and impertinence, and to force the wearied brain and overstrung nerves into patience and a kindly answer. And later on, the playful credence which he accorded to the myth deepened into a renewed sense of the possibility of spiritual realities, when he learnt to look, with those mediæval believers; once more as a little child upon the unfathomable mysteries of life.

But this anticipates the story; at the time, he found in Carpaccio the man who had touched the full chord of his feelings and his thoughts, just as, in his boyhood, Turner had led him, marvelling, through the fire and cloud to the mountain-altar; and as, in his youth, Tintoret had interpreted the storm and stress of a mind awakening to the terrible realities of the world. It was no caprice of a changeful taste, nor love of startling paradox, that brought him to "discover Carpaccio;" it was the logical sequence of his studies, and widening interests, and a view of art embracing far broader issues than the connoisseurship of "Modern Painters," or the didacticism of "Seven Lamps," or the historical research of "Stones of Venice."

Soon after the "Queen of the Air" was published Carlyle wrote:

"Last week I got y'r 'Queen of the Air,' and read it. *Euge, Ettge.* No such Book have I met with for long years past. The one soul now in the world who seems to feel as I do on the highest matters, and speaks *mir aus dem Herzen,* exactly what I wanted to hear!-As to the natural history of those old myths I remained here and there a little uncert'n; but as to the meanings you put into them, never anywhere. All these things I not only 'agree' with, but w'd use Thor's Hammer, if I had it, to enforce and put in action on this rotten world. Well done, well done!—and pluck up a heart, and continue ag'n and ag'n. And don't say 'most g't tho'ts are dressed *in shrouds*': many, many are the Phoebus Apollo celestial arrows you still have to shoot into the foul Pythons, and poisonous abominable Megatheriums and Plesiosaurians that go staggering ab't, large as cathedrals, in our sunk Epoch ag'n . . ."

NOTE:

16   Their "History of Painting in North Italy," containing a detailed account of Carpaccio, was published in 1871.

CHAPTER X

VERONA AND OXFORD (1869-1870)

The main object of this journey was, however, not to study mythology, but to continue the revision of old estimates of architecture, and after seventeen years to look with a fresh eye at the subjects of "Stones of Venice."

The churches and monuments of Verona had been less thoroughly studied than those of Venice, and now they were threatened with imminent restoration. On May 25th he wrote:—"It is very strange that I have just been in time—after 17 years' delay—to get the remainder of what I wanted from the red tomb of which my old drawing hangs in the passage"—(the Castelbarco monument). "To-morrow they put up scaffolding to retouch, and I doubt not, spoil it for evermore." He succeeded in getting a delay of ten days, to enable him to paint the tomb in its original state; but before he went home it "had its new white cap on and looked like a Venetian gentleman in a pantaloon's mask." He brought away one of the actual stones of the old roof.

On June 3 he wrote:

"I am getting on well with all my own work; and much pleased with some that Mr. Bunney is doing for me; so that really I expect to carry off a great deal of Verona . . . The only mischief of the place is its being too rich. Stones, flowers, mountains—all equally asking one to look at them; a history to every foot of ground, and a picture on every foot of wall; frescoes fading away in the neglected streets—like the colours of the dolphin."

As assistants in this enterprise of recording the monuments of Venice and Verona, and of recording them more fully and in a more interesting way than by photography, he took with him Arthur Burgess and John Bunney, his former pupils. Mr. Burgess was the subject of a memoir by Ruskin in the *Century Guild Hobby Horse* (April, 1887), appreciating his talents and lamenting his loss. Mr. Bunney, who had travelled with Ruskin in Switzerland in 1863, and had lately lived near Florence, thenceforward settled in Venice, where he died in 1882, after completing his great work, the St. Mark's now in the Ruskin Museum at Sheffield. A memoir of him by Mr. Wedderburn appeared in the catalogue of the Venice Exhibition, at the Fine Art Society's Gallery in November, 1882.

At Venice Ruskin had met his old friend Rawdon Brown[17], and Count Giberto Borromeo, whom he visited at Milan on his way home, with deep interest in the Luinis and in the authentic bust of St. Carlo; so closely resembling Ruskin himself. Another noteworthy encounter is recorded in a letter of May 4th.[18]

"As I was drawing in the square this morning, in a lovely, quiet, Italian, light, there came up the poet Longfellow with his little daughter—a girl of 12, or 13, with *springy*-curled flaxen hair,—curls, or waves, that wouldn't come out in damp, I mean. They stayed talking beside me some time. I don't think it was a very vain thought that came over me, that if a photograph could have been taken of the beautiful square of Verona, in that soft light, with Longfellow and his daughter talking to me at my work—some people both in England and America would have liked copies of it."

Readers of "Fors" will recognise an incident noted on the 18th of June.

"Yesterday, it being quite cool, I went for a walk; and as I came down from a rather quiet hillside, a mile or two out of town, I past a house where the women were at work spinning the silk off the cocoons. There was a sort of whirring sound as in an English mill; but at intervals they sang a long sweet chant, all together, lasting about two minutes—then pausing a minute and then beginning again. It was good and tender music, and the multitude of voices prevented any sense of failure, so that it was very lovely and sweet, and like the things that I mean to try to bring to pass."

For he was already meditating on the thoughts that issued in the proposals of St. George's Guild, and the daily letters of this summer are full of allusions to a scheme for a great social movement, as well as to his plans for the control of Alpine torrents and the better irrigation of their valleys. On the 2nd of June he wrote:—"I see more and more clearly every day my power of showing how the Alpine torrents may be—not subdued—but 'educated.' A torrent is just like a human creature. Left to gain full strength in wantonness and rage, no power can any more redeem it: but watch the channels of every early impulse, and fence *them*, and your torrent becomes the gentlest and most blessing of servants."

His mother was anxious for him to come home, being persuaded that he was overworking himself in the continued heat which his letters reported. But he was loath to leave Italy, in which, he said, his work for the future lay. He made two more visits to Venice, to draw some of the sculptured details, now quickly perishing, and to make studies of Tintoret and Carpaccio. Among other friends who met him there was Mr. Holman Hunt, with whom he went round his favourite Scuola di San Rocco (1st July). Two days later he wrote:

> "You will never believe it; but I have actually been trying to draw—a baby. *The* baby which the priest is holding in the little copy of Tintoret by Edward Jones which my father liked so much,

over the basin stand in his bedroom.[19] All the knowledge I have gained in these 17 years only makes me more full of awe and wonder at Tintoret. But it *is* so sad—so sad;—no one to care for him but me, and all going so fast to ruin. He has done that infant Christ in about five minutes—and I worked for two hours in vain, and could not tell *why* in vain—the mystery of his touch is so great."

Final farewell was said to Verona on the 10th August, for the homeward journey by the St. Gothard, and Giessbach, where he found the young friend of 1866 now near her end—and Thun, where he met Professor C.E. Norton. On the way he wrote:

"Lugano, *Saturday, 14th August,* 1869.

"My Dearest Mother,

"Yesterday—exactly three months from the day on which I entered Verona to begin work, I made a concluding sketch of the old Broletto of Como, which I drew first for the 7 lamps[20]—I know not how many years ago,—and left Italy, for this time—having been entirely well and strong every day of my quarter of a year's sojourn there.

"This morning, before breakfast, I was sitting for the first time before Luini's Crucifixion: for all religious-art qualities the greatest picture south of the Alps—or rather, in Europe.

"And just after breakfast I got a telegram from my cousin George announcing that I am Professor of Art—the first—at the University of Oxford.

"Which will give me as much power as I can well use—and would have given pleasure to my poor father—and therefore to me—once ... It will make no difference in my general plans, about travel, etc. I shall think quietly of it as I drive up towards St. Gothard to-day.

"Ever, my dearest mother, ever your loving son,
"J. Ruskin."

Six years earlier, while being examined before the Royal Academy commission, he had been asked: "Has it ever struck you that it would be advantageous to art if there were at the universities professors of art who might give lectures and give instruction to young men who might desire to avail themselves of it, as you have lectures on geology and botany?" To which he had replied: "Yes, assuredly. The want of interest on the part of the upper classes in art has been very much at the bottom of the abuses which have crept into all systems of education connected with it. If the upper classes could only be interested in it by being led into it when young, a great improvement might be looked for, therefore I feel the expediency of such an addition to the education of our universities." His interest in the first phase of University Extension, and his gifts of Turners to Oxford and Cambridge, had shown that he was ready to go out of his way to help in the cause he had promoted. His former works on art, and reputation as a critic, pointed to him as the best qualified man in the country for such a post. He had been asked by his Oxford friends, who were many and influential, to stand for the Professorship of Poetry, three years earlier. There was no doubt that the election would be a popular one, and creditable to the University. On the other hand, Ruskin as Professor would have a certain sanction for his teaching, he believed; the title and the salary of £358 a year were hardly an object to him; but the position, as accredited lecturer and authorised instructor of youth, opened up new vistas of usefulness, new worlds of work to conquer; and he accepted the invitation. On August 10th he was elected Slade Professor.

He returned home by the end of August to prepare himself for his new duties. During the last period he had been giving, on an average, half a dozen lectures a year, which amply filled his annual volume. Twelve lectures were required of the professor. Many another man would have read his twelve lectures and gone his way; but he was not going to work in that perfunctory manner. He undertook to revise his whole teaching; to write for his hearers a completely new series of treatises on art, beginning with first principles and broad generalisations, and proceeding to the different departments of sculpture, engraving, landscape-painting and so on; then taking up the history of art:—an encyclopædic scheme. He took this Oxford work not as a substitute for other occupation, exonerating him from further claims upon his energy and time; nor as a bye-play that could be slurred. He tried to do it thoroughly, and to do it in addition to the various work already in hand, under which, as it was, he used to break down, yearly, after each climax of effort.

This autumn and winter, with his first and most important course in preparation, he was still writing letters to the *Daily Telegraph*; being begged by Carlyle to come—"the sight of your face will be a comfort," says the poor old man—and undertaking lectures at the Royal Artillery Institution, Woolwich, and at the Royal Institution, London. The Woolwich lecture, given on December 14th, was that added to later editions of the "Crown of Wild Olive," under the title of "The Future of England." The other, February 4th, 1870, on "Verona and its Rivers," involved not only a lecture on art and history and contemporary political economy, but an exhibition of the drawings which he and his assistants had made during the preceding summer.

Four days later he opened a new period in his career with his inaugural Lecture in the Sheldonian Theatre at Oxford.

NOTES:

17 Whose book on the English in Italy (from Venetian documents) was shortly to be published, with funds supplied by Ruskin.
18 This date ought to be "June 4th," as Mr. E.T. Cook notices (Library Edn. XIX., p. liv.).
19 Mr. and Mrs Burne-Jones had been in Venice in June, 1862; the artist, then young and comparatively unknown, with a commission to copy for Ruskin.
20 "Stones of Venice," Vol. I., plate 5.

BOOK IV

PROFESSOR AND PROPHET (1870-1900)

CHAPTER I

FIRST OXFORD LECTURES (1870-1871)

On Tuesday, 8th February, 1870, the Slade Professor's lecture-room was crowded to over-flowing with members of the University, old and young, and their friends, who flocked to hear, and to see, the author of "Modern Painters." The place was densely packed long before the time; the ante-rooms were filled with personal friends, hoping for some corner to be found them at the eleventh hour; the doors were blocked open, and besieged outside by a disappointed multitude.

Professorial lectures are not usually matters of great excitement: it does not often happen that the accommodation is found inadequate. After some hasty arrangements Sir Henry Acland pushed his way to the table, announced that it was impossible for the lecture to be held in that place, and begged the audience to adjourn to the Sheldonian Theatre. At last, welcomed by all Oxford, the Slade Professor appeared, to deliver his inaugural address.[21]

It was not strictly academic, the way he used to come in, with a little following of familiars and assistants,—exchange recognition with friends in the audience, arrange the objects he had brought to show,—fling off his long sleeved Master's gown, and plunge into his discourse. His manner of delivery had not altered much since the time of the Edinburgh Lectures. He used to begin by reading, in his curious intonation, the carefully-written passages of rhetoric, which usually occupied only about the half of his hour. By-and-by he would break off, and with quite another air extemporise the liveliest interpolations, describing his diagrams or specimens, restating his arguments, re-enforcing his appeal. His voice, till then artificially cadenced, suddenly became vivacious; his gestures, at first constrained, became dramatic. He used to act his subject, apparently without premeditated art, in the liveliest pantomime. He had no power of voice-mimicry, and none of the ordinary gifts of the actor. A tall and slim figure, not yet shortened from its five feet ten or eleven by the habitual stoop, which ten years later brought him down to less than middle height; a stiff, blue frock-coat; prominent, half-starched wristbands, and tall collars of the Gladstonian type; and the bright blue stock which every one knows for his heraldic bearing: no rings or gewgaws, but a long thin gold chain to his watch:—plain old-English gentleman, neither fashionable bourgeois nor artistic mountebank.

But he gave himself over to his subject with such unreserved intensity of imaginative power, he felt so vividly and spoke so from the heart, that he became whatever he talked about, never heeding his professorial dignity, and never doubting the sympathy of his audience. Lecturing on birds, he strutted like the chough, made himself wings like the swallow; he was for the moment a cat, when he explained (not "in scorn") that engraving was the "art of scratch." If it had been an affectation of theatric display, we "emancipated school-boys," as the Master of University used to call us, would have seen through it at once, and scorned him. But it was so evidently the expression of his intense eagerness for his subject, so palpably true to his purpose, and he so carried his hearers with him, that one saw in the grotesque of the performance only the guarantee of sincerity.

If one wanted more proof of that, there was his face, still young-looking and beardless; made for expression, and sensitive to every change of emotion. A long head, with enormous capacity of brain, veiled by thick wavy hair, not affectedly lengthy but as abundant as ever, and darkened into a deep brown, without a trace of grey; and short, light whiskers growing high over his cheeks. A forehead not on the model of the heroic type, but as if the sculptor had heaped his clay in handfuls over the eyebrows, and then heaped more. A big nose, aquiline, and broad at the base, with great thoroughbred nostrils and the "septum" between them thin and deeply depressed; and there was a turn down at the corners of the mouth, and a breadth of lower lip, that reminded one of his Verona griffin, half eagle, half lion; Scotch in original type, and suggesting a side to his character not all milk and roses. And under shaggy eyebrows, ever so far behind, the fieriest blue eyes, that changed with changing expression, from grave to gay, from lively to severe; that riveted you, magnetised you, seemed to look through you and read your soul; and indeed, when they lighted on you, you felt you had a soul of a sort. What they really saw is a mystery. Some who had not persuaded them to see as others see, maintained that they only saw what they looked for; others, who had successfully deceived them, that they saw nothing. No doubt they might be deceived; but I know now that they often took far shrewder measurements of men—I do not say of women—than anybody suspected.

For the Inaugural Course, he was, so to speak, on his best behaviour, guarding against too hasty expression of individuality. He read careful orations, stating his maturest views on the general theory of art, in picked language, suited to the academic position. The little volume is not discursive or entertaining, like "Modern Painters," and contains no pictures either with pen or pencil; but it is crammed full of thought, and of the results of thought.

The Slade Professor was also expected to organise and superintend the teaching of drawing; and his first words in the first lecture expressed the hope that he would be able to introduce some serious study of Art into the University, which, he thought, would be a step towards realising some of his ideals of education. He had long felt that mere talking about Art was a makeshift, and that no real insight could be got into the subject without actual and practical dealing with it. He found a South Kensington School in existence at Oxford, with an able master, Mr. Alexander Macdonald; and though he did not entirely approve of the methods in use, tried to make the best of the materials to his hand, accepting but enlarging the scope of the system. The South Kensington method had been devised for industrial designing, primarily; Ruskin's desire was to get undergraduates to take up a wider subject, to familiarise themselves with the technical excellences of the great masters, to study nature, and the different processes of art,—drawing, painting and some forms of decorative work, such as, in especial, goldsmiths' work, out of which the Florentine school had sprung. He did not wish to train artists, but, as before in the Working Men's College, to cultivate the habit of mind that looks at nature and life, not analytically, as science does, but for the sake of external aspect and expression. By these means he hoped to breed a race of judicious patrons and critics, the best service any man can render to the cause of art.

And so he got together a mass of examples in addition to the Turners which he had already given to the University galleries. He placed in the school a few pictures by Tintoret, some drawings by Rossetti, Holman Hunt, and Burne-Jones, and a great number of fine casts and engravings. He arranged a series of studies by himself and others, as "copies," fitted, like the Turners in the National Gallery, with sliding frames in cabinets for convenient reference and removal. After spending most of his first Lent Term in this work, he went home for a month to prepare a catalogue, which was published the same year: the school not being finally opened until October, 1871. During these first visits to Oxford he was the guest of Sir Henry Acland; on April 29, 1871, Professor Ruskin, already honorary student of Christ Church, was elected to an honorary fellowship at Corpus, and enabled to occupy rooms, vacated by the Rev. Henry Furneaux, who gave up his fellowship on marrying Mr. Arthur Severn's twin-sister.[22]

After this work well begun, he went abroad for a vacation tour with a party of friends—as in 1866; Lady Trevelyan's sister, Mrs. Hilliard, to chaperone the same young ladies, and three servants with them. They started on April 27th; stayed awhile at Meurice's to see Paris; and at

Geneva, to go up the Salève, twice, in bitter black east wind. Then across the Simplon to Milan. After a month at Venice and Verona, where he recurred to his scheme against inundation, then ridiculed by *Punch*, but afterwards taken up seriously by the Italians, they went to Florence, and met Professor Norton. In the end of June they turned homewards, by Pisa and Lucca, Milan and Como, and went to visit their friend Marie of the Giessbach.

At the Giessbach they spent a fortnight, enjoying the July weather and glorious walks, in the middle of which war was suddenly declared between Germany and France. The summons of their German waiter to join his regiment brought the news home to them, as such personal examples do, more than columns of newspaper print; and as hostilities were rapidly beginning, Ruskin, with the gloomiest forebodings for the beautiful country he loved, took his party home straight across France, before the ways should be closed.

August was a month of feverish suspense to everybody; to no one more than to Ruskin, who watched the progress of the armies while he worked day by day at the British Museum preparing lectures for next term. This was the course on Greek relief-sculpture, published as "Aratra Pentelici."[23] It was a happy thought to illustrate his subject from coins, rather than from disputed and mutilated fragments; and he worked into it his revised theory of the origin of art—not Schiller's nor Herbert Spencer's, and yet akin to theirs of the "Spieltrieb,"—involving the notion of doll-play;—man as a child, re-creating himself, in a double sense; imitating the creation of the world and really creating a sort of secondary life in his art, to play with, or to worship. In the last lecture of the series (published separately) the Professor compared—as the outcome of classic art in Renaissance times—Michelangelo and Tintoret, greatly to the disadvantage of Michelangelo. This heresy against a popular creed served as text for some severe criticism; but as he said in a prefatory note to the pamphlet, readers "must observe that its business is only to point out what is to be blamed in Michael Angelo, and that it assumes the fact of his power to be generally known," and he referred to Mr. Tyrwhitt's "Lectures on Christian Art" for the opposite side of the question.

Meanwhile the war was raging. Ruskin was asked by his friends to raise his voice against the ravage of France; but he replied that it was inevitable. At last, in October, he read how Rosa Bonheur and Edouard Frère had been permitted to pass through the German lines, and next day came the news of the bombardment of Strasburg, with anticipations of the destruction of the Cathedral, library, and picture galleries, foretelling, as it seemed, the more terrible and irreparable ruin of the treasure-houses of art in Paris. His heart was with the French, and he broke silence in the bitterness of his spirit, upbraiding their disorder and showing how the German success was the victory of "one of the truest monarchies and schools of honour and obedience yet organised under heaven." He hoped that Germany, now that she had shown her power, would withdraw, and demand no indemnity. But that was too much to ask.

Before long Paris itself became the scene of action, and in January 1871 was besieged and bombarded. So much of Ruskin's work and affection had been given to French Gothic that he could not endure to think of his beloved Sainte Chapelle as being actually under fire—to say nothing of the horror of human suffering in a siege. He joined Cardinal (then Archbishop) Manning, Professor Huxley, Sir John Lubbock and James Knowles in forming a "Paris Food Fund," which shortly united with the Lord Mayor's committee for the general relief of the besieged. The day after writing on the Sainte Chapelle he attended the meeting of the Mansion House, and gave a subscription of £50. He followed events anxiously through the storm of the Commune and its fearful ending, angered at the fratricide and anarchy which no Mansion House help could avert or repair.

It was no time for talking on art, he felt: instead of the full course, he could only manage three lectures on landscape, and these not so completely prepared as to make them ready for printing. Before

Christmas he had been once more to Woolwich, where Colonel Brackenbury invited him to address the cadets at the prize-giving of the Science and Art Department, December 13, 1870, in which the Rev. W. Kingsley, an old friend of Ruskin's and of Turner's, was one of the masters. Two of the lectures of the "Crown of Wild Olive" had been given there, with more than usual animation, and enthusiastically received by crowded and distinguished audiences, among whom was Prince Arthur (the Duke of Connaught), then at the Royal Military Academy. This time it was the "Story of Arachne," an address on education and aims in life; opening with reminiscences of his own childhood, and pleasantly telling the Greek myths of the spider and the ant, with interpretations for the times.

In the three lectures on landscape, given January 20, February 9 and 23, 1871, he dwelt on the necessity of human and historic interest in scenery; and compared Greek "solidity and veracity" with Gothic "spirituality and mendacity," Greek chiaroscuro and tranquil activity with Gothic colour and "passionate rest." Botticelli's "Nativity" (now in the National Gallery) was then being shown at the Old Master's Exhibition, and Ruskin took it, along with the works of Cima, as a type of one form of Greek Art.

In April, 1871, his cousin, Miss Agnew, who had been seven years at Denmark Hill, was married to Mr. Arthur Severn. Ruskin, who had added to his other work the additional labour of "Fors Clavigera," went for a summer's change to Matlock. July opened with cold, dry, dark weather, dangerous for out-of-door sketching. One morning early—for he was always an early riser—he took a chill while painting a spray of wild roses before breakfast (the drawing now in the Oxford Schools). He was already overworked, and it ended in a severe attack of internal inflammation, which nearly cost him his life. He was a difficult patient to deal with. The local practitioner who attended him used to tell how he refused remedies, and in the height of the disease asked what would be *worst* for him. He took it; and to everybody's surprise, recovered.[24]

During the illness at Matlock his thoughts reverted to the old "Iteriad" times of forty years before, when he had travelled with his parents and cousin Mary from that same "New Bath Hotel," where he was now lying, to the Lakes; and again he wearied for "the heights that look adown upon the dale. The crags are lone on Coniston." If he could only lie down there, he said, he should get well again.

He had not fully recovered before he heard that W.J. Linton, the poet and wood-engraver, wished to sell a house and land at the very place: £1,500, and it could be his. Without question asked he bought it at once; and as it would be impossible to lecture at Oxford so soon after his illness, he set off, before the middle of September, with his friends the Hilliards to visit his new possession. They found a rough-cast country cottage, old, damp, decayed; smoky chimneyed and rat-riddled; but "five acres of rock and moor and streamlet; and," he wrote, "I think the finest view I know in Cumberland or Lancashire, with the sunset visible over the same."

The spot was not, even then, without its associations: Gerald Massey the poet, Linton, and his wife Mrs. Lynn Linton the novelist, Dr. G.W. Kitchin (Dean of Durham) had lived and worked there, and Linton had adorned it outside with revolutionary mottoes—"God and the people," and so on. It had been a favourite point of view of Wordsworth's; his "seat" was pointed out in the grounds. Tennyson had lived for a while close by: his "seat," too, was on the hill above Lanehead.

But the cottage needed thorough repair, and that cost more than rebuilding, not to speak of the additions of later years, which have ended by making it into a mansion surrounded by a hamlet. And there was the furnishing; for Denmark Hill, where his mother lived, was still to be headquarters. Ruskin gave carte-blanche to the London upholsterer with whom he had been accustomed to deal; and such expensive articles were sent that when he came down for a month next autumn, he reckoned that, all included, his country cottage had cost him not less than £4,000.

But he was not the man to spend on himself without sharing his wealth with others. On November 22nd, Convocation accepted a gift from the Slade Professor of £5,000 to endow a mastership of drawing at Oxford, in addition to the pictures and "copies" placed in the schools; he had set up a relative in business with £15,000, which was unfortunately lost; and at Christmas he gave £7,000, the tithe of his remaining capital, to the St. George's Fund; of which more hereafter.

On November 23rd he was elected Lord Rector of St. Andrew's University, by 86 votes against 79 for Lord Lytton. After the election it was discovered that, by the Scottish Universities Act of 1858, no one holding a professorship at a British University was eligible. Professor Ruskin was disqualified, and gave no address; and Lord Neaves was chosen in his place.

Mrs. Ruskin was now ninety years of age; her sight was nearly gone, but she still retained her powers of mind, and ruled with severe kindliness her household and her son. Her old servant Anne had died in March. Anne had nursed John Ruskin as a baby, and had lived with the family ever since, devoted to them, and ready for any disagreeable task—

"So that she was never quite in her glory," "Præterita" says, "unless some of us were ill. She had also some parallel speciality for *saying* disagreeable things, and might be relied upon to give the extremely darkest view of any subject, before proceeding to ameliorative action upon it. And she had a very creditable and republican aversion to doing immediately, or in set terms, as she was bid; so that when my mother and she got old together, and my mother became very imperative and particular about having her teacup set on one side of her little round table, Anne would observantly and punctiliously put it always on the other: which caused my mother to state to me, every morning after breakfast, gravely, that if ever a woman in this world was possessed by the Devil, Anne was that woman."

But this gloomy Calvinism was tempered with a benevolence quite as uncommon. It was from his parents that Ruskin learned never to turn off a servant, and the Denmark Hill household was as easy-going as the legendary "baronial" retinue of the good old times. A young friend asked Mrs. Ruskin, in a moment of indiscretion, what such a one of the ancient maids did—for there were several without apparent occupation about the house. Mrs. Ruskin drew herself up and said, "She, my dear, puts out the dessert."

And yet, in her blindness, she could read character unhesitatingly. That was, no doubt, why people feared her. When Mr. Secretary Howell, in the days when he was still the oracle of the Ruskin-Rossetti circle, had been regaling them with his wonderful tales, after dinner, she would throw her netting down and say, "How *can you* two sit there and listen to such a pack of lies?" She objected strongly, in these later years, to the theatre; and when sometimes her son would wish to take a party into town to see the last new piece, her permission had to be asked, and was not readily granted, unless to Miss Agnew, who was the ambassadress in such affairs of diplomacy. But while disapproving of some of his worldly ways, and convinced that she had too much indulged his childhood, the old lady loved him with all the intensity of the strange fierce lioness nature, which only one or two had ever had a glimpse of. And when (December 5th, 1871) she died, trusting to see her husband again—not to be near him, not to be so high in heaven but content if she might only *see* him, she said—her son was left "with a surprising sense of loneliness." He had loved her truly, obeyed her strictly and tended her faithfully; and even yet hardly realized how much she had been to him. He buried her in his father's grave, and wrote upon it, "Here beside my father's body I have laid my mother's: nor was dearer earth ever returned to earth, nor purer life recorded in heaven."

NOTES:

21 The inaugural course was given Feb. 8, 16, 23; March 3, 9, 16 and 23, 1870.
22 His rooms were in Fellows' buildings, No. 2 staircase, first floor right.
23 Delivered Nov. 24, 26, Dec. 1, 3, 8 and 10, 1870.
24 Mrs. Arthur Severn, in a note on the proof, says: "It was a slice of cold roast beef he hungered for, at Matlock (to our horror, and dear Lady Mount Temple's, who were nursing him): there was none in the hotel, and it was late at night; and Albert Goodwin went off to get some, somewhere, or anywhere. All the hotels were closed; but at last, at an eating-house in Matlock Bath, he discovered some, and came back triumphant with it, wrapped up in paper; and J.R. enjoyed his late supper thoroughly; and though we all waited anxiously till the morning for the result, it had done no harm! And when he was told pepper was bad for him, he dredged it freely over his food in defiance! It was directly after our return to Denmark Hill he got Linton's letter offering him this place (Brantwood). There are, I believe, ten acres of moor belonging to Brantwood." Mr. Albert Goodwin, R.W.S., the landscape painter, travelled, about this time, in Italy with Ruskin.

CHAPTER II

"FORS" BEGUN (1871-1872)

On January 1st, 1871, was issued a small pamphlet, headed "Fors Clavigera," in the form of a letter to the working men and labourers of England, dated from Denmark Hill, and signed "John Ruskin." It was not published in the usual way, but sold by the author's engraver, Mr. George Allen, at Heathfield Cottage, Keston, Kent. It was not advertised; press-copies were sent to the leading papers; and of course the author's acquaintance knew of its publication. Strangers, who heard of this curious proceeding, spread the report that in order to get Ruskin's latest, you had to travel into the country, with your sevenpence in your hand, and transact your business among Mr. Allen's beehives. So you had, if you wanted to see what you were buying; for no arrangements were made for its sale by the booksellers: sevenpence a copy, carriage paid, no discount, and no abatement on taking a quantity.

By such pilgrimages, but more easily through the post, the new work filtered out, in monthly instalments, to a limited number of buyers. After three years the price was raised to tenpence. In 1875 the first thousands of the earlier numbers were sold: "the public has a very long nose," Mr. Ruskin once said, "and scents out what it wants, sooner or later." A second edition was issued, bound up into yearly volumes, of which eight were ultimately completed. Meanwhile the work went on, something in the style of the old Addison *Spectator*, each part containing twenty pages, more or less, by Ruskin, with added contributions from various correspondents.

The charm of "Fors" is neither in epigram nor in anecdote, but in the sustained vivacity that runs through the texture of the work; the reappearance of golden threads of thought, glittering in new figures, and among new colours; and throughout all the variety of subject a unity of style unlike the style of his earlier works, where flowery rhetorical passages are tagged to less interesting chapters, separately studied sermonettes interposed among the geology, and Johnson, Locke, Hooker, Carlyle—or whoever happened to be the author he was reading at the time—frankly imitated. It was always clever, but often artificial; like the composition of a Renaissance painter who inserts his *bel corpo ignudo* to catch the eye. In "Fors," however, the web is of a piece, all sparkling with the same life; though as it is gradually unwound from the loom it is hard to judge the design. That can only be done when it is reviewed as a whole.

At the time, his mingling of jest and earnest was misunderstood even by friends. The author learnt too painfully the danger of seeming to trifle with cherished beliefs. He forswore levity, but soon relapsed into the old style, out of sheer sincerity: for he was too much in earnest not to be frankly himself in his utterances, without writing up to, or down to, any other person's standard.

Ruskin did not wish to lead a colony or to head a revolution. He had been pondering for fifteen years the cause of poverty and crime, and the conviction had grown upon him that modern commercialism was at the root of it all. But his attacks on commercialism—his analysis of its bad influence on all sections of society—were too vigorous and uncompromising for the newspaper editors who received "Fors," and even for most of his private friends. There were, however, some who saw what he was aiming at: and let it be remarked that his first encouragement came from the highest quarters. Just as Sydney Smith, the chief critic of earlier days, had been the first to praise "Modern Painters," in the teeth of vulgar opinion, so now Carlyle spoke for "Fors."

"5, Cheyne Row, Chelsea, *April 30th*, 1871.

"Dear Ruskin,

"This 'Fors Clavigera,' Letter 5th, which I have just finished reading, is incomparable; a quasi-sacred consolation to me, which almost brings tears into my eyes! Every word of it is as if spoken, not out of my poor heart only, but out of the eternal skies; words winged with Empyrean wisdom, piercing as lightning,—and which I really do not remember to have heard the like of. *Continue*, while you have such utterances in you, to give them voice. They will find and force entrance into human hearts, *whatever* the 'angle of incidence' may be; that is to say, whether, for the degraded and *in* human Blockheadism we, so-called 'men,' have mostly now become, you come in upon them at the broadside, at the top, or even at the bottom. Euge, Euge!—Yours ever,

"T. Carlyle."

Others, like Sir Arthur Helps, joined in this encouragement. But the old struggle with the newspapers began over again.

They united in considering the whole business insane, though they did not doubt his sincerity when Ruskin put down his own money, the tenth of what he had, as he recommended his adherents to do. By the end of the year he had set aside £7,000 toward establishing a company to be called of "St. George," as representing at once England and agriculture. Sir Thomas Dyke Acland and the Right Hon. W. Cowper-Temple (afterwards Lord Mount Temple), though not pledging themselves to approval of the scheme, undertook the trusteeship of the fund. A few friends subscribed; in June, 1872, after a year and a half of "Fors," the first stranger sent in his contribution, and at the end of three years £236 13s. were collected, to add to his £7,000, and a few acres of land were given.

Meanwhile Ruskin practised what he preached. He did not preach renunciation; he was not a Pessimist any more than an Optimist. Sometimes he felt he was not doing enough; he knew very well that others thought so. I remember his saying, in his rooms at Oxford in one of those years: "Here I am, trying to reform the world, and I suppose I ought to begin with myself, I am trying to do St. Benedict's work, and I ought to be a saint. And yet I am living between a Turkey carpet and a Titian, and drinking as much tea"—taking his second cup—"as I can *swig!*"

That was the way he put it to an undergraduate; to a lady friend he wrote later on, "I'm reading history of early saints, too, for my Amiens book, and feel that I ought to be scratched, or starved, or boiled, or something unpleasant; and I don't know if I'm a saint or a sinner in the least, in mediæval language. How did the saints feel themselves, I wonder, about their saintship!"

If he had forsaken all and followed the vocation of St. Francis,—he has discussed the question candidly in "Fors" for May, 1874—would not his work have been more effectual, his example more inspiring? Conceivably: but that was not his mission. His gospel was not one of asceticism; it called upon no one for any sort of suicide, or even martyrdom. He required of his followers that they should live their lives to the full in "Admiration, Hope and Love": and not that they should sacrifice themselves in fasting and wearing of camels'-hair coats. He wished them to work, to be honest, and just, in all things immediately attainable. He asked the tenth of their living—not the widow's two mites; and it was deeply painful to him to find, sometimes, that they had so interpreted his teaching: as when he wrote, later, to Miss Beever:

"One of my poor 'Companions of St. George' who has sent me, not a widow's but a parlour-maid's (an old schoolmistress) 'all her living,' and whom I found last night, dying, slowly and quietly, in a damp room, just the size of your study (which her landlord won't mend the roof of), by the light of a single tallow candle,—dying, I say, *slowly* of consumption, not yet near the end, but contemplating it with sorrow, mixed partly with fear lest she should not have done all she could for her children! The sight of this and my own shameful comforts, three wax candles and blazing fire and dry roof, and Susie and Joanie for friends! Oh me, Susie, what *is* to become of me in the next world, who have in this life all my good things!"

After carrying on "Fors" for some time his attention was drawn by Mr. W.C. Sillar to the question of "Usury." At first he had seen no crying sin in Interest. He had held that the "rights of capital" were visionary, and that the tools should belong to him that can handle them, in a perfect state of society; but he thought that the existing system was no worse in this respect than in others, and his expectation of reform in the plan of investment went hand-in-hand with his hope of a good time coming in everything else. So he quietly accepted his rents, as he accepted his Professorship, for example, thinking it his business to be a good landlord and spend his money generously, just as he thought it his business to retain the existing South Kensington drawing school, and the Oxford system of education—not at all his ideal—and to make the best use of them.

A lady who was his pupil in drawing, and a believer in his ideals of philanthropy, Miss Octavia Hill, undertook to help him in 1864 in efforts to reclaim part—though a very small part—of the lower-class dwellings of London. Half a dozen houses in Marylebone left by Ruskin's father, to which he added three more in Paradise Place, as it was euphemistically named, were the subjects of their experiment. They were ridiculed at first; but by the noblest endeavour they succeeded, and set an example which has been followed in many of our towns with great results. They showed what a wise and kind landlord could do by caring for tenants, by giving them habitable dwellings, recreation ground and fixity of tenure, and requiring in return a reasonable and moderate rent. He got five per cent. for his capital, instead of twelve or more, which such property generally returns, or at that time returned.

But when he began to write against rent and interest there were plenty of critics ready to cite this and other investments as a damning inconsistency. He was not the man to offer explanations at any time. It was no defence to say that he took less and did more than other landlords. And so he was glad to part with the whole to Miss Hill; nor did he care to spend upon himself the £3,500, which I believe was the price. It went right and left in gifts; till one day he cheerfully remarked:

"It's a' gane awa'
Like snaw aff a wa'."

"Is there really nothing to show for it?" he was asked. "Nothing," he said, "except this new silk umbrella."

He had talked so much of the possibility of carrying on honest and honourable retail trade, that he felt bound to exemplify his principles. He took a house No. 19, Paddington Street, with a corner shop, near his Marylebone property, and set himself up in business as a teaman. Mr. Arthur Severn painted the sign, in neat blue letters; the window was decked with fine old china, bought from a Cavaliere near Siena, whose unique collection had been introduced to notice by Professor Norton; and Miss Harrie Tovey, an old servant of Denmark Hill, was established there, like Miss Mattie in "Cranford," or rather like one of the salaried officials of "Time and Tide," to dispense the unadulterated leaf to all comers. No advertisements, no self-recommendation, no catchpenny tricks of trade were allowed; and yet the business went on, and, I am assured, prospered with legitimate profits. At first, various kinds of the best tea only were sold; but it seemed to the tenant of the shop that coffee and sugar ought to be included in the list. This was not at all in Ruskin's programme, and there were great debates at home about it. At last he gave way, on the understanding that the shop was to be responsible for the proper roasting of the coffee according to the best recipe. After some time Miss Tovey died. And when, in the autumn of 1876, Miss Octavia Hill proposed to take the house and business over and work it with the rest of the Marylebone property, the offer was thankfully accepted.

Another of his principles was cleanliness; "the speedy abolition of all abolishable filth is the first process of education." He undertook to keep certain streets, not crossings only, cleaner than the public seemed to care for, between the British Museum and St. Giles'. He took the broom himself, for a start, put on his gardener, Downes, as foreman of the job, and engaged a small staff of helpers. The work began, as he promised, in a humorous letter to the *Pall Matt Gazette* upon New Year's Day, 1872, and he kept his three sweepers at work for eight hours daily "to show a bit of our London streets kept as clean as the deck of a ship of the line."

There were some difficulties, too. One of the staff was an extremely handsome and lively shoeblack, picked up in St. Giles'. It turned out that he was not unknown to the world: he had sat to artists—to Mr. Edward Clifford, to Mr. Severn; and went by the name of "Cheeky." Every now and then Ruskin "and party" drove round to inspect the works. Downes could not be everywhere at once: and Cheeky used to be caught at pitch and toss or marbles in unswept Museum Street. Ruskin rarely, if ever, dismissed a servant; but street sweeping was not good enough for Cheeky, and so he enlisted. The army was not good enough, and so he deserted; and was last seen disappearing into the darkness, after calling a cab for his old friends one night at the Albert Hall.

One more escapade of this most unpractical man, as they called him. Since his fortune was rapidly melting away, he had to look to his works as an ultimate resource: they eventually became his only means of livelihood. One might suppose that he would be anxious to put his publishing business on the most secure and satisfactory footing; to facilitate sale, and to ensure profit. But he had views. He objected to advertising; though he thought that in his St. George's Scheme he would have a yearly Book Gazette drawn up by responsible authorities, indicating the best works. He distrusted the system of *unacknowledged* profits and percentages, though he fully agreed that the retailer should be paid for his work, and wished, in an ideal state, to see the shopkeeper a salaried official. He disliked the bad print and paper of the cheap literature of that day, and knew that people valued more highly what they did not get so easily. He had changed his mind with regard to one or two things—religion and glaciers chiefly—about which he had written at length in earlier works.

So he withdrew his most popular books—"Modern Painters" and the rest—from circulation, though he was persuaded by the publisher to reprint "Modern Painters" and "Stones of Venice" once more—"positively for the last time," as they said the plates would give no more good impressions. He had his later writings printed in a rather expensive style; at first through Smith & Elder, after two years by Messrs. Watson & Hazell (later Hazell, Watson & Viney, Ltd.), and the method of publication is illustrated in the history of "Sesame and Lilies," the first volume of these "collected works." It was issued by Smith & Elder, May, 1871, at 7s., to the trade only, leaving the retailer to fix the price to the public. In September, 1872, the work was also supplied by Mr. George Allen, and the price raised to 9s.6d., (carriage paid) to trade and public alike, with the idea that an extra shilling, or nearly ten per cent., might be added by the bookseller for his trouble in ordering the work. If he did not add the commission, that was his own affair; though with postage of order and payment, when only one or two copies at a time were asked for, this did not leave much margin. So it was doubled, by the simple expedient of doubling the price!—or, to be accurate, raising it to 18s. (carriage paid) for 20s. over the counter. It was freely prophesied by business men that this would not do: however, at the end of fifteen years the *sixth edition* of this work in this form was being sold, in spite of the fact that, five years before, a smaller reprint of the same book had been brought out at 5s., and was then in its fourth edition of 3,000 copies each.

Compared with the enormous sale of sensational novels and school books, this is no great matter; but for a didactic work, offered to the public without advertisement, and in the face of the almost universal opposition of the book-selling trade, it means not only that, as an author, Ruskin had made a secure reputation, but also that he deserved the curious tribute once paid him by the journal of a big modern shop (Compton House, Liverpool) as a "great tradesman."

CHAPTER III

OXFORD TEACHING (1872-1875)

Early in 1872, after bringing out "Munera Pulveris," the essays he had written ten years before for *Fraser* on economy; after getting those street-sweepers to work near the British Museum where he was making studies of animals and Greek sculpture; and after once more addressing the Woolwich cadets, this time[25] on the Bird of Calm (the mythology of the Halcyon), Professor Ruskin went to Oxford to give a course of ten lectures[26] on the Relation of Natural Science to Art, afterwards published under the title of "The Eagle's Nest." He wrote to Professor Norton:

"I am, as usual, unusually busy. When I get fairly into my lecture work at Oxford I always find the lecture would come better some other way, just before it is given, and so work from hand to mouth. I am always unhappy, and see no good in saying so. But I am settling to my work here—recklessly—to do my best with it: feeling quite sure that it is talking at hazard for what chance good may come. But I attend regularly in the schools as mere drawing-master, and the men begin to come in one by one, about fifteen or twenty already; several worth having as pupils in any way, being of temper to make good growth of."

Why was he always unhappy? It was not that Mr. W.B. Scott criticised "Ruskin's influence" in that March; or that by Easter he had to say farewell to his old home on Denmark Hill, and settle "for good" at Brantwood. Nor that he could go abroad again for a long summer in Italy with Mr. and Mrs. Severn and the Hilliards and Mr. Albert Goodwin. They started about the middle of April, and on the journey out he wrote, beside his "Fors" which always went on, a preface to the Rev. R. St. John Tyrwhitt's "Christian Art and Symbolism." He drew the Apse at Pisa, half-amused and half-worried by the little ragamuffin who varied the tedium of watching his work by doing horizontal-bar tricks on the railings of the Cathedral green. Then to Lucca, where, to show his friends something of Italian landscape, he took them for rambles through the olive farms and chestnut woods, among which Miss Hilliard lost her jewelled cross. Greatly to Ruskin's delight, as a firm believer in Italian peasant-virtue, it was found and returned without hint of reward.

At Rome they visited old Mr. Severn, and then went homeward by way of Verona, where Ruskin wrote an account of the Cavalli monuments for the Arundel society, and Venice, where he returned to the study of Carpaccio. At Rome he had been once more to the Sistine, and found that on earlier visits the ceiling and the Last Judgment had taken his attention too exclusively. Now that he could look away from Michelangelo he become conscious of the claims of Botticelli's frescoes, which represent, in the Florentine school, somewhat the same kind of interest that he had found in Carpaccio. He became enamoured of Botticelli's Zipporah, and resolved to study the master more closely. On reaching home he had to prepare "The Eagle's Nest" for publication; in the preface he gave special importance to Botticelli, and amplified it in lectures on early engraving, that Autumn;[27] in which I remember his quoting with appreciation the passage on the Venus Anadyomene from Pater's "Studies in the Renaissance" just published.

This sudden enthusiasm about an unknown painter amused the Oxford public: and it became a standing joke among the profane to ask who was Ruskin's last great man. It was in answer to that, and in expression of a truer understanding than most Oxford pupils attained, that Bourdillon of Worcester wrote on "the Ethereal Ruskin,"—that was Carlyle's name for him:—

"To us this star or that seems bright,
And oft some headlong meteor's flight
Holds for awhile our raptured sight.

"But he discerns each noble star;
The least is only the most far,
Whose worlds, may be, the mightiest are."

The critical value of this course however, to a student of art-history, is impaired by his using as illustrations of Botticelli, and of the manner of engraving which he took for standard, certain plates which were erroneously attributed to the artist. "It is strange," he wrote in despair to Professor Norton, "that I hardly ever get anything stated without some grave mistake, however true in my main discourse." But in this case a fate stronger than he had taken him unawares. The circumstances do not extenuate the error of the Professor, but they explain the difficulties under which his work was done. The cloud that rested on his own life was the result of a strange and wholly unexpected tragedy in another's.

It was an open secret—his attachment to a lady, who had been his pupil, and was now generally understood to be his *fiancée*. She was far younger than he; but at fifty-three he was not an old man; and the friends who fully knew and understood the affair favoured his intentions and joined in the hope, and in auguries for the happiness for which he had been so long waiting. But now that it came to the point the lady finally decided that it was impossible. He was not at one with her in religious matters. He could speak lightly of her evangelical creed—it seemed he scoffed in "Fors" at her faith. She could not be unequally yoked with an unbeliever. To her, the alternative was plain; the choice was terrible: yet, having once seen her path, she turned resolutely away.[28]

Meanwhile, in the bitterest despair he sought refuge as he had done before, in his work. He accepted the lesson, though he, too, could not recant; still he tried to correct his apparent levity in the renewed seriousness and more earnest tone of "Fors," speaking more plainly and more simply, but without concession. He wrote on the next Christmas Eve to an Aberdeen Bible-class teacher:

"If you care to give your class a word directly from me, say to them that they will find it well, throughout life, never to trouble themselves about what they ought *not* to do, but about what they *ought* to do. The condemnation given from the Judgment Throne—most solemnly described—is all for the *undones* and not for the *dones*. People are perpetually afraid of doing wrong; but unless they are doing its reverse energetically, they do it all day long, and the degree does not matter. Make your young hearers resolve to be honest in their work in this life. Heaven will take care of them for the other."

That was all he could say: he did not *know* there was another life: he *hoped* there was: and yet, if he were not a saint or a Christian, was there any man in the world who was nearer to the kingdom of Heaven than this stubborn heretic?

His heretical attitude was singular. He was just as far removed from adopting the easy antagonism of science to religion as from siding with religion against science. In a paper singularly interesting—and in his biography important—on the "Nature and Authority of Miracle," read to the Metaphysical Society (February 11, 1873), he tried to clear up his position and to state a qualified belief in the supernatural.

With that year expired the term for which he had been elected to the Slade Professorship, and in January 1873 he was re-elected. In his first three years he had given five courses of lectures designed to introduce an encyclopædic review and reconstruction of all he had to say upon art.

Beginning with general principles, he had proceeded to their application in history, by tracing certain phases of Greek sculpture, and by contrasting the Greek and the Gothic spirit as shown in the treatment of landscape, from which he went on to the study of early engraving. The application of his principles to theory was made in the course on Science and Art ("The Eagle's Nest"). Now, on his re-election, he proceeded to take up these two sides of his subject, and to illustrate this view of the right way to apply science to art, by a course on Birds, in Nature, Art and Mythology, and next year by a study of Alpine forms. The historical side was continued with lectures on Niccola Pisano and early Tuscan sculpture, and in 1874 with an important, though unpublished, course on Florentine Art.

It is to this cycle of lectures that we must look for that matured Ruskinian theory of art which his early works do not reach; and which his writings between 1860 and 1870 do not touch. Though the Oxford lectures are only a fragment of what he ought to have done, they should be sufficient to a careful reader; though their expression is sometimes obscured by diffuse treatment, they contain the root of the matter, thought out for fifteen years since the close of the more brilliant, but less profound, period of "Modern Painters."

The course on Birds[29] was given in the drawing school at the University Galleries. The room was not large enough for the numbers that crowded to hear Professor Ruskin, and each of these lectures, like the previous and the following courses, had to be repeated to a second audience. Great pains had been given to their preparation—much greater than the easy utterance and free treatment of his theme led his hearers to believe. For these lectures and their sequel, published as "Love's Meinie," he collected an enormous number of skins—to compare the plumage and wings of different species; for his work was with the *outside* aspect and structure of birds, not with their anatomy. He had models made, as large as swords, of the different quill-feathers, to experiment on their action and resistance to the air. He got a valuable series of drawings by H.S. Marks, R.A., and made many careful and beautiful studies himself of feathers and of birds at the Zoological Gardens, and the British Museum; and after all, he had to conclude his work saying, "It has been throughout my trust that if death should write on these, 'What this man began to build, he was not able to finish,' God may also write on them, not in anger, but in aid, 'A stronger than he cometh.'"

Two of the lectures on birds were repeated at Eton[30] before the boys' Literary and Scientific Society and their friends; and between this and 1880 Ruskin often went to address the same audience, with the same interest in young people that had taken him in earlier years to Woolwich.

After a long vacation at Brantwood, the first spent there, he went up to give his course on Early Tuscan Art ("Val d'Arno")[31]. The lectures were printed separately and sold at the conclusion and the first numbers were sent to Carlyle, whose unabated interest in his friend's work was shown in his letter of Oct. 31st: "*Perge, perge;*—and, as the Irish say, 'more power to your elbow!' I have yet read this 'Val d'Arno' only once. Froude snatched it away from me yesterday; and it has then to go to my brother at Dumfries. After that I shall have it back . . ."

During that summer and autumn Ruskin suffered from nights of sleeplessness or unnaturally vivid dreams and days of unrest and feverish energy, alternating with intense fatigue. The eighteen lectures in less than six weeks, a "combination of prophecy and play-acting," as Carlyle had called it in his own case, and the unfortunate discussion with an old-fashioned economist who undertook to demolish Ruskinism without understanding it, added to the causes of which we are already aware, brought him to New Year, 1874, in "failing strength, care, and hope." He sought quiet at the seaside, but found modern hotel-life intolerable; he went back to town and tried the pantomimes for distraction,—saw Kate Vaughan in Cinderella, and Violet Cameron in Jack in the Box, over and over again, and found himself:

"Now hopelessly a man of the world!—of that woeful outside one, I mean. It is now Sunday; half-past eleven in the morning. Everybody else is gone to church—and I am left alone with the cat, in the world of sin."

Thinking himself better, he went to Oxford, and announced a course on Alpine form; but after a week was obliged to retreat and go home to Coniston, still hoping to return and give his lectures. But it was no use. The gloom without deepened the gloom within; and he took the wisest course in trying Italy, alone this time with his old servant Crawley.

The greater part of 1874 was spent abroad—first travelling through Savoy and by the Riviera to Assisi, where he wrote to Miss S. Beever:

"The Sacristan gives me my coffee for lunch in his own little cell, looking out on the olive woods; then he tells me stories of conversions and miracles, and then perhaps we go into the sacristy and have a reverent little poke-out of relics. Fancy a great carved cupboard in a vaulted chamber full of most precious things (the box which the Holy Virgin's veil used to be kept in, to begin with), and leave to rummage in it at will! Things that are only shown twice in the year or so, with fumigation! all the congregation on their knees—and the sacristan and I having a great heap of them on the table at once, like a dinner service. I really looked with great respect on St. Francis's old camel-hair dress."

Thence he went to visit Colonel and Mrs. Yule at Palermo, deeply interested in Scylla and Charybdis, Etna and the metopes of Selinus. His interest in Greek art had been shown, not only in a course of lectures, but in active support to archæological explorations. He said once, "I believe heartily in diggings, of all sorts." Meeting General L.P. di Cesnola and hearing of the wealth of ancient remains in Cyprus then newly discovered, Mr. Ruskin placed £1,000 at his disposal. General di Cesnola was able, in April, 1875, to announce that in spite of the confiscation of half the treasure-trove by the local Government, he had shipped a cargo of antiquities, including many vases, terra-cottas, and fragments of sculpture. Whence, precisely, these relics came is now doubtful.

The landscape of Theocritus and the remains of ancient glories roused him to energetic sketching—a sign of returning strength, which continued when he reached Rome, and enabled him to make a very fine copy of Botticelli's Zipporah, and other details of the Sistine frescoes.

Late in October he reached England, just able to give the promised Lectures on Alpine forms,[32]—I remember his curious attempt to illustrate the névé-masses by pouring flour on a model;—and a second course on the Æsthetic and Mathematic schools of Florence;[33] and a lecture on Botticelli at Eton, of which the Literary and Scientific Society's minute-book contains the following report:

> "On Saturday, Dec. 12th (1874), Professor Ruskin lectured before a crowded, influential and excited audience, which comprised our noble Society and a hundred and thirty gentlemen and ladies, who eagerly accepted an invitation to hear Professor Ruskin 'talk' to us on Botticelli. It is utterly impossible for the unfortunate secretary of the Society to transmit to writing even an abstract of this address; and it is some apology for him when beauty of expression, sweetness of voice, and elegance in imagery defy the utmost efforts of the pen."

Just before leaving for Italy he had been told that the Royal Institute of British Architects intended to present him with their Gold Medal in acknowledgment of his services to the cause of architecture; and during his journey official announcement of the award reached him. He dictated from Assisi (June 12, 1874) a letter to Sir Gilbert Scott, explaining why he declined the honour intended him. He said in effect that if it had been offered at a time when he had been writing on architecture it would have been welcome; but it was not so now that he felt all his efforts to have been in vain and the profession as a body engaged in work—such as the "restoration" of ancient buildings—with which he had no sympathy. It had been represented to him that his refusal to accept a Royal Medal would be a reflection upon the Royal donor. To which he replied:

> "Having entirely loyal feelings towards the Queen, I will trust to her Majesty's true interpretation of my conduct; but if formal justification of it be necessary for the public, would plead that if a Peerage or Knighthood may without disloyalty be refused, surely much more the minor grace proceeding from the monarch may be without impropriety declined by any of her Majesty's subjects who wish to serve her without reward, under the exigency of peculiar circumstances."

It was only the term before that Prince Leopold had been at Oxford, a constant attendant on Ruskin's lectures, and a visitor to his drawing school. The gentle prince, with his instinct for philanthropy, was not to be deterred by the utterances of "Fors" from respecting the genius of the Professor; and the Professor, with his old-world, cavalier loyalty, readily returned the esteem and affection of his new pupil. A sincere friendship was formed, lasting until the Prince's death.

In June, 1875, Princess Alice and her husband, with Prince Arthur and Prince Leopold, were at Oxford. Ruskin had just made arrangements completing his gifts to the University galleries and schools. The Royal party showed great interest in the Professor and his work. The Princess, the Grand Duke of Hesse, and Prince Leopold acted as witnesses to the deed of gift, and Prince Arthur and Prince Leopold accepted the trusteeship.

With all the Slade Professor's generosity, the Ruskin drawing school, founded in these fine galleries to which he had so largely contributed, in a palatial hall handsomely furnished, and hung with Tintoret and Luini, Burne-Jones and Rossetti, and other rare masters, ancient and modern; with the most interesting examples to copy—at the most convenient of desks, we may add—yet in spite of it all, the drawing school was not a popular institution. When the Professor was personally teaching, he got some fifteen or twenty—if not to attend, at any rate to join. But whenever the chief attraction could not be counted on, the attendance sank to an average of two or three. The cause was simple. An undergraduate is supposed to spend his morning in lectures, his afternoon in taking exercise, and his evening in college. There is simply no time in his scheme for going to a drawing school. If it were recognised as part of the curriculum, if it counted in any way along with other studies, or contributed to a "school" akin to that of music, practical art might become teachable at Oxford; and Professor Ruskin's gifts and endowments—to say nothing of his hopes and plans—would not be wholly in vain.

As he could not make the undergraduates draw, he made them dig. He had noticed a very bad bit of road on the Hinksey side, and heard that it was nobody's business to mend it: meanwhile the farmers' carts and casual pedestrians were bemired. He sent for his gardener Downes, who had been foreman of the street-sweepers; laid in a stock of picks and shovels; took lessons in stone-breaking himself, and called on his friends to spend their recreation times in doing something useful.

Many of the disciples met at the weekly open breakfasts at the Professor's rooms in Corpus; and he was glad of a talk to them on other things beside drawing and digging. Some were attracted chiefly by the celebrity of the man, or by the curiosity of his humorous discourse; but there were a few who partly grasped one side or other of his mission and character. The most brilliant undergraduate of the time, seen at this breakfast table, but not one of the diggers, was W.H. Mallock, afterwards widely known as the author of "Is Life Worth Living?" He was the only man. Professor Ruskin said, who really understood him—referring to "The

New Republic." But while Mallock saw the reactionary and pessimistic side of his Oxford teacher, there was a progressist and optimistic side which does not appear in his "Mr. Herbert." That was discovered by another man whose career, short as it was, proved even more influential. Arnold Toynbee was one of the Professor's warmest admirers and ablest pupils: and in his philanthropic work the teaching of "Unto this Last" and "Fors" was illustrated—not exclusively—but truly. "No true disciple of mine will ever be a Ruskinian" (to quote "St. Mark's Rest"); "he will follow, not me, but the instincts of his own soul, and the guidance of its Creator."

Like all energetic men, Ruskin was fond of setting other people to work. One of his plans was to form a little library of standard books ("Bibliotheca Pastorum") suitable for the kind of people who, he hoped, would join or work under his St. George's Company. The first book he chose was the "Economist" of Xenophon, which he asked two of his young friends to translate. To them and their work he would give his afternoons in the rooms at Corpus, with curious patience in the midst of pre-occupying labour and severest trial; for just then he was lecturing at the London Institution on the Alps[34]— reading a paper to the Metaphysical Society[35]—writing the Academy Notes of 1875, and "Proserpina," etc.—as well as his regular work at "Fors," and the St. George's Company was then taking definite form;—and all the while the lady of his love was dying under the most tragic circumstances, and he forbidden to approach her.

At the end of May she died. On the 1st of June the Royal party honoured the Slade Professor with their visit—little knowing how valueless to him such honours had become. He went north[36] and met his translators at Brantwood to finish the Xenophon,—and to help dig his harbour and cut coppice in his wood. He prepared a preface; but the next term was one of greater pressure, with the twelve lectures on Sir Joshua Reynolds to deliver. He wrote, after Christmas:

"Now that I have got my head fairly into this Xenophon business, it has expanded into a new light altogether; and I think it would be absurd in me to slur over the life in one paragraph. A hundred things have come into my head as I arrange the dates, and I think I can make a much better thing of it—with a couple of days' work. My head would not work in town—merely turned from side to side—never nodded (except sleepily). I send you the proofs just to show you I'm at work. I'm going to translate all the story of Delphic answer before Anabasis: and his speech after the sleepless night."

Delphic answers—for he was then again brought into contact with "spiritualism"; and sleepless nights—for the excitement of overwork was telling upon him—were becoming too frequent in his own experience; and yet the lectures on Reynolds went off with success.[37] The magic of his oratory transmuted the scribbled jottings of his MS. into a magnificent flow of rolling paragraph and rounded argument that thrilled a captious audience with unwonted emotion, and almost persuaded many a hearer to accept the gospel of "the Ethereal Ruskin." In spite of a sense of antagonism to his surroundings, he did useful work which none other could do in the University. That this was acknowledged was proved by his re-election, early in 1876: but his third term of three years was a time of weakened health. Repeated absence from his post and inability to fulfil his duties made it obviously his wisest course, at the end of that term, to resign the Slade Professorship.

NOTES:

25   January 13, 1872.
26   Feb. 8, 10, 15, 17, 22, 24. 29; March 2, 7, and 9.

27   "Ariadne Florentina," delivered on Nov. 2, 9, 16, 23, 30, and Dec. 7, and repeated on the following Thursdays. Ruskin's first mention of Botticelli was in the course on Landscape, Lent Term, 1871.
28   In former editions the following sentence was added: "Three years after, as she lay dying, he begged to see her once more. She sent to ask whether he could yet say that he loved God better than he loved her; and when he said 'No,' her door was closed upon him for ever." The statement was suggested by information from Ruskin in later days. I must, however, have misrepresented the facts, as the lady's mother has left it in writing that no such incident occurred.
29   March 15, May 2 and 9; repeated March 19, May 5, and 12, 1873.
30   May 10 and 17.
31   On Mondays and Thursdays, Oct. 21, 23, 27, 30, Nov. 3, 6, 10, 13, 17, 20; repeated on the Wednesdays and Fridays following.
32   Oct. 27, 30; Nov. 3 and 6, 1874.
33   Nov. 10, 13, 17, 20, 24, 27; Dec. 1 and 4, 1874.
34   "The Simple Dynamic Conditions of Glacial Action among the Alps," March 11, 1875.
35   "Social Policy based on Natural Selection," May 11.
36   "On a posting tour through Yorkshire". He made three such tours in 1875—southward in January, northward in June and July, and southward in September: and another northward in April and May, 1876.
37   Nov. 2, 4, 6, 9, 11, 13, 16, 18, 20, 23, 25, and 27; 1875.

CHAPTER IV

ST. GEORGE AND ST. MARK (1875-1877)

In the book his Bertha of Canterbury was reading at twilight on the Eve of St. Mark, Keats might have been describing "Fors." Among its pages, fascinating with their golden broideries of romance and wit, perplexing with mystic vials of wrath as well as all the Seven Lamps and Shekinah of old and new Covenants commingled, there was gradually unfolded the plan of "St. George's Work."

The scheme was not easy to apprehend; it was essentially different from anything then known, though superficially like several bankrupt Utopias. Ruskin did not want to found a phalanstery, or to imitate Robert Owen or the Shakers. That would have been practicable—and useless.

He wanted much more. He aimed at the gradual introduction of higher aims into ordinary life: it giving true refinement to the lower classes, true simplicity to the upper. He proposed that idle hands should reclaim waste lands; that healthy work and country homes should be offered to townsfolk who would "come out of the gutter." He asked land-owners and employers to furnish opportunities for such reforms;—which would involve no elaborate organization nor unelastic rules;—simply the one thing needful, the refusal of Commercialism.

As before, he scorned the idea that real good could be done by political agitation. Any government would work, he said, if it were an efficient government. No government was efficient unless it saw that every one had the necessaries of life, for body and soul; and that every one earned them by some work or other. Capital—that is, the means and material of labour, should therefore be in the hands of the Government, not in the hands of individuals: this reform would result easily and necessarily from the forbidding of loans on interest. Personal property would still be in private hands; but as it could not be invested and turned into capital, it would necessarily be restricted to its actual use, and great accumulation would be valueless.

This is, of course, a very sketchy statement of the ground-work of "Fors," but to most readers nowadays as comprehensible as, at the time of its publication, it was incomprehensible. For when, long after "Fors" had been written, Ruskin found other writers advocating the same principles and calling themselves Socialists, he said that he too was a Socialist.

But the Socialists of various sects have complicated, and sometimes confused, their simple fundamental principles with various ways and means; to which he could not agree. He had his own ways and means. He had his private ideals of life, which he expounded, along with his main doctrine. He thought, justifiably, that theory was useless without practical example; and so he founded St. George's Company (in 1877 called St. George's Guild) as his illustration.

The Guild grew out of his call, in 1871, for adherents: and by 1875 began to take definite form. Its objects were to set the example of a common capital as opposed to a National debt, and of co-operative labour as opposed to competitive struggle for life. Each member was required to do some work for his living—without too strict limits as to the kind—and to practice certain precepts of religion and morality, broad enough for general acceptance. He was also required to obey the authority of the Guild, and to contribute a tithe of his income to a common fund, for various objects. These objects were—first: to buy land for the agricultural members to cultivate, paying their rent, not to the other members, but to the company; not refusing machinery, but preferring manual labour. Next, to buy mills and factories, to be likewise owned by the Guild and worked by members—using water power in preference to steam (steam at first not forbidden)—and making the lives of the people employed as well spent as might be, with a fair wage, healthy work, and so forth. The loss on starting was to be made up from the Guild store, but it was anticipated that the honesty of the goods turned out would ultimately make such enterprises pay, even in a commercial world. Then, for the people employed and their families, there would be places of recreation and instruction, supplied by the Guild, and intended to give the agricultural labourer or mill-hand, trained from infancy in Guild schools, some insight into Literature, Science and Art—and tastes which his easy position would leave him free to cultivate.

So far the plan was simple. It was not a *colony*—but merely the working of existing industries in a certain way. Anticipating further development of the scheme, Ruskin looked forward to a guild coinage, as pretty as the Florentines had; a costume as becoming as the Swiss: and other Platonically devised details, which were not the essentials of the proposal, and never came into operation. But some of his plans were actually realised.

The chief objects of "St. George" come under three heads, as we have just noticed: agricultural, industrial, and educational. The actual schools would not be needed until the farms and mills had been so far established as to secure a permanent attendance. But meanwhile provision was being made for them, both in literature and in art. The "Bibliotheca Pastorum," was to be a comprehensive little library—far less than the 100 books of the *Pall Mall Gazette*—and yet bringing before the St. George's workman standard and serious writing of all times. It was to include, in separate volumes, the Books of Moses and the Psalms of David and the Revelation of St. John. Of Greek, the Economist of Xenophon, and Hesiod, which Ruskin undertook to translate into prose. Of Latin the first two Georgics and sixth Æneid of Virgil, in Gawain Douglas' translation. Dante; Chaucer, excluding the "Canterbury Tales"—but including the "Romance of the Rose"; Gotthelf's "Ulric the Farmer," from the French version which Ruskin had loved ever since his father used to read it him on their first tours in Switzerland; and an early English history by an Oxford friend. Later were published Sir Philip Sidney's psalter, and Ruskin's own biography of Sir Herbert Edwardes, under the title of "A Knight's Faith."

These books were for the home library; reference works were bought to be deposited in central libraries, along with objects of art and science. It was not intended to keep the Guild property centralised; but rather to spread it, as its other work was spread, broad-cast. A number of books and other objects were bought with the Guild money, and lent or given to various schools and colleges and institutions where work akin to the objects of the Guild was being done. But for the time Ruskin fixed upon Sheffield as the place of his first Guild Museum—being the home of the typical English industry—central to all parts of England, near beautiful hill-country, and yet not far from a number of manufacturing towns in which, if St. George's work went on, supporters and recruits might be found.

The people of Sheffield were already, in 1875, building a museum of their own, and naturally thought that the two might be conveniently worked together. But that was not at all what Ruskin wished. Not only was his museum to be primarily the storehouse of the Guild, rather than one among many means of popular education; but the objects which he intended to place there were not such as the public expected to see. He had no interest in a vast accumulation of articles of all kinds. He wanted to provide for his friends' common treasury a few definitely valuable and interesting examples—interesting to the sort of people that he hoped would join the Guild or be bred up in it; and valuable according to his own standard and experience.

In September 1875, Ruskin stayed a couple of days at Sheffield to inspect a cottage at Walkley, in the outskirts of the town, and to make arrangements for founding the museum—humbly to begin with, but hoping for speedy increase. He engaged as curator, at a salary of £40 a year and free lodging on the premises, his former pupil at the Working Men's College, Henry Swan, who had done occasional work for him in drawing and engraving. Swan was a Quaker, and a remarkable man in his way; enthusiastic in his new vocation, and interested in the social questions which were being discussed in "Fors." Under his care the Museum remained at Walkley, accumulating material in the tiny and hardly accessible cottage—being so to speak in embryo, until the way should be clear for its removal or enlargement, which took place in 1890.

When Ruskin came back on his posting tour of April 1876, he stayed again at Sheffield, to meet a few friends of Swan's—Secularists, Unitarians, and Quakers, who professed Communism. They had an interview (reported in the Sheffield *Daily Telegraph*, April 28th, 1876), which brought out rather curiously the points of difference between their opinions and his. They refused to join the Guild because they would not promise obedience, and help in its objects. Ruskin, however, was willing to advance theirs. A few weeks afterwards he invited them to choose a piece of ground for their Communist experiment. They chose a farm of over thirteen acres at Abbeydale, which the Guild bought in 1877 at a cost of £2,287 16s.6d. for their use—the communists agreeing to pay the money back in instalments, without interest, by the end of seven years: when the farm should be their own.

When it was actually in their hands they found that they knew nothing of farming—and besides, were making money at trades they did not really care to abandon. They engaged a man to work the farm for them: and then another. They were told that the land they had chosen was—for farming purposes—worthless. Their capital ran short; and they tried to make money by keeping a tea-garden. The original proposer of the scheme wrote to Ruskin, who sent £100:— the others returned the money. Ruskin declined to take it back, and began to perceive that the Communists were trifling. They had made no attempt to found the sort of community they had talked about;

neither their plans nor his were being carried out. So when the original proposer and a friend of his named Riley approached Ruskin again, they found little difficulty in persuading him to try them as managers. The rest, finding themselves turned out by Riley, vainly demanded "explanations" from Ruskin, who then was drifting into his first attack of brain fever. So they declined further connection with the farm; the Guild accepted their resignation, and undertook for the time nothing more than to get the land into good condition again.

This was not the only land held by the St. George's Guild. It acquired the acre of ground on which the Sheffield Museum stood, and a cottage with a couple of acres near Scarborough. Two acres of rock and moor at Barmouth had been given by Mrs. Talbot in 1872; and in 1877 Mr. George Baker, then Mayor of Birmingham, gave twenty acres of woodland at Bewdley in Worcestershire, to which at one time Mr. Ruskin thought of moving the museum, before the present building was found for it by the Sheffield Corporation at Meersbrook Park. On the resignation of the original Trustees, in 1877, Mr. Q. Talbot and Mr. Baker were offered the trust: and on the death of Mr. Talbot the trust was accepted by Mr. John Henry Chamberlain. After he died it was taken by Mr. George Thomson of Huddersfield, whose woollen mills, transformed into a co-operative concern, though not directly in connection with the Guild, have given a widely known example of the working of principles advocated in "Fors."

In the middle of 1876, Egbert Rydings, the auditor of the accounts which, in accordance with his principles of "glass pockets," Ruskin published in "Fors," proposed to start a homespun woollen industry at Laxey, in the Isle of Man, where the old women who formerly spun with the wheel had been driven by failure of custom to work in the mines. The Guild built him a water mill, and in a few years the demand for a pure, rough, durable cloth, created by this and kindred attempts, justified the enterprise. Ruskin set the example, and had his own grey clothes made of Laxey stuffs—whose chief drawback was that they never wore out. A little later a similar work was done, with even greater success, by Mr. Albert Fleming, another member of the Guild; who introduced old-fashioned spinning and hand-loom weaving at Langdale.

The story of Ruskin's posting tour was told many years afterwards, at the opening of the new Sheffield museum, by Mr. Arthur Severn, a famous *raconteur*, whose description of the adventures of their cruise upon wheels includes so bright a picture of Ruskin, that I must use his words as they were reported on the occasion in the magazine *Igdrasil*:

"... With the Professor, who dislikes railways very much, it was not a question of travelling by rail. He said, 'I will take you in a carriage and with horses, and we will drive the whole way from London to the North of England. And I will not only do that, but I will do the best in my power to get a postilion to ride, and we will go quite in the old-fashioned way...' The Professor went so far that he actually built a carriage for this drive. It was a regular posting carriage, with good strong wheels, a place behind for the luggage, and cunning drawers inside it for all kinds of things that we might require on the journey. We started off one fine morning from London—I must say without a postilion—but when we arrived at the next town, about twenty miles off, having telegraphed beforehand that we were coming, there was a gorgeous postilion ready with the fresh horses, and we started off in a right style, according to the Professor's wishes.

"After many pleasant days of travelling, we at last arrived at Sheffield, and I well remember that we created no small sensation as we clattered up to the old posting inn. I think it was the King's Head. We stayed a few days, and visited the old Museum at Walkley; and I remember the look of regret on the Professor's face when he saw how cramped the space was there for the things he had to show. However, with his usual kindliness, he did not say much about it at the time, and he did not complain of the considerable amount of room it was necessary for the curator and his family to take up in that place. We stayed about two days looking at the beautiful country,— and I am glad to say there was a good deal still left,—and then the Professor gave orders that the carriage should be got ready to take us on our journey, and that a postilion should be forthcoming, if possible. I remember leaving the luncheon table and going outside to see if the necessary arrangements were complete. Sure enough, there was the carriage at the door, and a still more gorgeous postilion than any we had had so far on our journey. His riding breeches were of the tightest and whitest I ever saw; his horses were an admirable pair, and looked like going. A very large crowd had assembled outside the inn, to see what extraordinary kind of mortals could be going to travel in such a way.

"I went to the room where the Professor was still at luncheon, and told him that everything was ready, but that there was a very large crowd at the door. He seemed rather amused; and I said, 'You know, Professor, I really don't know what the people expect—whether it is a bride and bridegroom, or what.' He said, 'Well, Arthur, you and Joan shall play at being bride and bridegroom inside the carriage, and I will get on the box.' He got Mrs. Severn on his arm, and had to hold her pretty tightly as he left the door, because when she saw the crowd outside she tried to beat a retreat. At last he got her into the carriage, I was put in afterwards, and he jumped up on the box. The crowd closed in, and looked at us as if we were a sort of menagerie. I was much amused when I thought how little these eager people knew that the real attraction was on the box; I felt inclined to put my head out of the window, and say, 'My good people, there is the man you should look at,—not us.' I did not like to do so; and the Professor gave the word to be off, the postilion cracked his whip, and we went off in grand style, amidst the cheers of the crowd . . ."

On one of these posting excursions, they came to Hardraw; Mrs. Alfred Hunt tells the story in her edition of Turner's "Richmondshire"; Mr. Severn's account is somewhat different. After examining the Fall, Mrs. Severn and Mr. Ruskin left Mr. Severn to sketch, and went away to Hawes to order their tea. When they were gone, a man who had been standing by came up and asked if that were Professor Ruskin. "Yes," said Mr. Severn, "it was; he is very fond of the Fall, and much puzzled to know why the edge of the cliff is not worn away by the water, as he expected to find it after so many years." "Oh," said the other, "there are twelve feet of masonry up there to protect the rock. I'm a native of the place, and know all about it." "I wish," said Mr. Severn, absently, as he went on drawing, "Mr. Ruskin knew that; he would be so interested." And the stranger ran off. When the sketcher came in to tea he felt there was something wrong. "You're in for it!" said his wife. "Let us look at his sketch first," said Mr. Ruskin; and luckily it was a very good one. By and by it all came out;—how the Yorkshireman had caught the Professor, and eagerly described the horrible Vandalism, receiving in reply some very emphatic language. Upon which he took off his hat and bowed low: "But, sir," he faltered, "the gentleman up there said I was to tell you, and you would be so interested!" The Professor, suddenly mollified, took off his hat in turn, and apologised for his reception of the news: "but," said he, "I shall never care for Hardraw Waterfall again."

"The Professor," said Mr. Severn, "dislikes railways very much:" and on his arrival at Brantwood after that posting journey he wrote a preface to "A Protest against the Extension of Railways in the Lake District," by Mr. Robert Somervell. Ruskin's dislike of railways has been the text of a great deal of misrepresentation, and his use of them, at all, has been often quoted as an inconsistency. As a matter of fact, he never objected to main lines of railway communication; but he strongly objected, in common with a vast number of people, to the introduction of railways into districts whose chief interest is in their scenery; especially where, as in the English Lake district, the scenery is in miniature, easily spoiled by embankments and viaducts, and by the rows of ugly buildings which usually grow up round a station; and where the beauty of the landscape can only be felt in quiet walks or drives through it. Many years later, after he had said all he had to say on the subject again and again, and was on the brink of one of his illnesses, he wrote in violent language to a correspondent who tried to "draw" him on the subject of another proposed railway to Ambleside. But his real opinions were simple enough, and consistent with a practicable scheme of life.

In August 1876 he left England for Italy. He travelled alone, accompanied only by his new servant Baxter, who had lately taken the place vacated by Crawley, Mr. Ruskin's former valet of twenty years' service. He crossed the Simplon to Venice, where he was welcomed by an old friend, Rawdon Brown, and a new friend, Prof. C.H. Moore, of Harvard. He met two Oxford pupils, Mr. J. Reddie Anderson, whom he set to work on Carpaccio; and Mr. Whitehead—"So much nicer they all are," he wrote in a private letter, "than I was at their age;"—also his pupil Mr. Bunney, at work on copies of pictures and records of architecture, the legacy of St. Mark to St. George. Two young artists were brought into his circle, during that winter—both Venetians, and both singularly interesting men: Giacomo Boni, now a celebrated antiquary, then capo d'opera of the Ducal Palace, and doing his best to preserve, instead of "restoring," the ancient sculptures; and Angelo Alessandri, a painter of more than usual seriousness of aim and sympathy with the fine qualities of the old masters.

Ruskin had been engaged on a manual of drawing for his Oxford schools, which he now meant to complete in two parts: "The Laws of Fésole"—teaching the principles of Florentine draughtsmanship; and "The Laws of Rivo Alto"—about Venetian colour. Passages for this second part were written. But he found himself so deeply interested in the evolution of Venetian art, and in tracing the spirit of the people as shown by the mythology illustrated in the pictures and sculptures, that his practical manual became a sketch of art history, "St. Mark's Rest"—as a sort of companion to "Mornings in Florence," which he had been working at during his last visit to Italy. His intention was to supersede "Stones of Venice" by a smaller book, giving more prominence to the ethical side of history, which should illustrate Carpaccio as the most important figure of the transition period, and do away with the exclusive Protestantism of his earlier work.

He set himself to this task, with Tintoret's motto—*Sempre si fa il mare maggiore*, and worked with feverish energy, recording his progress in letters home.

"13 *Nov.*—I never was yet, in my life, in such a state of hopeless confusion of letters, drawings, and work: chiefly because, of course, when one is old, one's *done* work seems all to tumble in upon one, and want rearranging, and everything brings a thousand old as well as new thoughts. My head seems less capable of accounts every year. I can't *fix* my mind on a sum in addition—it goes off, between seven and nine, into a speculation on the seven deadly sins or the nine muses. My table is heaped with unanswered letters,—MS. of four or five different books at six or seven different parts of each,—sketches getting rubbed out,—others getting smudged in,—parcels from Mr. Brown unopened, parcels *for* Mr. Moore unsent; my inkstand in one place,—too probably upset,—my pen in another; my paper under a pile of books, and my last carefully written note thrown into the waste-paper basket.

"3 *Dec.*—I'm having nasty foggy weather just now,—but it's better than fog in London,—and I'm really resting a little, and trying not to be so jealous of the flying days. I've a most *cumfy* room [at the Grand Hotel]—I've gone out of the very expensive one, and only pay twelve francs a day; and I've two windows, one with open balcony and the other covered in with glass. It spoils the look of the window dreadfully, but gives me a view right away to Lido, and of the whole sunrise. Then the bed is curtained off from rest of room like that [sketch of window and room] with fine flourishing white and gold pillars—and the black place is where one goes out of the room beside the bed.

"*9 Dec.*—I hope to send home a sketch or two which will show I'm not quite losing my head yet . . . I must show at Oxford some reason for my staying so long in Venice."

Beside studies in the Chapel of St. George, he copied Carpaccio's "Dream of St. Ursula" which was taken down—it had been "skied" at the Academy until then—and placed in the sculpture gallery; and be laboured to produce a facsimile.

"*24 Dec.*—I do think St. Ursula's lips are coming pretty—and her eyelids—but oh me, her hair. Toni, Mr. Brown's gondolier, says she's all right—and he's a grave and close looking judge, you know."

Christmas Day was a crisis in his life. He was attacked by illness; severe pain, followed by a dreamy state in which the vividly realized presence of St. Ursula mingled with memories of his dead lady, whose "spirit" had been shown him a year before by a "medium" met at a country house. Since then he had watched eagerly for evidences of another life: and the sense of its conceivability grew upon him, in spite of the doubts which he had entertained of the immortality of the soul. At last, after a year's earnest desire for some such assurance, it seemed to come to him. What others call coincidences, and accidents, and states of mind flashed, for him, into importance; times and seasons, names and symbols, took a vivid meaning. His intense despondency changed for a while into a singular happiness—it seemed a renewed health and strength: and instead of despair, he rejoiced in the conviction of guarding Providences and helpful influences.

Readers of "Fors" had traced for some years back the re-awakening of a religious tone, now culminating in a pronounced mysticism which they could not understand, and in a recantation of the sceptical judgments of his middle period. He found, now, new excellences in the early Christian painting; he depreciated Turner and Tintoret, and denounced the frivolous art of the day. He searched the Bible more diligently than ever for its hidden meanings; and in proportion as he felt its inspiration, he recoiled from the conclusions of modern science, and wrapped the prophet's mantle more closely round him, as he denounced with growing fervour the crimes of our unbelieving age.

CHAPTER V

DEUCALION AND PROSERPINA
(1877-1879)

In the summer of 1875, Ruskin had written:

"I begin to ask myself, with somewhat pressing arithmetic, how much time is likely to be left me, at the age of fifty-six, to complete the various designs for which, until past fifty, I was merely collecting material. Of these materials I have now enough by me for a most interesting (in my own opinion) history of fifteenth century Florentine Art, in six octavo volumes; an analysis of the Attic art of the fifth century B.C. in three volumes; an exhaustive history of northern thirteenth-century art, in ten volumes; a life of Sir Walter Scott, with analysis of modern epic art, in seven volumes; a life of Xenophon, with analysis of the general principles of education, in ten volumes; a commentary on Hesiod, with final analysis of the principles of Political Economy, in nine volumes; and a general description of the geology and botany of the Alps, in twenty-four volumes."

The estimate of volumes was—perhaps—in jest; but the plans for harvesting his material were in earnest.

"Proserpina"—so named from the Flora of the Greeks, the daughter of Demeter, Mother Earth—grew out of notes already begun in 1866.

275

It was little like an ordinary botany book;—that was to be expected. It did not dissect plants; it did not give chemical or histological analysis: but with bright and curious fancy, with the most ingenious diagrams and perfect drawings—beautifully engraved by Burgess and Allen—illustrated the mystery of growth in plants and the tender beauty of their form. Though this was not science, in strict terms it was a field of work which no one but Ruskin had cultivated. He was helped by a few scientific men like Professor Oliver, who saw a value in his line of thought, and showed a kindly interest in it.

"Deucalion"—from the mythical creator of human life out of stones—was begun as a companion work: to be published in parts, as the repertory of Oxford lectures on Alpine form, and notes on all kinds of kindred subjects. For instance, before that hasty journey to Sheffield he gave a lecture at the London Institution on "Precious Stones" (February 17th, repeated March 28th, 1876. A lecture on a similar subject was given to the boys of Christ's Hospital on April 15th). This lecture, called "The Iris of the Earth," stood first in Part III. of "Deucalion": and the work went on, in studies of the forms of silica, on the lines marked out ten years before in the papers on Banded and Brecciated Concretions; now carried forward with much kind help from the Rev. J. Clifton Ward, of the Geological Survey, and Mr. Henry Willett, F.G.S., of Brighton.

On the way home over the Simplon in May and June, 1877, travelling first with Signor Alessandri, and then with Mr. G. Allen, Professor Ruskin continued his studies of Alpine flowers for "Proserpina." In the autumn he gave a lecture at Kendal (Oct. 1st, repeated at Eton College Dec. 8th) on "Yewdale and its Streamlets."

"Yewdale"—reprinted as Part V. of "Deucalion"—took an unusual importance in his own mind, not only because it was a great success as a lecture—though some Kendalians complained that there was not enough "information" in it:—but because it was the first given since that Christmas at Venice, when a new insight had been granted him, as he felt, into spiritual things, and a new burden laid on him, to withstand the rash conclusions of "science falsely so called," and to preach in their place the presence of God in nature and in man.

Writing to Miss Beever about his Oxford course of that autumn, "Readings in Modern Painters,"[38] he said, on the 2nd December:

> "I gave yesterday the twelfth and last of my course of lectures this term, to a room crowded by six hundred people, two-thirds members of the University, and with its door wedged open by those who could not get in; this interest of theirs being granted to me, I doubt not, because for the first time in Oxford I have been able to speak to them boldly of immortal life. I intended when I began the course only to have read 'Modern Painters' to them; but when I began, some of your favourite bits[39] interested the men so much, and brought so much larger a proportion of undergraduates than usual, that I took pains to re-inforce and press them home; and people say I have never given so useful a course yet. But it has taken all my time and strength."

He wrote again, on Dec. 16th, from Herne Hill:

> "It is a long while since I've felt so good-for-nothing as I do this morning. My very wristbands curl up in a dog's-eared and disconsolate manner; my little room is all a heap of disorder. I've got a hoarseness and wheezing and sneezing and coughing and choking. I can't speak and I can't think; I'm miserable in bed and useless out of it; and it seems to me as if I could never venture to open a window or go out of a door any more. I have the dimmest sort of diabolical pleasure in thinking how miserable I shall make Susie by telling her all this; but in other respects I seem entirely devoid of all moral sentiments. I have arrived at this state of things, first by catching cold, and since trying to 'amuse myself' for three days."

He goes on to give a list of his amusements—Pickwick, chivalric romances, the *Daily Telegraph*, Staunton's games of chess, and finally analysis of the Dock Company's bill of charges on a box from Venice.

Ten days after he wrote from Oxford, in his whimsical style:

"Yesterday I had two lovely services in my own cathedral. You know the *Cathedral* of Oxford is the chapel of Christ Church College, and I have my high seat in the chancel, as an honorary student, besides being bred there, and so one is ever so proud and ever so pious all at once, which is ever so nice you know: and my own dean, that's the Dean of Christ Church, who is as big as any bishop, read the services, and the psalms and anthems were lovely; and then I dined with Henry Acland and his family . . . but I do wish I could be at Brantwood too." Next day it was "Cold quite gone."

But he was not to be quit so easily this time of the results of overwork and worry.

He had been passing through the unpleasant experience of a misunderstanding with one of his most trusted friends and helpers. His work on behalf of the St. George's Guild had been energetic and sincere: and he had received the support of a number of strangers, among whom were people of responsible station and position. But he was surprised to find that many of his personal friends held aloof. He was still more surprised to learn, on returning from Venice, full of new hope and stronger convictions in his mission, that the caution of one upon whom he had counted as a firm ally had dissuaded an intending adherent from joining in the work. A man of the world, accustomed to overreach and to be overreached, would have taken the discovery coolly, and accepted an explanation. But Ruskin was never a man of the world; and now, much less than ever. He took it as treason to the great work of which he felt himself to be the missionary. Throughout the autumn and winter the discovery rankled, and preyed on his mind. As for the sake of absolute candour he had published in "Fors" everything that related to the Guild work,—even his own private affairs and confessions, whatever they risked,—he felt that this too must out; in order that his supporters might judge of his conduct and that nothing affecting the enterprise might be kept back. And so, at Christmas, he sent the correspondence to his printers.

Years afterwards, by the intervention of friends, this breach was healed: but what suffering it cost can be learnt from the sequel. To Ruskin it was the beginning of the end. His Aberdeen correspondent asked just then for the usual Christmas message to the Bible class: and instead of the cheery words of bygone years, received the couplet from Horace:

"Inter spem curamque, timores inter et iras,
Omnem crede diem tibi diluxisse supremum."

"Amid hope and sorrow, amid fear and wrath, believe
every day that has dawned on thee to be thy last."

From Oxford, early in January, 1878, he went on a visit to Windsor Castle, whence he wrote: "I came to see Prince Leopold, who has been a prisoner to his sofa lately, but I trust he is better; he is very bright and gentle under severe and almost continual pain." No less gentle, in spite of the severe justice he was inflicting upon himself even more than upon his friend, was the author of "Fors," as the letters of the time to his invalid neighbour in "Hortus Inclusus" show. How ready to own himself in the wrong,—at that very moment when he was being pointed at as the most obstinate and egotistic of men—how placable he really was and open to rebuke, he showed, when, from Windsor, he went to Hawarden. Nearly three years before he had written roughly of Mr. Gladstone; as a Conservative, he was not predisposed in favour of the leader of the party to whom he attributed most of the evils he was combating. Mr. Gladstone and he had often met, and by no means agreed together in conversation. But this visit convinced him that he had misjudged Mr. Gladstone; and he promptly made the fullest apology in the current number of "Fors," saying that he had written under a complete misconception of his character. In reprinting the old pages he not only cancelled the offending passage, but he left the place blank, with a note in the middle of it, as "a memorial of rash judgment."

He went slowly northward, seeking rest at Ingleton; whence he wrote, January 17:—"I've got nothing done all the time I've been away but a few mathematical figures [crystallography, no doubt, for 'Deucalion,'] and the less I do the less I find I can do it; and yesterday, for the first time these twenty years, I hadn't so much as a 'plan' in my head all day." Arrived at Brantwood, as rest was useless, he tried work. Mr. Willett had asked him to reprint "The Two Paths," and he got that ready for press, and wrote a short preface. At Venice, Mr. J.R. Anderson had been working out for him the myths illustrated by Carpaccio in the Chapel of S. Giorgio de' Schiavoni; and the book had been waiting for Ruskin's introduction until he was surprised by the publication of an almost identical inquiry by M. Clermont-Ganneau. He tried to fulfil his duty to his pupil by writing the preface immediately; most sorrowfully feeling the inadequacy of his strength for the tasks he had laid upon it. He wrote:

> "My own feeling, now, is that everything which has hitherto happened to me, and been done by me, whether well or ill, has been fitting me to take greater fortune more prudently, and to do better work more thoroughly. And just when I seem to be coming out of school,—very sorry to have been such a foolish boy, yet having taken a prize or two, and expecting now to enter upon some more serious business than cricket,—I am dismissed by the Master I hoped to serve, with a—'That's all I want of you, sir.'"

In such times he found relief by reverting to the past. He wrote in the beginning of February a paper for the *University Magazine* on "My First Editor," W.H. Harrison, and forgot himself—almost—in bright reminiscences of youthful days and early associations. Next, as Mr. Marcus Huish, who had shown great friendliness and generosity in providing prints for the Sheffield museum, was now proposing to hold an Exhibition of Mr. Ruskin's "Turners" at the Fine Art Galleries in New Bond Street, it was necessary to arrange the exhibits and to prepare the catalogue. For the next fortnight he struggled on with this labour, and with his last "Fors"—the last he was to write in the long series of more than seven years.[40] How little the thousands who read the preface to his catalogue, with its sad sketch of Turner's fate, and what they supposed to be its "customary burst of terminal eloquence," understood that it was indeed the cry of one who had been wounded in the house of his friends, and was now believing every day that dawned on him to be his last. He told of Turner's youthful picture of the Coniston Fells and its invocation to the mists of morning, bidding them "in honour to the world's great Author, rise,"—and then how Turner's "health, and with it in great degree his mind, failed suddenly with a snap of some vital chord," after the sunset splendours of his last, dazzling efforts . . .

> "Morning breaks, as I write, along those Coniston Fells, and the level mists, motionless and grey beneath the rose of the moorlands, veil the lower woods, and the sleeping village, and the long lawns by the lake-shore. Oh that some one had but told me, in my youth, when all my heart seemed to be set on these colours and clouds, that appear for a little while and then vanish away, how little my love of them would serve me, when the silence of lawn and wood in the dews of morning should be completed; and all my thoughts should be of those whom, by neither, I was to meet more!"

The catalogue was finished, and hurried off to the printers. A week of agitating suspense at home, and then it could no longer be concealed. Friends and foes alike were startled and saddened with the news of his "sudden and dangerous illness,"—some form of inflammation of the brain—the result of overwork, but still more immediately of the emotional strain from which he had been suffering.

On March 4th, the Turner Exhibition opened, and day by day the bulletins from Brantwood announcing his condition were read by multitudes of visitors with eager and sorrowful interest. Newspapers all the world over copied the daily reports: in the Far West of America the same telegrams were posted, and they say even a more demonstrative sympathy was shown. Nor was the feeling confined to the English speaking public. The Oxford Proctor in Convocation of April 24th, when the patient, after the first burst of the storm was slowly drifting back into calmer waters, thought it worth while, in the course of his speech, to mention that in Italy, where he had lately been on an Easter vacation tour, he had witnessed a widespread anxiety about Ruskin, and prayers put up for his recovery.

By May 10th he was so much better that he could complete the catalogue with some gossip about those Alpine drawings of 1842 which he regarded as the climax of Turner's work. The first—and best in some ways—of the series was the Splügen. Without any word to him, the diligence of kind friends and the help of a wide circle of admirers traced the drawing, and subscribed its price—1,000 guineas, to which Mr. Agnew generously added his commission—and it was presented to Mr. Ruskin as a token of sympathy and respect. He was not insensible to the personal compliment implied, and by way of some answer he spent the first few days of his convalescence in arranging and annotating a series of drawings by himself, and engravings, illustrating the Turners, to add to his show during the remainder of the season. When they were sent off (early in June) to Bond Street, he left home with the Severns to complete his recovery at Malham.

There was another reason why that spontaneous testimonial was welcome at the moment, for a curious and unaccustomed ordeal was impending for his claims as an art critic. On his return from Venice after months of intercourse with the great Old Masters, he found the Grosvenor Gallery just opened for the first time, with its memorable exhibition of the different extra-academical schools. It placed before the public, in sharp contrast, the final outcome of the Pre-Raphaelitism for which he had fought many a year before, and samples of the last new fashion from Paris. The maturer works of Burne-Jones had been practically unseen by the public, and Ruskin took the opportunity of their exhibition to write his praise of the youngest of the Old Masters in the current numbers of "Fors," and afterwards in two papers on the "Three Colours of Pre-Raphaelitism" (*Nineteenth Century Magazine*, November and December, 1878). But in the same "Fors" he dismissed with half a paragraph of contempt Mr. Whistler's eccentric sketch of Fireworks at Cremorne. Long before, in 1863, when he was working with various artists connected with the Pre-Raphaelite circle, Mr. Whistler had made overtures to the great critic through Mr. Swinburne the poet; but he had not been taken seriously. Now he had become the missionary in England of the new French gospel of "impressionism," which to Ruskin was one of those half-truths which are ever the worst of heresies. Mr. Whistler appealed to the law. He brought an action for libel, which was tried on November 25th and 26th before Baron Huddleston, and recovered a farthing damages. Ruskin's costs—amounting to £386 12s. 4d.—were paid by a public subscription to which one hundred and twenty persons, including many strangers, contributed.

By that time he was fully recovering from his illness, back at Coniston, after a short visit to Liverpool. It was forbidden to him to attempt any exciting work. He had given up "Fors" and Oxford lecturing, and was devoting himself again to quiet studies for "Proserpina" and "Deucalion." On the first day of the trial the St. George's Guild was registered as a Company; on the second day he wrote to Miss Beever:

"I have entirely resigned all hope of ever thanking you rightly for bread, sweet odours, roses and pearls, and must just allow myself to be fed, scented, rose-garlanded and be-pearled, as if I were a poor little pet dog, or pet pig. But my cold is better, and I *am* getting on with this botany; but it is really too important a work to be pushed for a week or fortnight."

Early in 1879 his resignation of the Slade Professorship was announced; followed by what was virtually his election to an honorary doctor's degree; or, as officially worded—"the Hebdomadal Council resolved on June 9, 1879, to propose to Convocation to confer the degree of D.C.L. *honoris causa* upon John Ruskin, M.A., of Ch. Ch., at the enænia of that year; but the proposal, though notified in the *Gazette* of June 10, was not submitted to vote owing to the inability of Mr. Ruskin to be present at the encænia." The degree was conferred, in his absence, in 1893.

NOTES:

38 Nov. 6, 8, 10, 13, 15, 17, 20, 22, 24, 27, 29 and Dec. 1, 1877. These lectures were never prepared for publication as a course; the last lecture was printed in the *Nineteenth Century* for January, 1878.
39 Miss Beever had published early in 1875 the extracts from "Modern Painters," so widely known as "Frondes Agrestes."
40 "Fors" was taken up again, at intervals, later on; but never with the same purpose and continuity.

CHAPTER VI

THE DIVERSIONS OF BRANTWOOD
(1879-1881)

Sixty years of one of the busiest lives on record were beginning to tell upon Ruskin. He would not confess to old age, but his recent illness had shaken him severely. The next three years were spent chiefly at Coniston, in comparative retirement; but neither in despair, nor idleness, nor loneliness. He had always lived a sort of dual life, solitary in his thoughts, but social in his habits; liking company, especially of young people; ready, in the intervals of work, to enter into their employments and amusements, and curiously able to forget his cares in hours of relaxation. Sometimes, when earnest admirers made the pilgrimage to their Mecca—"holy Brantwood" as a scoffing poet called it—they were surprised and even shocked, to find the prophet of "Fors" at the head of a merry dinner-table, and the Professor of Art among surroundings which a London or a Boston "æsthete" would have ruled to be in very poor taste.

Shall I take you for a visit there,—to Brantwood as it was in those old times?

It is a weary way to Coniston, whatever road you choose. The inconvenience of the railway route was perhaps one reason of Ruskin's preference for driving on so many occasions. After changing and changing trains, and stopping at many a roadside station, at last you see, suddenly, over the wild undulating country, the Coniston Old Man and its crags, abrupt on the left, and the lake, long and narrow, on the right. Across the water, tiny in the distance and quite alone amongst forests and moors, there is Brantwood; and beyond it everything seems uncultivated, uninhabited, except for one grey farmhouse high on the fell, where gaps in the ragged larches show how bleak and storm-swept a spot it is.

To come out of the station after long travel is to find yourself face to face with magnificent rocks, and white cottages among the fir-trees. As you are whirled down through the straggling village, and along the shore round the head of the lake, the panorama, though not Alpine in magnitude, is almost Alpine in character. The valley, too, is not yet built up; it is still the old-fashioned lake country, almost as it was in the days of the "Iteriad." You drive up and down a narrow, hilly lane, catching peeps of mountains and sunset, through thick, overhanging trees; you turn sharp up through a gate under dark firs and larches, and the carriage stops in what seems in the twilight a sort of court,—a gravelled space, one side formed by a rough stone wall crowned with laurels and almost precipitous coppice, the *brant* (or steep) wood above, and the rest is Brantwood, with a capital B.[41]

You expect that Gothic porch you have read of in "Lectures on Architecture and Painting," and you are surprised to find a stucco classic portico in the corner, painted and *grained*, and heaped around with lucky horseshoes, brightly blackleaded, and mysterious rows of large blocks of slate and basalt and trap—a complete museum of local geology, if only you knew it—very unlike an ideal entrance; still more unlike an ordinary one. While you wait you can see through the glass door a roomy hall, lit with candles, and hung with large drawings by Burne-Jones and by the master of the house. His soft hat, and thick gloves, and chopper, lying on the marble table, show that he has come in from his afternoon's woodcutting.

But if you are expected you will hardly have time to look round, for Brantwood is nothing if not hospitable. The honoured guest—and all guests are honoured there—after welcome, is ushered up a narrow stair, which betrays the original cottage, into the "turret room." It had been "the Professor's" until after his illness, and he papered it with naturalistic pansies, to his own taste, and built out at one corner a projecting turret to command the view on all sides, with windows strongly latticed to resist the storms. There is old-fashioned solid comfort in the way of furniture; and pictures,—a Dürer engraving, some Prouts and Turners, a couple of old Venetian heads, and Meissonier's "Napoleon," over the fireplace—a picture which Ruskin bought for one thousand guineas, showed for a time at Oxford, and hung up here in a shabby little frame to be out of the way.[42]

If you are a man, you are told not to dress; if you are a lady, you may put on your prettiest gown. They dine in the new room, for the old dining-room was so small that the waitress could not get round the table. The new room is spacious and lofty compared with the rest of the house; it has a long window with thick red sandstone mullions—there at last is a touch of Gothicism—to look down the lake, and a bay window open on the narrow lawn sloping steeply down to the road in front, and the view of the Old Man. The walls, painted "duck egg," are hung with old pictures; the Doge Gritti, a bit saved from the great Titian that was burnt in the fire at the Ducal Palace in 1574; a couple of Tintorets; Turner and Reynolds, each painted by himself in youth; Raphael by a pupil, so it is said; portraits of old Mr. and Mrs. Ruskin, and little John and his "boo hills." There he sits, no longer little, opposite: and you can trace the same curve and droop of the eyebrows prefigured in the young face and preserved in the old, and a certain family likeness to his handsome young father.

Since Mr. Ruskin's illness his cousin, Mrs. Arthur Severn, has become more and more indispensable to him: she sits at the head of the table and calls him "the coz." An eminent visitor was once put greatly out of countenance by this apparent irreverence. After obvious embarrassment, light dawned upon him towards the close of the meal. "Oh!" said he, "it's 'the coz' you call Mr. Ruskin. I thought you were saying' the cuss!'"

There are generally two or three young people staying in the house, salaried assistants[43] or amateur, occasional helpers; but though there is a succession of visitors from a distance, there is not very frequent entertainment of neighbours.

A Brantwood dinner is always ample; there is no asceticism about the place; nor is there any affectation of "intensity" or of conversational cleverness. The neat things you meant to say are forgotten—you must be hardened indeed to say them to Mr. Ruskin's face; but if you were shy, you soon feel that there was no need for shyness; you have fallen among friends; and before dessert comes in, with fine old sherry—the pride of your host, as he explains—you feel that nobody understands you so well, and that all his books are nothing to himself.

They don't sit over their wine, and smoking is not allowed. Ruskin goes off to his study after dinner—it is believed for a nap, for he was at work early and has been out all the afternoon. In the drawing-room you see pictures—water-colours by Turner and Hunt, drawings by Prout and Ruskin, an early Burne-Jones, a sketch in oil by Gainsborough. The furniture is the old mahogany of Mr. Ruskin's childhood, with rare things interspersed—like the cloisonné vases on the mantelpiece.

Soon after nine Ruskin comes in with an armful of things that are going to the Sheffield museum, and while his cousin makes his tea and salted toast, he explains his last acquirements in minerals or missals, eager that you should see the interest of them; or displays the last studies of Mr. Rooke or Mr. Fairfax Murray, copies from Carpaccio or bits of Gothic architecture.

Then, sitting in the chair in which he preached his baby-sermon, he reads aloud a few chapters of Scott or Miss Edgeworth, or, with judicious omissions, one of the older novelists; or translates, with admirable facility, a scene of Scribe or George Sand. When his next work comes out you will recognise this evening's reading in his allusions and quotations, perhaps even in the subjects of his writing, for at this time he is busy on the articles of "Fiction, Fair and Foul."

After the reading, music; a bit of his own composition, "Old Aegina's Rock," or "Cockle-hat and Staff"; his cousin's Scotch ballads or Christy Minstrel songs; and if you can sing a new ditty, fresh from London, now is your chance. You are surprised to see the Prophet clapping his hands to "Camptown Races," or the "Hundred Pipers"—chorus given with the whole strength of the company; but you are in a house of strange meetings.

By about half-past ten his day is over; a busy day, that has left him tired out. You will not easily forget the way he lit his candle—no lamps allowed, and no gas—and gave a last look lovingly at a pet picture or two, slanting his candlestick and shading the light with his hand, before he went slowly upstairs to his own little room, literally lined with the Turner drawings you have read about in "Modern Painters."

You may be waked by a knock at the door, and "Are you looking out?" And pulling up the blind, there is one of our Coniston mornings, with the whole range of mountains in one quiet glow above the cool mist of the valley and lake. Going down at length on a voyage of exploration, and turning in perhaps at the first door, you intrude upon "the Professor" at work in his study, half sitting, half kneeling at his round table in the bay window, with the early cup of coffee, and the cat in his crimson arm-chair. There he has been working since dawn, perhaps, or on dark mornings by candlelight. And he does not seem to mind the interruption; after a welcome he asks you to look round while he finishes his paragraph, and writes away composedly.

A long, low room, evidently two old cottage-rooms thrown into one; papered with a pattern specially copied from Marco Marziale's "Circumcision" in the National Gallery; and hung with Turners. A great early Turner[44] of the Lake of Geneva is over the fireplace. You are tempted to make a mental inventory. Polished steel fender, very unæsthetic; curious shovel—his design, he will stop to remark, and forged by the village smith. Red mahogany furniture, with startling shiny emerald leather chair-cushions; red carpet and green curtains. Most of the room crowded with bookcases and cabinets for minerals. Scales in a glass case; heaps of mineral specimens; books on the floor; rolls of diagrams; early Greek pots from Cyprus; a great litter of things and yet not disorderly nor dusty. "I don't understand," he once said, "why you ladies are always complaining about the dust; my bookcases are never dusty!" The truth being that, though he rose early, the housemaid rose earlier.

Before you have finished your inventory he breaks off work to show you a drawer or two of minerals, fairy-land in a cupboard; or some of his missals, King Hakon's Bible, or the original MS. of the Scott he was reading last night; or, opening a door in a sort of secrétaire, pulls out of their sliding cases frame after frame of Turners—the Bridge of Narni, the Falls of Terni, Florence, or Rome, and many more—to hold in your hand, and take to the light, and look into with a lens—quite a different thing from seeing pictures in a gallery.

At breakfast, when you see the post-bag brought in, you understand why he tries to get his bit of writing done early. The letters and parcels are piled in the study, and after breakfast, at which, as in old times, he reads his last-written passages—how much more interesting they will always look to you in print!—after breakfast he is closeted with an assistant, and they work through the heap. Private friends, known by handwriting, he puts aside; most of the morning will go in answering them. Business he talks over, and gives brief directions. But the bulk of the correspondence is from strangers in all parts of the world—admirers' flattery; students' questions; begging-letters for money, books, influence, advice, autographs, criticism on enclosed MS. or accompanying picture; remonstrance or abuse from dissatisfied readers, or people who object to his method of publication, or wish to convert him to their own religion. And so the heap is gradually cleared, with the help of the waste-paper basket; the secretary's work cut out, his own arranged; and by noon a long row of letters and envelopes have been set out to dry—Mr. Ruskin uses no blotting-paper, and, as he dislikes the vulgar method of fastening envelopes, the secretary's work will be to seal them all with red wax, and the seal with the motto "To-day" cut in the apex of a big specimen of chalcedony.

If you take, as many do, an interest in the minutiæ of portrait painting, and think the picture more finished for its details, you may notice that he writes on the flat table, not on a desk; that he uses a cork penholder and a fine steel pen, though he is not at all a slave to his tools, and differs from others rather in the absence of the *sine quâ non* from his conditions. He can write anywhere, on anything, with anything; wants no pen-wiper, no special form of paper, or other "fad." Much of his work is written in bound notebooks, especially when he *is* abroad, to prevent the loss and disorder of multitudinous foolscap. He generally makes a rough syllabus of his subject, in addition to copious notes and extracts from authorities, and then writes straight off; not without a noticeable hesitation and revision, even in his letters. His rough copy is transcribed by an assistant, and he often does not see it again until it is in proof.[45]

Printers' proofs are always a trial, and he is glad to shift the work on to an assistant's shoulders, such as Mr. Harrison was, who saw all his early works through the press. But he is extremely particular about certain matters, such as the choice of type and arrangements of the page; though his taste does not coincide with that of the leaders of recent fashions. Mr. Jowett (of Messrs. Hazell, Watson & Viney, Limited) said in *Hazell's Magazine* for September; 1892, that Ruskin made the size of the page a careful study, though he adopted many varieties. The "Fors" page is different from, and not so symmetrical as that of the octavo "Works Series," although both are printed on the same sized paper—medium 8vo. Then there is the "Knight's Faith" and "Ulric," in both of which the type (pica *modern*—"this delightful type," wrote Ruskin) and the size of the page are different from any other; yet both were his choice. The "Ulric" page was imitated from an old edition of Miss Edgeworth. The first proof he criticised thus: "Don't you think a quarter inch off this page, as enclosed, would look better? The type is very nice. How delicious a bit of Miss Edgeworth's is, like this!" "Ida" was another page of his choice, and greatly approved. His title pages, too, were arranged with great care; he used to draw them out in pen and ink, indicating the size and position of the lines and letters. He objected to ornaments and to anything like blackness and heaviness, but he was very particular about proportions and spacing, and about the division of words.

In the morning everybody is busy. There are drawings and diagrams to be made, MS. to copy, references to look up, parcels to pack and unpack. Someone is told off to take you round, and you visit the various rooms and see the treasures, inspect the outhouse with its workshop for carpentry, framing and mounting, casting leaves and modelling; one work or another is sure to be going on; perhaps one of the various sculptors who have made Ruskin's bust is busy there. Down at the Lodge, a miniature Brantwood, turret and all, the Severn children live when they are at Coniston. Then there are the gardens, terraced in the steep, rocky slope, and some small hot-houses, which Ruskin thinks a superfluity, except that they provide grapes for sick neighbours.

Below the gardens a path across a field takes you to the harbour, begun in play by the Xenophon translators and finished by the village mason, with its fleet of boats—chief of them the "Jumping Jenny" (called after Nanty Ewart's boat in "Redgauntlet"), Ruskin's own design and special private water-carriage. Outside the harbour the sail-boats are moored, Mr. Severn's *Lily of Brantwood*. Milliard's boat, and his *Snail*, an unfortunate craft brought from Morecambe Bay with great expectations that were never realized; though Ruskin always professed to believe in her, as a *real sea-boat* (see "Harbours of England") such as he used to steer with his friend Huret, the Boulogne fisherman, in the days when he, too, was smitten with sea-fever.

After luncheon, if letters are done, all hands are piped to the moor. With billhooks and choppers the party winds up the wood paths, "the Professor" first, walking slowly, and pointing out to you his pet bits of rock-cleavage, or ivied trunk, or nest of wild strawberry plants. You see, perhaps, the ice-house—tunnelled at vast expense into the rock and filled at more expense with the best ice; opened at last with great expectations and the most charitable intent—for it was planned to supply invalids in the neighbourhood with ice, as the, hothouses supplied them with grapes; and revealing, after all, nothing but a puddle of dirty water. You see more successful works—the Professor's little private garden, which he is supposed to cultivate with his own hands; various little wells and watercourses among the rocks, moss-grown and fern-embowered; and so you come out on the moor.

There great works go on. Juniper is being rooted up; boggy patches drained and cultivated cranberries are being planted, and oats grown; paths engineered to the best points of view; rocks bared to examine the geology—though you cannot get the Professor to agree that every inch of his territory has been glaciated. These diversions have their serious side, for he is really experimenting on the possibility of reclaiming waste land; perhaps too sanguine, you think, and not counting the cost. To which he replies that, as long as there are hands unemployed and misemployed, a government such as he would see need never be at a loss for labourers. If corn can be made to grow where juniper grew before, the benefit is a positive one, the expense only comparative. And so you take your pick with the rest, and are almost persuaded to become a companion of St. George.

Not to tire a new comer, he takes you away after a while to a fine heathery promontory, where you sit before a most glorious view of lake and mountains. This, he says, is his "Naboth's vineyard";[46] he would like to own so fine a point of vantage. But he is happy in his country retreat, far happier than you thought him; and the secret of his happiness is that he has sympathy with all around him, and hearty interest in everything, from the least to the greatest.

Coming down from the moor after the round, when you reach the front door you must see the performance of the waterfall: everybody must see that. On the moor a reservoir has been dug and dammed, with ingenious flood-gates—Ruskin's device, of course—and a channel led down through the wood to a rustic bridge in the rock. Some one has stayed behind to let out the water, and down it comes; first a black stream and then a white one, as it gradually clears; and the rocky wall at the entrance becomes for ten minutes a cascade. This too has it uses; not only is there a supply of water in case of fire (the exact utilisation of which is yet undecided), but it illustrates one of his doctrines about the simplicity with which works of irrigation could be carried out among the hills of Italy.

And so you go in to tea and chess, for he loves a good game of chess with all his heart. He loves many things, you have found. He is different from other men you know, by the breadth and vividness of his sympathies, by power of living as few other men can live, in Admiration, Hope and Love.

NOTES:

41   The archway supporting a great pile of new buildings did not exist in the time when this visit is supposed to be made. Since that time new stables and greenhouses also have been built; with other additions somewhat altering the cottage-like house of Ruskin's working days.

42   Sold in 1882 for 5,900 guineas.

43   The face most familiar at Brantwood in those times was "Laurie's." A strange, bright, gifted boy—admirable draughtsman, ingenious mechanician, marvellous actor; the imaginer of the quaintest and drollest humours that ever entered the head of man; devoted to boats and boating, but unselfishly ready to share all labours and contribute to all diversions; painstaking and perfect in his work, and brilliant in his wit,—Laurence Hilliard was dearly loved by his friends, and is still loved by them dearly. He was Ruskin's chief secretary at Brantwood from Jan., 1876 to 1882, when the death of his father, and ill-health, led him to resign the post, which was then filled by Miss Sara D. Anderson. Hilliard continued to live at Coniston, and was just beginning to succeed as a painter of still life and landscape when he died of pleurisy on board a friend's yacht in the Aegean, April 11th, 1887, aged thirty-two.

44   Since sold, and replaced by a della Robbia Madonna.

45   In later years he sometimes had his copy type-written.

46   Since then become part of the Brantwood estate.

CHAPTER VII

"FORS" RESUMED (1880-1881)

Retirement at Brantwood was only partial. Ruskin's habits of life made it impossible for him to be idle, much as he acknowledged the need of thorough rest. He could not be wholly ignorant of the world outside Coniston; though sometimes for weeks together he tried to ignore it, and refused to read a newspaper. The time when General Gordon went out to Khartoum was one of these periods of abstraction, devoted to mediæval study. Somebody talked one morning at breakfast about the Soudan. "And who *is* the Soudan?" he earnestly inquired, connecting the name, as it seemed, with the Soldan of Babylon, in crusading romance.

"Don't you know," he wrote to a friend (January 8th, 1880):

"That I am entirely with you in this Irish misery, and have been these thirty years?—only one can't speak plain without distinctly becoming a leader of Revolution? I know that Revolution *must come* in all the world—but I can't act with Dan ton or Robespierre, nor with the modern French Republican or Italian one. I *could* with you and your Irish, but you are only at the beginning of the end. I have spoken,—and plainly too,—for all who have ears, and hear."

The author of "Fors" had tried to show that the nineteenth-century commercialist spirit was not new; that the tyranny of capital was the old sin of usury over again; and he asked why preachers of religion did not denounce it—why, for example, the Bishop of Manchester did not, on simply religious grounds, oppose the teaching of the "Manchester School," who were the chief supporters of the commercialist economy. Not until the end of 1879 had Dr. Fraser been aware of the challenge; but at length he wrote, justifying his attitude. The popular and able bishop had much to say on the expediency of the commercial system and the error of taking the Bible literally; but he seemed unaware of the revolution in economical thought which "Unto this Last" and "Fors" had been pioneering.

"I'm not gone to Venice yet," wrote Ruskin to Miss Beever, "but thinking of it hourly. I'm very nearly done with toasting my bishop; he just wants another turn or two, and then a little butter." The toasting and the buttering appeared in the *Contemporary Review* for February 1880; and this incident led him to feel that the mission of "Fors" was not finished. If bishops were still unenlightened, there was yet work to do. He gave up Venice, and resumed his crusade.

Brantwood life was occasionally interrupted by short excursions to London or elsewhere. In the autumn he had heard Professor Huxley on the evolution of reptiles; and this suggested another treatment of the subject, from his own artistic and ethical point of view, in a lecture oddly called "A Caution to Snakes," given at the London Institution, March 17th, 1880 (repeated March 23rd, and printed in "Deucalion"). He was not merely an amateur zoologist and F.Z.S., but a devoted lover and keen observer of animals. It would take long to tell the story of all his dogs, from the spaniel Dash, commemorated in his earliest poems, and Wisie, whose sagacity is related in "Præterita," down through the long line of bulldogs, St. Bernards, and collies, to Bramble, the reigning favourite; and all the cats who made his study their home, or were flirted with abroad. To Miss Beever, from Bolton Abbey (January 24th, 1875) he describes the Wharfe in flood, and then continues: "I came home (to the hotel) to quiet tea, and a black kitten called Sweep, who lapped half my creamjugful (and yet I had plenty), sitting on my shoulder." Grip, the pet rook at Denmark Hill, is mentioned in "My First Editor," as celebrated in verse by Mr. W.H. Harrison.

Ruskin had not Thoreau's intimate acquaintance with the details of wild life, but his attitude towards animals and plants was the same; hating the science that murders to dissect; resigning his Professorship at Oxford, finally, because vivisection was introduced into the University; and supporting the Society for the Prevention of Cruelty to Animals with all his heart. But, as he said at the Annual Meeting in 1877, he objected to the sentimental fiction and exaggerated statements which some of its members circulated. "They had endeavoured to prevent cruelty to animals," he said, "but they had not enough endeavoured to promote affection for animals. He trusted to the pets of children for their education, just as much as to their tutors."

It was to carry out this idea (to anticipate a little) that he founded the Society of Friends of Living Creatures, which he addressed, May 23rd, 1885, at the club, Bedford Park, in his capacity of—not president—but "papa." The members, boys and girls from seven to fifteen, promised not to kill nor hurt any animal for sport, nor tease creatures; but to make friends of their pets and watch their habits, and collect facts about natural history.

I remember, on one of the rambles at Coniston in the early days, how we found a wounded buzzard—one of the few creatures of the eagle kind that our English mountains still breed. The rest of us were not very ready to go near the beak and talons of the fierce-looking, and, as we supposed, desperate bird. Ruskin quietly took it up in his arms, felt it over to find the hurt, and carried it, quite unresistingly, out of the way of dogs and passers-by, to a place where it might die in solitude or recover in safety. He often told his Oxford hearers that he would rather they learned to love birds than to shoot them; and his wood and moor were harbours of refuge for hunted game or "vermin;" and his windows the rendezvous of the little birds.

He had not been abroad since the spring of 1877, and in August 1880 felt able to travel again. He went for a tour among the northern French cathedrals, staying at old haunts,—Abbeville, Amiens, Beauvais, Chartres, Rouen,—and then returned with Mr. A. Severn and Mr. Brabazon to Amiens, where he spent the greater part of October. He was writing a new book—the "Bible of Amiens"—which was to be to the "Seven Lamps" what "St. Mark's Rest" was to "Stones of Venice."

Before he returned, the secretary of the Chesterfield Art School had written to ask him to address the students. Mr. Ruskin, travelling without a secretary, and in the flush of new work and thronging ideas, put the letter aside; he carried his letters about in bundles in his portmanteau, as he said in his apology, "and looked at them as Ulysses at the bags of Aeolus." Some wag had the impudence to forge a reply, which was actually read at the meeting in spite of its obviously fictitious style and statements:

"HARLESDEN(!), LONDON, *Friday*.

"MY DEAR SIR,

"Your letter reaches me here. Have just returned [commercial English, not Ruskin] from Venice [where he had meant to go, but did not go] where I have ruminated(!) in the pasturages of the home of art(!); the loveliest and holiest of lovely and holy cities, where the very stones cry out, eloquent in the elegancies of iambics" (!!)—and so forth.

However, it deceived the newspapers, and there was a fine storm, which Mr. Ruskin rather enjoyed. For though the forgery was clumsy enough, it embodied some apt plagiarism from a letter to the Mansfield Art School on a similar occasion.

Not long before, a forgery of a more serious kind had been committed by one of the people connected with St. George's Guild, who had put Mr. Ruskin's name to cheques. The bank authorities were long in tracing the crime. They even sent a detective to Brantwood to watch one of the assistants, who never knew—nor will ever know—that he was honoured with such attentions; and none of his friends for a moment believed him guilty. He had sometimes imitated Mr. Ruskin's hand; a dangerous jest. The real culprit was discovered at last, and Mr. Ruskin had to go to London as a witness for the prosecution. "Being in very weak health," the *Times* report said (April 1st, 1879), "he was allowed to give evidence from the bench." He had told the Sheffield communists that "he thought so strongly on the subject of the repression of crime that he dare not give expression to his ideas for fear of being charged with cruelty"; but no sooner was the prisoner released than he gave the help needed to start him again in a better career.

Though he did not feel able to lecture to strangers at Chesterfield, he visited old friends at Eton, on November 6th, 1880, to give an address on Amiens. For once he forgot his MS., but the lecture was no less brilliant and interesting. It was practically the first chapter of his new work, the "Bible of Amiens,"—itself intended as the first volume of "Our Fathers have Told us: Sketches of the History of Christendom, for Boys and Girls who have been held at its Fonts." The distinctly religious tone of the work was noticed as marking, if not a change, a strong development of a tendency which had been strengthening for some time past.

Early in 1879 the Rev. F.A. Malleson, vicar of Broughton, near Coniston, had asked him to write, for the Furness Clerical Society's Meetings, a series of letters on the Lord's Prayer. In them he dwelt upon the need of living faith in the Fatherhood of God, and childlike obedience to the commands of old-fashioned religion and morality. He criticised the English liturgy as compared with mediæval forms of prayer; and pressed upon his hearers the strongest warnings against evasion, or explaining away of stern duties and simple faiths. He concluded:

> "No man more than I has ever loved the place where God's honour dwells, or yielded truer allegiance to the teaching of His evident servants. No man at this time grieves more for the damage of the Church which supposes him her enemy, while she whispers procrastinating *pax vobiscum* in answer to the spurious kiss of those who would fain toll curfew over the last fires of English faith, and watch the sparrows find nest where she may lay her young, around the altars of the Lord."

But if the Anglican Church refused him, the Roman Church was eager to claim him. His interest in mediævalism seemed to point him out as ripe for conversion. Cardinal Manning, an old acquaintance, showed him special attention, and invited him to charming *tête-à-tête* luncheons. It was commonly reported that he had gone over, or was going. But two letters (of a later date) show that he was not to be caught. To a Glasgow correspondent he wrote in 1887:

> "I shall be entirely grateful to you if you will take the trouble to contradict any news gossip of this kind, which may be disturbing the minds of any of my Scottish friends. I was, am, and can be, only a Christian Catholic in the wide and eternal sense. I have been that these five-and-twenty years at least. Heaven keep me from being less as I grow older! But I am no more likely to become a Roman Catholic than a Quaker, Evangelical, or Turk."

To another, next year, he wrote:

> "I fear you have scarcely read enough of 'Fors' to know the breadth of my own creed or communion. I gladly take the bread, water, wine, or meat of the Lord's Supper with members of my own family or nation who obey Him, and should be equally sure

it was His giving, if I were myself worthy to receive it, whether the intermediate mortal hand were the Pope's, the Queen's, or a hedge-side gipsy's."

At Coniston he was on friendly terms with Father Gibson, the Roman Catholic priest, and gave a window to the chapel, which several of the Brantwood household attended. But though he did not go to Church, he contributed largely to the increase of the poorly-endowed curacy, and to the charities of the parish. The religious society of the neighbourhood was hardly of a kind to attract him, unless among the religious society should be included the Thwaite, where lived the survivors of a family long settled at Coniston—Miss Mary Beever, scientific and political; and Miss Susanna, who won Mr. Ruskin's admiration and affection by an interest akin to his own in nature and in poetry, and by her love for animals, and bright, unfailing wit. Both ladies were examples of sincerely religious life, "at once sources and loadstones of all good to the village," as he wrote in the preface to "Hortus Inclusus," the collection of his letters to them since first acquaintance in the autumn of 1873. The elder Miss Beever died at an advanced age on the last day of 1883; Miss Susanna survived until October, 29, 1893.

In children he took a warm and openly-expressed interest. He used to visit the school often, and delighted to give them a treat. On January 13th, 1881, he gave a dinner to 315 Coniston youngsters, and the tone of his address to his young guests is noteworthy as taken in connection with the drift of his religious tendency during this period. He dwelt on a verse of the Sunday School hymn they had been singing: "Jesu, here from sin deliver." "That is what we want," he said; "to be delivered from our sins. We must look to the Saviour to deliver us from our sin. It is right we should be punished for the sins which we have done; but God loves us, and wishes to be kind to us, and to help us, that we may not wilfully sin."

At this time he used to take the family prayers himself at Brantwood: preparing careful notes for a Bible-reading, which sometimes, indeed, lasted longer than was convenient to the household; and writing collects for the occasion, still existing in manuscript, and deeply interesting as the prayers of a man who had passed through so many wildernesses of thought and doubt, and had returned at last—not to the fold of the Church, but to the footstool of the Father.

CHAPTER VIII

THE RECALL TO OXFORD (1882-1883)

This Brantwood life came to an end with the end of 1881. Early in the next year he went for change of scene to stay with the Severns at his old home on Herne Hill. He seemed much better, and ventured to reappear in public. On March 3rd he went to the National Gallery to sketch Turner's Python. On the unfinished drawing is written: "Bothered away from it, and never went again. No light to work by in the next month." An artist in the Gallery had been taking notes of him for a surreptitious portrait—an embarrassing form of flattery.

He wrote: "No—I won't believe any stories about overwork. It's impossible, when one's in good heart and at really pleasant things. I've a lot of nice things to do, but the heart fails—after lunch, particularly!" Heart and head did, however, fail again; and another attack of brain fever followed. Sir William Gull brought him through, and won his praise as a doctor and esteem as a friend. Ruskin took it as a great compliment when Sir William, in acknowledging his fee, wrote that he should keep the cheque as an autograph.

By Easter Monday the patient was better again, and plunging into work in spite of everybody. He wrote:

"I was not at all sure, myself, till yesterday, whether I *would* go abroad; also I should have told you before. But as you have had the (sorrowful?) news broken to you—and as I find Sir William

Gull perfectly fixed in his opinion, I obey him, and reserve only some liberty of choice to myself—respecting, not only climate,—but the general appearance of the—inhabitants, of the localities, where for antiquarian or scientific research I may be induced to prolong my sojourn.—Meantime I send you—to show you I haven't come to town for nothing, my last bargain in beryls, with a little topaz besides . . ."

But the journey was put off week after week. There was so much to do, buying diamonds for Sheffield museum, and planning a collection of models to show the normal forms of crystals, and to illustrate a subject which he thought many people would find interesting, if they could be got over its first difficulties. Not only Sheffield was to receive these gifts and helps: Ruskin had become acquainted with the Rev. J.P. Faunthorpe, Principal of Whitelands College for Pupil Teachers, and had given various books and collections to illustrate the artistic side of education. Now he instituted there the May Queen Festival, in some sort carrying out his old suggestion in "Time and Tide." Mr. A. Severn designed a gold cross, and it was presented, with a set of volumes of Ruskin's works, sumptuously bound, to the May Queen and her maidens. The pretty festival became a popular feature of the school, "patronised by royalty," and Ruskin continued his annual gift to Whitelands, and kept up a similar institution at the High School at Cork.

At last, in August, he started for the Continent and stayed a while at Avallon in central France, a district new to him. There he met Mr. Frank Randal, one of the artists working for St. George's Guild, and explored the scenery and antiquities of a most interesting neighbourhood. He drove over the Jura in the old style, revisited Savoy, and after weeks of bitter *bise* and dark weather, a splendid sunset cleared the hills. He wrote to Miss Beever:—"I saw Mont Blanc again to-day, unseen since 1877; and was very thankful. It is a sight that always redeems me to what I am capable of at my poor little best, and to what loves and memories are most precious to me."

At Annecy he was pleased to find the waiter at the Hôtel Verdun remembered his visit twenty years before;—everywhere he met old friends, and saw old scenes that he had feared he never would revisit. After crossing the Cenis and hastening through Turin and Genoa, he reached Lucca, to be awaited at the Albergo Reale dell' Universo by a crowd, every one anxious to shake hands with Signor Ruskin. No wonder!—for instead of allowing himself to be a mere Number-so-and-so in a hotel, wherever he felt comfortable—and that was everywhere except at pretentious modern hotels—he made friends with the waiter, chatted with the landlord, found his way into the kitchen to compliment the cook, and forgot nobody in the establishment—not only in "tips," but in a frank and sympathetic address which must have contrasted curiously, in their minds, with the reserve and indifference of other English tourists.

At Florence he met Mr. Henry Roderick Newman, an American artist who had been at Coniston and was working for the Guild. He introduced Ruskin to Mrs. and Miss Alexander. In these ladies' home he found his own aims, in religion, philanthropy, and art, realised in an unexpected way. Miss Alexander's drawing at first struck him by its sincerity. Not only did she draw beautifully, but she also wrote a beautiful hand; and it had been one of his old sayings that missal-writing, rather than missal-painting, was the admirable thing in mediæval art. The legends illustrated by her drawings were collected by herself, through an intimate acquaintance with Italians of all classes, from the nobles to the peasantry, whom she understood and loved, and by whom she was loved and understood. By such intercourse she had learned to look beneath the surface. In religious matters her American common-sense saw through her neighbours—saw the good in them as well as the weakness—and she was as friendly, not only in social intercourse, but in spiritual things, with the worthy village priest as with T.P. Rossetti,[47] the leader of the Protestant "Brethren," whom she called her pastor. And Ruskin, who had been driven away from Protestantism by the poor Waldensian at Turin, and had wandered through many realms of doubt and voyaged through strange seas of thought, alone, found harbour at last with the disciple of a modern evangelist, the frequenter of the little meeting-house of outcast Italian Protestants.

One evening before dinner he brought back to the hotel at Florence a drawing of a lovely girl lying dead in the sunset; and a little note-book. "I want you to look over this," he said, in the way, but not quite in the tone, with which the usual MS. "submitted for criticism" was tossed to a secretary to taste. It was "The True Story of Ida; written by her Friend."

An appointment to meet Mr. E.R. Robson, who was making plans for an intended Sheffield museum, took him back to Lucca, to discuss Romanesque mouldings and marble facings. Mr. Charles Fairfax Murray also came to Lucca with drawings commissioned for St. George's Guild. But Ruskin soon returned to his new friends, and did not leave Florence finally until he had purchased the wonderful collection of 110 drawings, with beautifully written text, in which Miss Alexander had enshrined "The Roadside Songs of Tuscany."

Returning homewards by the Mont Cenis he stayed a while at Talloires, a favourite haunt, extremely content to be among romantic scenery, and able to work steadily at a new edition of his books in a much cheaper form, of which the first volumes were at this time in hand. He had been making further studies also, in history and Alpine geology; but at last the snow drove him away from the mountains. So he handed over the geology to his assistant, who compiled "The Limestone Alps of Savoy" (supplementary to "Deucalion") "as he could, not as he would," while Ruskin wrote out the new ideas suggested by his visit to Cîteaux and St. Bernard's birthplace. These notes he completed on the journey home, and gave as a lecture on "Cistercian Architecture" (London Institution,

December 4th, 1882), in place of the previously advertised lecture on crystallography.

He seemed now to have quite recovered his health, and to be ready for re-entry into public life. What was more, he had many new things to say. The attacks of brain fever had passed over him like passing storms, leaving a clear sky.

After his retirement from the Oxford Professorship, a subscription had been opened for a bust by Sir Edgar Boehm, in memorial of a University benefactor; and the model (now in the Sheffield Museum) was placed in the Drawing School pending the collection of the necessary £220. *The Oxford University Herald*, in its article of June 5th, 1880, no doubt expressed the general feeling in reciting his benefactions to the University with becoming appreciation.

It was natural, therefore, that on recovering his health he should resume his post. Professor (now Sir) W.B. Richmond, the son of his old friend Mr. George Richmond, gracefully retired, and the *Oxford University Gazette* of January 16th, 1883, announced the re-election. On March 2nd he wrote that he was "up the Old Man yesterday"; as much as to say that he defied catechism, now, about his health; and a week later he gave his first lecture. The *St. James's Budget* of March 16th gave an account of it in these terms:

> "Mr. Ruskin's first lecture at Oxford attracted so large an audience that, half-an-hour before the time fixed for its delivery, a greater number of persons were collected about the doors than the lecture-room could hold. Immediately after the doors were opened the room was so densely packed that some undergraduates found it convenient to climb into the windows and on to the cupboards. The audience was composed almost equally of undergraduates and ladies; with the exception of the vice-chancellor, heads of houses, fellows, and tutors were chiefly conspicuous by their absence."

I omit an abstract of the lecture, which can be read in full in the "Art of England." The reporter continued:

"He had made some discoveries: two lads and two lasses, who[48] . . . could draw in a way to please even him. He used to say that, except in a pretty graceful way, no woman can draw; he had now almost come to think that no one else can. (This statement the undergraduates received with gallant, if undiscriminating, applause.) To many of his prejudices, Mr. Ruskin said, in the last few years the axe had been laid. He had positively found an American, a young lady, whose life and drawing were in every way admirable. (Again great and generous applause on the part of the undergraduates, stimulated, no doubt, by the knowledge that there were then in the room two fair Americans, who have lately graced Oxford by their presence.) At the end of his lecture Mr. Ruskin committed himself to a somewhat perilous statement. He had found two young Italian artists in whom the true spirit of old Italian art had yet lived. No hand like theirs had been put to paper since Lippi and Leonardo."

Three more lectures of the course were given in May, and each repeated to a second audience. Coming to London, he gave a private lecture on June 5th to some two hundred hearers at the house of Mrs. W.H. Bishop, in Kensington, on Miss Kate Greenaway and Miss Alexander. The *Spectator* shared his enthusiasm for the pen and ink drawings of Miss Alexander's "Roadside Songs of Tuscany," and concluded a glowing account of the lecture by saying: "All Professor Ruskin's friends must be glad to see how well his Oxford work has agreed with him. He has gifts of insight and power of reaching the best feelings and highest hopes of our too indifferent generation which are very rare."

With much encouragement in his work, he returned to Brantwood for the summer, and resolved upon another visit to Savoy for more geology, and another breath of health-giving Alpine air. But he found time only for a short tour in Scotland before returning to Oxford to complete the series of lectures on recent English Art. During this term he was prevailed upon to allow himself to be nominated as a candidate for the Rectorship of the University of Glasgow. He had been asked to stand in the Conservative interest in 1880, and he had been worried into a rather rough reply to the Liberal party, when after some correspondence they asked him whether he sympathised with Lord Beaconsfield or Mr. Gladstone. "What, in the devil's name," he exclaimed, "have *you* to do with either Mr. D'Israeli or Mr. Gladstone? You are students at the University, and have no more business with politics than you have with rat-catching. Had you ever read ten words of mine with understanding, you would have known that I care no more either for Mr. D'Israeli or Mr. Gladstone than for two old bagpipes with the drones going by steam, but that I hate all Liberalism as I do Beelzebub, and that, with Carlyle, I stand, we two alone now in England, for God and the Queen." After that, though he might explain[49] that he never under any conditions of provocation or haste, would have said that he hated Liberalism as he did *Mammon*, or Belial, or Moloch; that he "chose the milder fiend of Ekron as the true exponent and patron of Liberty, the God of Flies," still the matter-of-fact Glaswegians were minded to give the scoffer a wide berth. He was put up as an independent candidate in the three-cornered duel; and, as such candidates usually fare, he fared badly. The only wonder is that three hundred and nineteen students were found to vote for him, instead of siding, in political orthodoxy, with Mr. Fawcett or the Marquis of Bute.

At last a busy and eventful year came to a close at Coniston, with a lecture at the village Institute on his old friend Sir Herbert Edwardes (December 22nd). His interest in the school and the schoolchildren was unabated, and he was always planning new treats for them, or new helps to their lessons. He had set one of the assistants to make a large hollow globe, inside of which one could sit and see the stars as luminous points pricked through the mimic "vault of heaven," painted blue and figured with the constellations. By a simple arrangement of cogs and rollers the globe revolved, the stars rose and set, and the position of any star at any hour of the year could be roughly fixed. But the inclement climate of Coniston, and the natural roughness of children, soon wrecked the new toy.

About this time he was anxious to get the village children taught music with more accuracy of tune and time than the ordinary singing-lessons enforced. He made many experiments with different simple instruments, and fixed at last upon a set of bells, which he wanted to introduce into the school. But it was difficult to interfere with the routine of studies prescribed by the Code. Considering that he scorned "the three R's," a school after his own heart would have been a very different place from any that earns the Government grant; and he very strongly believed that if a village child learnt the rudiments of religion and morality, sound rules of health and manners, and a habit of using its eyes and ears in the practice of some good handicraft or art and simple music, and in natural philosophy, taught by object lessons—then book-learning would either come of itself, or be passed aside as unnecessary or superfluous. This was his motive in a well-known incident which has sometimes puzzled his public. Once, when new buildings were going on, the mason wanted an advance of money, which Mr. Ruskin gave him, and then held out the paper for him to sign the receipt. "A great deal of hesitation and embarrassment ensued, somewhat to Mr. Ruskin's surprise, as he knows a north-country-man a great deal too well to expect embarrassment from him. At last the man said, in dialect: 'Ah mun put ma mark!' He could not write. Mr. Ruskin rose at once, stretched out both hands to the astonished rustic, with the words: 'I am proud to know you. Now I understand why you are such an entirely good workman.'"

NOTES:

47 A cousin of the artist, and in his way no less remarkable a man. A short account of his life is given in "D.G. Rossetti, his family letters," Vol. I., p. 34. The circumstances of his death are touchingly related by Miss Alexander in "Christ's Folk; in the Apennine."
48 Referring to Misses Alexander and Greenaway, and Messrs. Boni and Alessandri.
49 Epilogue to "Arrows of the Chace."

CHAPTER IX

THE STORM-CLOUD (1884-1888)

The sky had been a favourite subject of study with the author of "Modern Painters." His journals for fifty years past had kept careful account of the weather, and effects of cloud. He had noticed since 1871 a prevalence of chilly, dark *bise*, as it would be called in France; but different in its phenomena from anything of his earlier days. The "plague wind," so he named it—tremulous, intermittent, blighting grass and trees—blew from no fixed point of the compass, but always brought the same dirty sky in place of the healthy rain-cloud of normal summers; and the very thunder-storms seemed to be altered by its influence into foul and powerless abortions of tempest. We should now be disposed to call this simply "the smoke nuisance," but feeling as he did the weight of human wrong against which it was his mission to prophesy, believing in a Divine government of the world in all its literalness, he had the courage to appear before a London audience,[50] like any seer of old, and to tell them that this eclipse of heaven was—if not a judgment—at all events a symbol of the moral darkness of a nation that had "blasphemed the name of God deliberately and openly; and had done iniquity by proclamation, every man doing as much injustice to his brother as it was in his power to do."

In the autumn, at Oxford, he took up his parable again. His lectures on "The Pleasures of England" he intended as a sketch of the main stream of history from his own religious standpoint. It was a noble theme, and one which his breadth of outlook and detailed experience would have fitted him to handle; but he was already nearing the limit of his vital powers. He had been suffering from depression throughout the summer, unrelieved by the energetic work for St. George's Museum, which in other days might have been a relaxation from more serious thought. He had been editing Miss Alexander's "Roadside Songs of Tuscany," and recasting earlier works of his own, incessantly busy; presuming upon the health he had enjoyed, and taking no hints nor advice from anxious friends, who would have been glad to have seen the summer spent in change of scene and holiday-making.

At Oxford he was watched with concern—restless and excited, too absorbed in his crusade against the tendencies of the modern scientific party, too vehement and unguarded in his denunciations of colleagues, too bitter against the new order of things which, to his horror, was introducing vivisection in the place of the old-fashioned natural history he loved, and speculative criticism instead of "religious and useful learning."

He was persuaded to cancel his last three attacks on modern life and thought—"The Pleasures of Truth," of "Sense," and of "Nonsense"— and to substitute readings from earlier works, hastily arranged and re-written; and his friends breathed more freely when he left Oxford without another serious attack of brain-disease. He wrote on December 1st, 1884, to Miss Beever:

> "I gave my fourteenth, and last for this year, lecture with vigour and effect, and am safe and well (D.G.) after such a spell of work as I never did before."

To another correspondent, a few days later:

> "Here are two lovely little songs for you to put tunes to, and sing to me. You'll have both to be ever so good to me, for I've been dreadfully bothered and battered here. I've bothered other people a little, too,—which is some comfort!"

But in spite of everything, the vote was passed to establish a physiological laboratory at the museum; to endow vivisection—which to him meant not only cruelty to animals, but a complete misunderstanding of the purpose of science, and defiance of the moral law. He resigned his Professorship, with the sense that all his work had been in vain, that he was completely out of touch with the age, and that he had best give up the unequal fight.

In former times when he had found himself beaten in his struggles with the world, he had turned to geology for a resource and a relief; but geology, too, was part of the field of battle now. The memories of his early youth and the bright days of his boyhood came back to him as the only antidote to the distress and disappointments of his age, and he strove to forget everything in "bygones"—"Præterita."

It was Professor Norton who had suggested that he should write his own life. He had begun to tell the story, bit by bit, in "Fors." On the journey of 1882 he made a point of revisiting most of the scenes of youthful work and travel, to revive his impressions; but the meeting with Miss Alexander gave him new interests, and his return to Oxford put the autobiography into the background.

Now, at last he collected the scattered notes, and completed his first volume, which brings the account up to the time of his coming of age. It is not a connected and systematic biography; it omits many points of interest, especially the steps of his early successes and mental development; but it is the brightest conceivable picture of himself and his surroundings—"scenes and thoughts perhaps worthy of memory," as the title modestly puts it—told with inimitable ease and graphic power.

We have traced a life which was—even more than might be gathered from "Præterita"—a battle with adversities from the beginning. Not to discuss the influences of heredity, there was over-stimulus in childhood; intense application to work in youth and middle-age, under conditions of discouragement, both public and private, which would have been fatal to many another man; and this, too, not merely hard work, but work of an intense emotional nature, involving—in his view at least—wide issues of life and death, in which he was another Jacob wrestling with the angel in the wilderness, another Savonarola imploring reconciliation between God and man.

Without a life of singular temperance, without unusual moral principle and self-command, he would long ago have fallen like other men of genius of his passionate type. He outlived "consumptive" tendencies in youth; and the repeated indications of over-strain in later life, up to the time of his first serious break-down in 1878, had issued in nothing more than the depression and fatigue with which most busy men are familiar. He had been accustomed to hear himself called mad—the defence of Turner was thought by the *dilettanti* of the time to be possible only to a lunatic; the author of "Stones of Venice," we saw, was insane in the eyes of his critic, the architect; it was seriously whispered when he wrote on Political Economy that Ruskin was out of his mind; and so on. Every new thing he put forward "made Quintilian stare and gasp," and *soi-disant* friends shake their heads, until a still newer nine-days' wonder appeared from his pen. The break-down of 1878, so difficult to explain to his public, made it appear that the common reproach might after all be coming true. The recurrence of a similar illness in 1881 and 1882 made it still more to be feared. It seemed as though his life's work was to be invalidated by his age's failure; it seemed that the stale, shallow reproach might only too easily be justifiable.

These attacks of mental disease, which at his recall to Oxford seemed to have been safely distanced, after his resignation began again at more and more frequent intervals. Crash after crash of tempest fell upon him—clearing away for a while only to return with fiercer fury, until they left him beaten down and helpless at last, to learn that he must accept the lesson and bow before the storm. Like another prophet who had been very jealous for the Lord God of Hosts, he was to feel tempest and earthquake and fire pass over him, before hearing the still small voice that bade him once more take courage, and live in quietness and in confidence, for the sake of those whom he had forgotten, when he cried, "I, even I only, am left."

From one who has been out in the storm the reader will not expect a cool recital of its effects. The delirium of brain-fever brings strange things to pass; and, no doubt, afforded ground for the painful gossip, of which there has been more than enough—much of it absurdly untrue, the romancing of ingenious newspaper-correspondents; some of it, the lie that is half a truth. For in these times there were not wanting parasites such as always prey upon creatures in disease, as well as weak admirers who misunderstood their hero's natural character, and entirely failed to grasp his situation.

Let such troubles of the past be forgotten: all that I now remember of many a weary night and day is the vision of a great soul in torment, and through purgatorial fires the ineffable tenderness of the real man emerging, with his passionate appeal to justice and baffled desire for truth. To those who could not follow the wanderings of the wearied brain it was nothing but a horrible or a grotesque nightmare. Some, in those trials, learnt as they could not otherwise have learnt to know him, and to love him as never before.

There were many periods of health, or comparative health, even in those years. While convalescent from the illness of 1885 he continued "Præterita" and "Dilecta," the series of notes and letters illustrating his life. In connection with early reminiscences, he amused himself by reproducing his favourite old nursery book, "Dame Wiggins of Lee." He edited the works of one or two friends, wrote occasionally to newspapers—notably on books and reading, to the *Pall Mall Gazette*, in the "Symposium" on the best hundred books. He continued his arrangements for the Museum, and held an exhibition (June, 1886) of the drawings made under his direction for the Guild.

He was already drifting into another illness when he sent the famous reply to an appeal for help to pay off the debt on a chapel at Richmond. The letter is often misquoted for the sake of raising a laugh, so that it is not out of place to reprint it as a specimen of the more vehement expressions of this period. The reader of his life must surely see, through the violence of the wording, a perfectly consistent and reasonable expression of Mr. Ruskin's views:—

"BRANTWOOD, CONISTON, LANCASHIRE.
"*May 19th*, 1886.

"SIR,

"I am scornfully amused at your appeal to me, of all people in the world the precisely least likely to give you a farthing! My first word to all men and boys who care to hear me is 'Don't get into debt. Starve and go to heaven—but don't borrow. Try first begging,—I don't mind, if it's really needful, stealing! But don't buy things you can't pay for!'

"And of all manner of debtors, pious people building churches they can't pay for are the most detestable nonsense to me. Can't you preach and pray behind the hedges—or in a sandpit—or a coal-hole—first?

"And of all manner of churches thus idiotically built iron churches are the damnablest to me.

"And of all the sects of believers in any ruling spirit—Hindoos, Turks, Feather Idolaters, and Mumbo Jumbo, Log and Fire worshippers, who want churches, your modern English Evangelical sect is the most absurd, and entirely objectionable and unendurable to me! All which they might very easily have found out from my books—any other sort of sect would!—before bothering me to write it to them.

"Ever, nevertheless, and in all this saying, your faithful servant,
"JOHN RUSKIN."

The recipient of the letter promptly sold it. Only three days later, Ruskin was writing one of the most striking passages in "Præterita" (vol. ii., chap. 5)—indeed, one of the daintiest landscape pieces in all his works, describing the blue Rhone as it flows under the bridges of Geneva.

This energetic letter-writing made people stare; but a more serious result of these periods between strength and helplessness was the tendency to misunderstanding with old friends. Ruskin had spoiled many of them, if I may say so, by too uniform forbearance and unselfishness: and now that he was not always strong enough to be patient, difficulties ensued which they had not always the tact to avert. "The moment I have to scold people they say I'm crazy," he said, piteously, one day. And so, one hardly knows how, he found himself at strife on all sides. Before he was fully recovered from the attack of 1886 there were troubles about the Oxford drawing school; and he withdrew most of the pictures he had there on loan. How little animosity he really felt against Oxford is shown from the fact that early in the next year (February, 1887) he was planning with his cousin, Wm. Richardson, to give £5,000 to the drawing school, as a joint gift in memory of their two mothers. Mr. Richardson's death, and Ruskin's want of means—for he had already spent all his capital—put an end to the scheme. But the remaining loans, including important and valuable drawings by himself, he did not withdraw, and it is to be hoped they may stay there to show not only the artist's hand but the friendly heart of the founder and benefactor.

In April, 1887, came the news of Laurence Hilliard's death in the Aegean, with a shock that intensified the tendency to another recurrence of illness. For months the situation caused great anxiety. In August he posted with Mrs. A. Severn towards the south, and took up his quarters at Folkestone, moving soon after to Sandgate, where he remained, with short visits to town, until the following summer—better, or worse, from week to week—sometimes writing a little for "Præterita," or preparing material for the continuation of unfinished books; but bringing on his malady with each new effort. In June, 1888, he went with Mr. Arthur

Severn to Abbeville, and made his headquarters for nearly a month at the Tête de Boeuf. Here he was arrested for sketching the fortifications and examined at the police station, much to his amusement. At Abbeville, too, he met Mr. Detmar Blow, a young architect, whom he asked to accompany him to Italy. They stayed awhile at Paris,—drove, as in 1882, over the Jura, and up to Chamouni, where Ruskin wrote the epilogue to the reprint of "Modern Painters"; then, by Martigny and the Simplon, they went to visit Mrs. and Miss Alexander at Bassano; and thence to Venice. They returned by the St. Gothard, reaching Herne Hill early in December.

But this journey did not, as it had been hoped, put him in possession of his strength like the journey of 1882. Then, he had returned to public life with new vigour; now, his best hours were hours of feebleness and depression; and he came home to Brantwood in the last days of the year, wearied to death, to wait for the end.

NOTES:

50   "The Storm-Cloud of the Nineteenth Century," London Institution, February 4th, 1884; repeated with variations and additions a week later.

CHAPTER X

DATUR HORA QUIETI (1889-1900)

In the summer of 1889, at Seascale, on the Cumberland coast, Ruskin was still busy upon "Præterita." He had his task planned out to the finish: in nine more chapters he meant to conclude his third volume with a review of the leading memories of his life, down to the year 1875, when the story was to close. Passages here and there were written, material collected from old letters and journals, and the contents and titles of the chapters arranged; but the intervals of strength had become fewer and shorter, and at last, in spite of all his courage and energy, he was brought face to face with the fact that his powers were ebbing away, and that head and hand would do their work no more.

He could not finish "Præterita"; but he could not leave it without record of one companionship of his life, which was, it seemed, all that was left to him of the old times and the old folks at home. And so, setting aside the plans he had made, he devoted the last chapter, as his forebodings told him it must be, to his cousin, Mrs. Arthur Severn, and wrote the story of "Joanna's Care."

In his bedroom at Seascale, morning after morning, he still worked, or tried to work, as he had been used to do on journeys farther afield in brighter days. But now he seemed lost among the papers scattered on his table; he could not fix his mind upon them, and turned from one subject to another in despair; and yet patient, and kindly to those with him whose help he could no longer use, and who dared not show—though he could not but guess—how heart-breaking it was.

They put the best face upon it, of course: drove in the afternoons about the country—to Muncaster Castle, to Calder Abbey, where he tried to sketch once more; and when the proofs of "Joanna's Care" were finally revised, to Wastwater. But travelling now was no longer restorative.

It added not a little to the misfortunes of the time that two of his best friends in the outside world were disputing over a third. By nobody was Carlyle's reputation more valued, and yet he acknowledged that Froude was but telling the truth in the revelations which so surprised the public; and much as he admired Norton, he deprecated the attack on Carlyle's literary executor, whose motives he understood and approved.

In August, after his return to Coniston, the storm-cloud came down upon him once more. It was only in the summer of 1890 that he was able to get about. But firmly convinced that his one chance lay in absolute rest and quiet, he wisely refused any sort of exertion, and was rewarded by a temporary improvement in health and strength.

In the meantime he was obliged to hand over to others such parts of his work as others could do. The St. George's Guild still continued in existence, though it naturally lost much of its interest, and the whole of its distinctive mission, when he ceased to be able to direct it. The Museum had quite outgrown its cottage at Walkley, never intended for more than temporary premises; and for ten years there had been talk of new buildings, at first on the spot, then on the Guild's ground at Bewdley, where, at one time, Ruskin planned a fairy palace in the woods, with cloistered hostelries for the wandering student. Such schemes were stopped less by his illness than by want of means.

Sheffield, however, did not wish to lose the Museum, and offered to house it if the Guild would present it to the town. That was, of course, out of the question. But a new offer to take over the collection on loan, the Guild paying a curator, was another matter, and was thankfully accepted. The Corporation fulfilled their share of the bargain with generosity. An admirable site was assigned at Meersbrook Park, in a fine old hall surrounded with trees, and overlooking a broad view of the town and country. On April 15th, 1890, the Museum was opened by the Earl of Carlisle, in presence of the Corporation, the Trustees of the Guild, and a large assembly of friends and Sheffield townspeople. Since then the attendance of visitors and students shows that the collection is appreciated by the public; and it is to be hoped that though nominally a loan it will remain there in perpetuity, and that it will be maintained and used with due regard to the intentions of the founder.

Many other plans had to be modified, as he found himself less able to work, and was obliged to hand over his business to others. With his early books he had been dissatisfied, as expressing immature views. "The Stones of Venice" had been recast into two small volumes, and "St. Mark's Rest" written in the attempt to supplement and correct it. But the original book was obviously in demand, and a new edition was brought out in 1886.

"Modern Painters" had been also on the condemned list. The aggressive Protestantism and the geological theories involved in his description of mountains he condemned as errors; moreover, at the time of the last edition published by Messrs. Smith & Elder (1873), he had been told that the plates, which he considered a very important part of the work, would not stand another impression; and so he destroyed nine of them, in order that no subsequent edition might be brought out in the original form. He reprinted vol. ii. in a cheap edition, and began to recast the rest, with annotations and additions, as "In Montibus Sanctis," and "Coeli Enarrant", while Miss S. Beever's selections ("Frondes Agrestes") found a ready sale. But this did not satisfy the public, and there was a continual cry for a reprint, to which, at last, he yielded. Early in 1889 the "Complete Edition" appeared; with the cancelled plates reproduced.

He had always felt it a grievance that the enormous popularity of his works in America meant an enormous piracy. Towards the end of the "Fifties," Mr. Wiley of New York had begun to print cheap Ruskins;

not, indeed, illegally, but without proper acknowledgment to the author, and without any reference to the author's wishes as to form and style of production. An artist and writer on art, insisting on delicacy and refinement as the first necessity of draughtsmanship, and himself sparing no trouble or expense in the illustrations of his own works, was naturally dissatisfied with the wretched "Artotypes" with which the American editions caricatured his beautiful plates. Not only that, but it was a common practice to smuggle these editions, recommended by their cheapness, into other countries. Mr. Wiley sent, on an average, five hundred sets of "Modern Painters" to Europe every year, the greater number to England. His example was followed by other American publishers, so that in New York alone there came to be half a dozen houses advertising Ruskin's works, and many more throughout the cities of the States. Mr. Wiley, the first in the field, proposed to pay up a royalty upon all the copies he had sold if Ruskin would recognise him as accredited publisher in America. The offer of so large a sum would have been tempting, had it not meant that Ruskin must condone what he had for years denounced, and sanction what he strongly disapproved. The case would have been different if proposals had been made to reproduce his books in his own style, under competent supervision. This was done in 1890, when arrangements were made with Messrs. Charles E. Merrill & Co., of New York, to bring out the "Brantwood" edition of Ruskin, under the editorship of Professor C.E. Norton.

Though the sale of Ruskin's books in America had never, until so recently, brought him any profit, his own business in England, started in 1871 with the monthly pamphlet of "Fors," and in 1872 with the volume of "Sesame and Lilies," prospered singularly. Mr. George Allen, who, while building up an independent connection, still remained the sole publisher of Mr. Ruskin's works, said that the venture was successful from its earliest years. It was found that the booksellers were not indispensable, and that business could be done through the post as well as over the counter. In spite of occasional difficulties, such as the bringing out of works in parts, appearing irregularly or stopping outright at the author's illnesses, there was a steady increase of profit, rising in the author's later years (according to Mr. Allen) to an average of £4,000.

Fortunate it was that this bold attempt succeeded. The £200,000 he inherited from his parents had gone,—chiefly in gifts and in attempts to do good. The interest he used to spend on himself; the capital he gave away until it totally disappeared, except what is represented by the house he lived in and its contents. The sale of his books was his only income, and a great part of that went to pensioners to whom in the days of his wealth he pledged himself, to relatives and friends, discharged servants, institutions in which he took an interest at one time or other. But he had sufficient for his wants, and no need to fear poverty in his old age.

In this quiet retreat at Brantwood the echoes of the outer world did not sound very loudly. Ruskin had been too highly praised and too roundly abused, during fifty years of public life, to care what magazine critics and journalists said of him. Other men of his standing could solace themselves, if it be solace, in the consciousness that a grateful country has recognised their talents or their services. But civic and academic honours were not likely to be showered on a man who had spent his life in strenuous opposition to academicism in art and letters, and in vigorous attacks upon both political parties, and upon the established order of things.

And yet Oxford and Cambridge awarded him the highest honours in their gift. In 1873 the Royal Society of Painters in Watercolours voted him honorary member, a recognition which gave him great pleasure at the time. At different dates he was elected to various societies—Geological, Zoological, Architectural, Horticultural, Historical, Anthropological, Metaphysical; and to the Athenæum and Alpine Clubs. He was elected Hon. Member of the Academy of Florence in 1862, of the Academy of Venice, 1877, of the Royal Academies of Antwerp and Brussels in 1892; and was also an Hon. Member of the American Academy. But he did not seek distinctions, and he even declined them, as in the case of the medal of the Royal Institute of British Architects.

A more striking form of distinction than such titles is the fact that he was the first writer whose contemporaries, during his lifetime, formed societies to study his work. The first Ruskin Society was founded in 1879 at Manchester, and was followed by the Societies of London, Glasgow and Liverpool. In 1887 the Ruskin Reading Guild was formed in Scotland, with many local branches in England and Ireland, and a journal, subsequently re-named *Igdrasil*, to promote study of literary and social subjects in Ruskin, and in writers like Carlyle and Tolstoi taking a standpoint similar to his. In 1896, Ruskin Societies were formed at Birmingham and in the Isle of Man. Many classes and clubs for the study of Ruskin were also in operation throughout America during his lifetime.

His eightieth birthday was the signal for an outburst of congratulations almost greater than even admirers had expected. The post came late and loaded with flowers and letters, and all day long telegrams arrived from all parts of the world, until they lay in heaps, unopened for the time being. A great address had been prepared, with costly illumination on vellum, and binding by Mr. Cobden Sanderson.

"Year by year," it said, "in ever widening extent, there is an increasing trust in your teaching, an increasing desire to realize the noble ideals you have set before mankind in words which we feel have brought nearer to our hearts the kingdom of God upon earth. It is our hope and prayer that the joy and peace you have brought to others may return in full measure to your own heart filling it with the peace which comes from the love of God and the knowledge of the love of your fellow-men."

Among those who subscribed to these sentiments were various people of importance, such as Royal Academicians, the Royal Society of Painters in Watercolours, the Trustees of the British Museum and of the National Gallery, the St. George's Guild and Ruskin Societies, with many others; and the address was presented by a deputation who reported that they had found him looking well "and extremely happy."

A similar illuminated address from the University of Oxford ran thus:

> "We venture to send you, as you begin your eighty-first year, these few words of greeting and good-will, to make you sure that in Oxford the gratitude and reverence with which men think of you is ever fresh. You have helped many to find in life more happiness than they thought it held; and we trust there is happiness in the latter years of your long life. You have taught many to see the wealth of beauty in nature and in art, prizing the remembrance of it; and we trust that the sights you have best loved come back to your memory with unfading beauty. You have encouraged many to keep a good heart through dark days, and we trust that the courage of a constant hope is yours."

The London Ruskin Society sent a separate address; and to show that if not a prophet in his own country he was at any rate a valued friend, the Coniston Parish Council resolved "and carried unanimously," says the local journal, "with applause,"

> "That the congratulations of this council be offered to Mr. John Ruskin, on the occasion of his eightieth birthday, together with the warm thanks which they and all their neighbours feel for the kindness he has shown, and the many generous acts he has done to them and theirs during twenty-seven years of residence at Coniston, where his presence is most truly appreciated, and his name will always be most gratefully remembered."

But as the year went on he did not regain his usual summer strength. Walking out had become a greater weariness to him, and he had to submit to the humiliation of a bath-chair. To save himself even the labour of creeping down to his study, he sat usually in the turret-room upstairs, next to his bed-chamber, but still with the look of health in his face, and the fire in his eyes quite unconquered. He would listen while Baxter read the news to him, following public events with interest, or while Mrs. Severn or Miss Severn read stories, novel after novel; but always liking old favourites best, and never anything that was unhappy. Some pet books he would pore over, or drowse over by the hour. The last of these was one in which he had a double interest, for it was about ships of war, and it was written by the kinsman of a dear friend. Some of the artists he had loved and helped had failed him or left him, but Burne-Jones was always true. One night, going up to bed, the old man stopped long to look at the photograph from Philip Burne-Jones's portrait of his father. "That's my dear brother, Ned," he said, nodding good-bye to the picture as he went. Next night the great artist died, and of all the many losses of these later years this one was the hardest to bear.

So when a little boy lent him "A Fleet in Being" he read and re-read it; then got a copy for himself, and might have learnt it by heart, so long he pored over it. But when the little boy or his sisters went to visit the "Di Pa" (Dear Papa), as he liked children to call their old friend, he had now scarcely anything to talk about. "He just looked at us, and smiled," they would report; "and we couldn't think what to say."

He had his "bright days," when he would hear business discussed, though a very little of it was wearisome. It was impossible to bring before him half the wants and wishes of his correspondents, who could not yet realise his weakness, and besought the notice they fancied so easily given. Yet in that weakness one could trace no delusions, none of the mental break-down which was taken for granted. If he gave an opinion it was clear and sound enough; of course with the old Ruskinian waywardness of idea which always puzzled his public. But he knew what he was about, and knew what was going on. He was like the aged Queen Aud in the saga, who "rose late and went to bed early, and if anyone asked after her health she answered sharply."

But all the love and care spent on him could not keep him with us. There came the Green Yule that makes a fat kirkyard, and in January of 1900 hardly a house in the neighbourhood was free from the plague of influenza. In spite of strictest precautions it invaded Brantwood.

On the 18th of January he was remarkably well, as people often are before an illness—"fey," as the old Northern folk-lore has it. Towards evening, when Mrs. Severn went to him for the usual reading—it was Edna Lyall's "In the Golden Days"—his throat was irritable and he "ached all over." They put him to bed and sent for Dr. Parsons, his constant medical attendant, who found his temperature as high as 102°, and feared the consequences. But the patient, as he always did, refused to be considered ill, and ate his dinner, and seemed next day to be really better. There was no great cause for alarm, though naturally some for anxiety; and in reasonable hopes of amendment, the slight attack was not made public.

On Saturday morning, the 20th, all appeared to be going well until about half-past ten. Suddenly he collapsed and became unconscious. It was the dreaded failure of heart after influenza. His breathing weakened, and through the morning and through the afternoon in that historic little room, lined with his Turners, he lay, falling softly asleep. No efforts could revive him. There was no struggle; there were no words. The bitterness of death was spared him. And when it was all over, and those who had watched through the day turned at last from his bedside, "sunset and evening star" shone bright above the heavenly lake and the clear-cut blue of Coniston fells.

Next morning brought messages of hurried condolence, and the Monday such a chorus from the press as made all the praises of his lifetime seem trifling and all its blame forgotten. If only, in his years of struggle and despair, he had known the place he should win!

On the Tuesday came a telegram offering a grave in Westminster Abbey, the highest honour our nation can give to its dead. But his own mind had long since been made plain on that point, and his wishes had not been forgotten. "If I die here," he used to say, "bury me at Coniston. I should have liked, if it happened at Herne Hill, to lie with my father and mother in Shirley churchyard, as I should have wished, if I died among the Alps, to be buried in the snow."

We carried him on Monday night down from his bed-chamber and laid him in the study. There was a pane of glass let into the coffin-lid, so that the face might be kept in sight; and there it lay, among lilies of the valley, and framed in the wreath sent by Mr. Watts, the great painter, a wreath of the true Greek laurel, the victor's crown, from the tree growing in his garden, cut only thrice before, for Tennyson and Leighton and Burne-Jones. It would be too long to tell of all such tokens of affection and respect that were heaped upon the coffin,—from the wreath of the Princess Louise down to the tributes of humble dependants,—above a hundred and twenty-five, we counted; some of them the costliest money could buy, some valued no less for the feeling they expressed. I am not sure that the most striking was not the village tailor's, with this on its label—"There was a man sent from God, and his name was John."

On the Wednesday we made our sad procession to the church, through storm and flood. The village was in mourning, and round the churchyard gates men, women, and children stood in throngs. The coffin was carried in by eight of those who had been in his employ, and the church filled noiselessly with neighbours and friends, who after a hymn, and the Lord's prayer, and a long silence, passed up the aisles for their last look, and to heap more offerings of wreaths and flowers around the bier. At dusk tall candles were lit, and so through the winter's night watch was kept.

Thursday, the 25th, brought together a great assembly, great for the remoteness of the place and the inclemency of the weather. The country folk have a saying "Happy is the dead that the rain rains on;" and the fells were darkly clouded and the beck roared by, swollen to a torrent. The church was far too small to hold the congregation, which included most of his personal friends and the representatives of many public bodies. A crowd stood outside in the storm while the service went on.

It began with a hymn written for the occasion by Canon Rawnsley who with the Vicar of Hawkshead, Brantwood's parish church, read the Psalms. A hymn, "Comes at times a stillness as of even," was sung by his friend Miss Wakefield; and the lesson read by Canon Richmond, arrived officially to represent the Bishop of Carlisle, but to most of us representing old times and the comradeships of his youth and early manhood. The Vicar of Coniston and the Rev. Reginald Meister, on behalf of the Dean of Christ Church, also took part in the service. When the Dead March sounded the coffin was covered with a pall given by the Ruskin Linen Industry of Keswick, lined with bright crimson silk, and embroidered with the motto, "Unto This Last," and with his favourite wild roses showered over the gray field, just as they fall in the *Primavera* of Botticelli. There was no black about his burying, except what we wore for our own sorrow; it was remembered how he hated black, so much that he would even have his mother's coffin painted blue; and among the white and green and violet of the wreaths that filled the chancel, none was more significant in its sympathy than Mrs. Severn's great cross of red roses.

As we carried him down the churchyard path, a drop or two fell from the boughs, but a gleam of sunshine, the first after many days, shot along the crags from under the cloud, and the wind paused. Standing there by the graveside, who could help being thankful that he had found so lovely a resting-place after so tranquil a falling to sleep? At his feet, parted only by the fence and the garden, is the village school; and who does not know how he loved the children of Coniston? At his right hand are the graves of the Beevers; his last old friend, Miss Susan Beever, lies next to him. Over the spot hang the thick boughs of a fir-tree—who does not know what he has written of his favourite mountain-pine? And behind the church, shut in with its dark yews', rise the crags of Coniston, those that he wearied for in his boyhood, beneath which he prayed, in sickness, to lie down and rest. "The crags are lone on Coniston."

Milton Keynes UK
Ingram Content Group UK Ltd.
UKHW021845180823
427137UK00004B/133